The Emergence of the Digital World

Elsie Ong
Editor

The Emergence of the Digital World

Friend or Foe to Young Adults in the Post-pandemic Era?

Springer

Editor
Elsie Ong
Department of Psychology and Human Development
IOE—UCL's Faculty of Education and Society
University College London
London, UK

ISBN 978-981-97-3097-1 ISBN 978-981-97-3098-8 (eBook)
https://doi.org/10.1007/978-981-97-3098-8

This Springer imprint is published by the registered company Springer Nature Singapore Pte Ltd.
The registered company address is: 152 Beach Road, #21-01/04 Gateway East, Singapore 189721, Singapore

The Editorial Board

Elsie Ong, hailing from the UK, and Kevin Conn, representing the United States, have been appointed as the co-editors for the forthcoming book titled *The Emergence of the Digital World: Friend or Foe to Young Adults in the Post-pandemic Era?* With their extensive backgrounds in academia and research, Ong and Conn bring a wealth of knowledge and expertise to the project. Their collaborative effort aims to explore the multifaceted impacts of the digital age on young adults, particularly in the context of the post-pandemic landscape. Through this endeavor, Ong and Conn seek to foster a comprehensive understanding of the opportunities and challenges presented by digital technologies, offering valuable insights for scholars, educators, policymakers, and practitioners alike.

Preface

In the maze of existence, the transition from teenage to early adulthood is a time of profound change and upheaval. As these young individuals navigate this uncharted territory, their mental well-being is a guiding light through the intricate web of emotions, self-discovery, and personal development. This book is a testament to the strength of resilience, compassion, and self-understanding in the lives of young people who have weathered the pandemic storm. Within the chapters, we have assembled a diverse group of experts (students, educators, and policymakers) to delve into and share the varied experiences of youth from all walks of life. Their narratives not only reflect the trials, victories, and perseverance of young people during challenging times in China and England, but also offer a glimpse into the collective resilience that defines our generation. We delve into the intricacies of student learning, depression, anxiety, and other mental health hurdles that touch countless lives, often in silence.

Our journey leads us beyond the shadows of mental health challenges. We delve into the strategies, resilience, healing, and empowerment that have emerged from the experiences of those who have confronted these obstacles. We explore coping mechanisms, emotional regulation, and transformative educational opportunities that guide those seeking understanding and solace. This book is not a prescription, but a dialogue. It aims to foster understanding, reduce stigma, and awaken empathy for the struggles of young people. It is a testament to the resilience and strength inherent in all of us.

Through this collective exploration of young people's mental health, we aim to convey to readers that these individuals are not alone in their battles. As part of a larger community, we can contribute to a tapestry of experiences and emotions that shape our lives. We hope this book will be a companion to a healthier, happier, and more empathetic world for young people and those who support them. Thank you for joining us on this journey. Your dedication to understanding and supporting youth mental health shines as a beacon of hope in the often-challenging landscape of adolescence.

London, UK Elsie Ong

Acknowledgements

Firstly, I would also like to thank my publisher for their belief in my work and their unwavering support throughout the process. Your professionalism and commitment to excellence have made this journey a rewarding one. You have not only guided me through the publishing process but also inspired me with your passion for bringing ideas to life. Having a team of educators, students, and parents from different countries in this book, I have had the privilege of witnessing the incredible resilience and strength of individuals who have faced the challenges brought about by the COVID-19 pandemic. I am constantly inspired by the unwavering determination and perseverance shown by students, parents, and colleagues as we navigated through these unprecedented times. I am deeply grateful for the support and understanding of my family especially Ambrose and Fiona, who stood by me as I balanced the demands of work and home in this new normal. Their love and encouragement have been my anchor during the storm. I also extend my heartfelt appreciation to my colleagues and fellow educators who have worked tirelessly to adapt to the rapidly changing landscape of education. Your dedication and innovative spirit have not only kept the flame of learning alive but have also ignited a new wave of creativity and collaboration in our field. To all the students who have embraced new technologies and modes of learning with grace and resilience, I commend your adaptability and eagerness to explore new horizons. Your enthusiasm and willingness to learn have been a source of inspiration for me. Lastly, I want to express my gratitude to the readers of this book. Your interest and support drive me to continue my journey as an educator and a lifelong learner. May we all continue to grow stronger, adapt to new technologies, and make life easier in education, together. In conclusion, I recognize that this book, *The Emergence of the Digital World: Friend or Foe to the Young Adults in the Post-pandemic Era?* would not have been possible without the support and inspiration from each one of you. I am eternally grateful for your contributions and feel incredibly fortunate to have had you by my side on this journey.

Overview of This Book/The Purpose, Structure, and Content of This Volume

This book consists of seven chapters focusing on (1) the transition from adolescence to adulthood; (2) the world in the pandemic; (3) students' learning experience; (4) mental health of students during and after the pandemic; (5) the importance of digital technology; (6) implementation of digital technology as a mental health service; (7) the concluding chapter and future directions.

In response to the global COVID-19 pandemic, higher education institutions were compelled to transition from traditional in-person instruction to online learning due to the implementation of social distancing measures aimed at curbing the spread of the virus (Ali 2020; Adedoyin and Soykan 2020; Bao 2020). This unprecedented shift has raised concerns regarding the adequacy of students' resources and facilities for online education, and their capacity for self-regulated learning (Chiu 2022; Meeter et al. 2020). As an educator, addressing the need to provide students with an optimal online learning experience is a pressing and significant issue. Building upon the general introduction in Chap. 1 of this book, Chap. 2 will examine the global impact of COVID-19, focusing specifically on its effects on young people, and will elucidate the pandemic's educational implications for young individuals in a university context. We will specifically examine the perspectives of students to the changes in their learning and the resulting impact on their engagement, motivation, and other significant academic outcomes. In Chap. 3, we will investigate the coping mechanisms employed by university students during challenging circumstances through two distinct studies conducted in different countries. The first study will analyze coping strategies among UK university students by quantitatively correlating this variable with various mental health indicators. Conversely, the second study will involve a qualitative examination of university students residing in the residential halls of a Hong Kong university during the pandemic. This study will delve into the experiences of Chinese students and the effects of COVID-19 on them. Both studies will aim to identify the stressors associated with COVID-19 and comprehend how students from diverse backgrounds adopted varying coping strategies in response to the pandemic.

In Chap. 4, we aim to expand the investigation of students' mental health in the post-COVID-19 Era. We examined various factors such as levels of depression, intrapersonal well-being, loneliness, self-efficacy, interpersonal support, and social support. The potential of digital technologies to transform clinical research and treatment is significant, and it is imperative to explore recent advancements in this field and their potential relevance to young individuals facing mental health challenges. This encompasses examining the internet as a source of information and its capacity to facilitate help-seeking behaviour among young people. In Chap. 5, we will present empirical evidence regarding the influence of digital technologies on young individuals' learning and psychological well-being, drawing from two research studies. Additionally, we will analyze the potential application of recent interventions for young adults grappling with mental health challenges, including the use of the internet as an information resource and its capacity to facilitate help-seeking behaviour among youth. Furthermore, we will explore recent advancements in using mobile phones for intervention.

Chapter 6 encompasses various considerations essential for developing, utilizing, and assessing digital mental health interventions. One study sought to investigate students' mental health status in the post-pandemic era, as well as the barriers hindering their help-seeking behaviour, while also aiming to enhance the current comprehension of digital interventions by examining student experiences with them. Another study employed a mixed-methods approach to explore student encounters with digital interventions and their self-management of mental health. The concluding chapter will summarize the challenges confronting the current educational system and the changes that have transpired in the aftermath of a global crisis. Drawing from the amalgamation of research findings and experiential insights, we will endeavor to outline the expectations for the future development of higher education in addressing the needs of individuals in the twenty-first century.

References

Adedoyin OB, Soykan E (2020) COVID-19 pandemic and online learning: the challenges and opportunities. Interactive learning environments, pp 1–13. https://doi.org/10.1080/10494820.2020.1813180

Ali W (2020) Online and remote learning in higher education institutes: A necessity in light of COVID-19 pandemic. High Educ Stud, 10(3):16–25. https://doi.org/10.5539/hes.v10n3p16

Bao W (2020) COVID-19 and online teaching in higher education: A case study of Peking University. Hum Behav Emerg Technol 2(2):113–115. https://doi.org/10.1002/hbe2.191

Chiu TK (2022) Applying the self-determination theory (SDT) to explain student engagement in online learning during the COVID-19 pandemic. J Res Technol Educ 54(sup1):S14–S30. https://doi.org/10.1080/15391523.2021.1891998

Meeter M, Bele T, den Hartogh C, Bakker T, de Vries RE, Plak S (2020) College students' motivation and study results after COVID-19 stay-at-home orders

Contents

Editor and Contributors

About the Editor

Dr. Elsie Ong is a Lecturer and a Dissertation Supervisor in UCL. She has worked in many universities in Asia and the UK for over ten years. Elsie is active in leading research that focuses on the mental health of young adults, especially those going through university transitions. Her expertise in cognitive neuroscience and psychology has also initiated further exploration on the underlying causes of mental health problems and later sparkles potentials for suicide preventions and interventions. Elsie is devoted to the study of psychological well-being in young adults and has published her research through internationally renowned conferences and reputed journals such as Frontiers in psychiatry. These experiences have helped to keep her most up to date on the latest development in preventions and interventions in mental health.

Contributors

Molly Bass Faculty of Health, Education and Society, University of Northampton, Northampton, UK

Kevin Conn Executive Director Student Housing and Residential Life California State University Northridge, Northridge, CA, United States

Taran Dale IOE—Psychology and Human Development, UCL Institute of Education, University College London, London, WC, UK

Bethany Finch IOE—Psychology and Human Development, UCL Institute of Education, University College London, London, WC, UK

Can He IOE—Psychology and Human Development, UCL Institute of Education, University College London, London, WC, UK

Yuefei Jiang IOE—Psychology and Human Development, UCL Institute of Education, University College London, London, WC, UK

Jing Ma IOE—Psychology and Human Development, UCL Institute of Education, University College London, London, WC, UK

Elsie Ong Department of Psychology and Human Development, IOE—UCL's Faculty of Education and Society, University College London, London, WC, UK

Wan San Wendy Wang Department of Psychology and Human Development, IOE—UCL's Faculty of Education and Society, University College London, London, WC, UK

Carol Zheng IOE—Psychology and Human Development, UCL Institute of Education, University College London, London, WC, UK

Chapter 1
Introduction

Elsie Ong

The World Under the Pandemic

Coronavirus-19 (COVID-19) was first reported in Wuhan, China, in December 2019. The public quickly learned through social media that this virus is a transmissible new infectious disease characterised by respiratory and digestive tract symptoms. Symptoms ranged from entirely asymptomatic for severe pneumonia, acute respiratory distress syndrome, septic shock, and systemic multi-organ failure. This unknown and deadly viral disease spread rapidly across 114 countries within two months (Liang et al. 2020), leading to the World Health Organisation's (WHO) decision to declare COVID-19 a global pandemic on the 11 March 2020 (Fig. 1.1; WHO 2020).

The COVID-19 pandemic, caused by the severe acute respiratory syndrome coronavirus 2 (SARS-CoV-2), was first reported in Wuhan, China, in December 2019. Over the subsequent ten months, the virus spread rapidly, with more than 30 million confirmed cases worldwide. This public health emergency of international concern, as declared by the World Health Organization (WHO), has had far-reaching effects. Since the first case was reported, the pandemic has significantly influenced our behaviour, work environments, social interactions, and daily routines. It has also had substantial impacts on various aspects of mental and physical health (Arora and Grey 2020). On March 23, 2020, the UK Government responded to the escalating crisis by declaring a lockdown. This resulted in a 'stay at home' order, where individuals were instructed to remain indoors and avoid non-essential social contact, work, or travel (UK Government 2020). This directive led to the immediate closure of schools and universities across the UK. Consequently, all teaching and examinations transitioned to an online format, marking a significant shift in the educational landscape (Fig. 1.2).

E. Ong (✉)
Department of Psychology and Human Development, IOE—UCL's Faculty of Education and Society, University College London, London, WC 1E 6BT, UK
e-mail: Elsie.ong@ucl.ac.uk

E. Ong (ed.), *The Emergence of the Digital World*,
https://doi.org/10.1007/978-981-97-3098-8_1

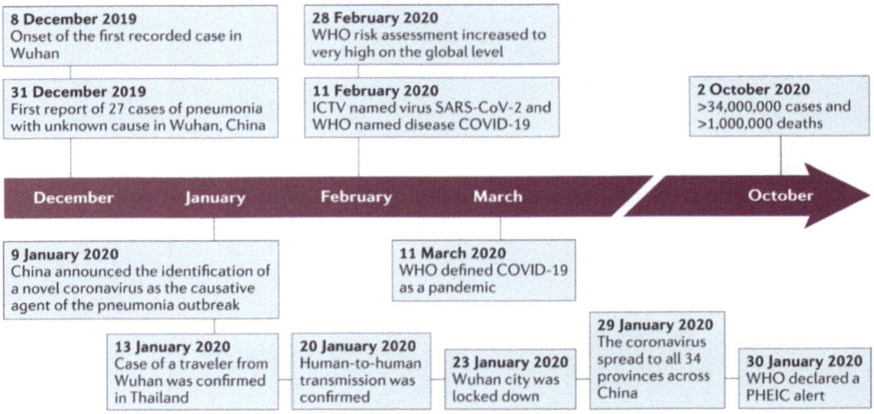

Fig. 1.1 Obtained from https://www.nature.com/articles/s41579-020-00459-7/figures/1

Fig. 1.2 Obtained from https://www.ageuk.org.uk/ealing/about-us/news/articles/2021/national-lockdown---stay-at-home/

The restrictions and orders imposed by the government have undoubtedly placed a heavy financial burden on society and individuals. The use of public transportation has drastically decreased, followed by a reduction in the food supply chain (Ebrahim et al. 2020). This exacerbated the situation and led to a shortage of many essential resources, food, and personal protective equipment. Subsequently, this triggered a general feeling of helplessness and restlessness among the people living under the order. This postulation was substantiated by several studies showing how the COVID-19 outbreak has been seen as a disaster for mental health (Chang et al. 2020). Psychosocial responses to such a global stressor + include overestimating the likelihood of infection and mortality (Koh 2020), feelings of fear, shame and weakness, feelings of personal and social failure, taking excessive and inappropriate preventive measures, and increasing demand for health services in a time of shortages (Dong et al. 2020; Koh 2020).

The psychological and physical impacts of COVID-19 on individuals have been more severe and enduring compared to everyday life stressors such as divorce, relocation, and job loss, as the pandemic represents an acute, widespread, and uncontrollable stressor (Chang et al. 2020). Psychosocial effects include feelings of isolation, distrust, stress, anxiety, reduced social interaction, and a compromised immune system (Moghe et al. 2020). A study by Qiu et al. (2020) found that approximately 35% of the general population in China reported experiencing psychological distress due to the COVID-19 epidemic. While numerous studies have examined the impact of COVID-19 on mental health issues, most have focused on healthcare workers, patients, children, and the general population (Lai et al. 2020). There is comparatively less evidence (Cao et al. 2020; Liang et al. 2020) focusing on how the pandemic has affected university students, who are considered vulnerable, particularly when living away from home. For instance, many students have experienced the closure of educational institutions, suspension of face-to-face classes, and significant disruption to their university accommodation and lives due to drastically reduced public transportation (Liang et al. 2020). A rising number of research on the mental health implications of the COVID-19 pandemic has indicated high levels of depression among university student populations. Therefore, it is important to investigate how the pandemic changed in the global population (Fig. 1.3).

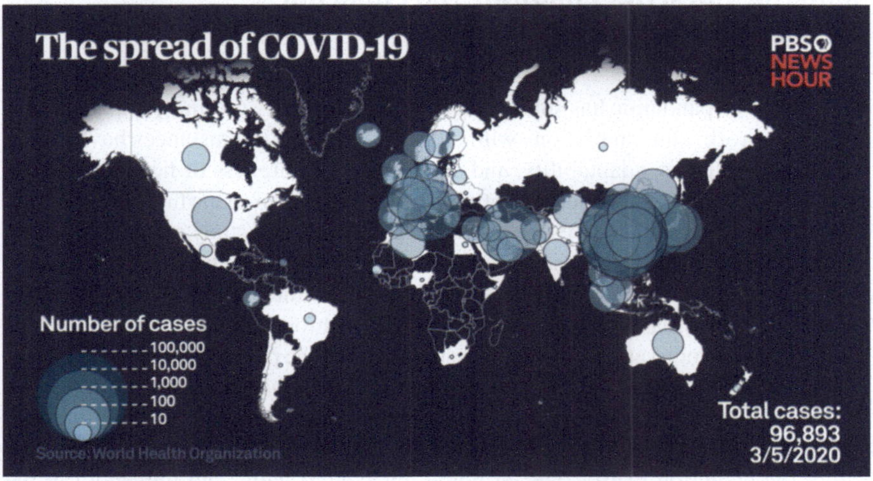

Fig. 1.3 Map of COVID spreading around the world. (Obtained from https://www.pbs.org/newshour/health/map-watch-how-covid-19-traveled-the-world)

Digital World Defined

The term "digital world" denotes the interconnected web of digital devices, systems, and platforms that facilitate digital data creation, storage, transmission, and retrieval (Brynjolfsson and McAfee 2014). This world permeates various aspects of human life, including communication, commerce, entertainment, education, and more, all made possible by digital technologies. In this digitally connected world, individuals can establish global connections via social media platforms, instant messaging apps, and video conferencing tools (Castells 2010). The advent of online marketplaces and e-commerce platforms has transformed our approach to business and shopping (Turban et al. 2018). Digital content, such as music, films, and books, can be accessed and enjoyed through streaming services and e-readers.

Education has also seen significant changes due to the digital world, with online learning platforms and educational resources providing new avenues for remote and self-paced learning (Means et al. 2014). Moreover, the digital world has enabled the gathering and analysing big data, leading to progress in fields like artificial intelligence and data analytics (Mayer-Schoenberger and Cukier 2013). In the post-pandemic era, the digital world has become integral to our daily routines, influencing how we communicate, work, learn, and interact with our surroundings. It continues to evolve rapidly, presenting opportunities and challenges as society navigates the digital age.

Change of Lifestyles Following the Pandemic (The Post-pandemic Era)

The COVID-19 pandemic has substantially altered our daily routines, impacting our way of life, work, and interactions with the world. These circumstances have necessitated these changes, adaptability, and a heightened awareness of health and well-being. These evolving lifestyles are anticipated to continue to shape the "new normal" across various facets of our lives long after the pandemic. In a study conducted by van der Werf et al. (2021) during the initial wave of the pandemic in the Netherlands, it was found that 19.3% of adult respondents adopted healthier habits, such as improved dietary choices, increased physical activity, and relaxation. Most individuals (56.2%) expressed strong motivation to sustain these changes in the post-COVID-19 era, while 12.3% indicated a shift towards unhealthier lifestyles. The global health concerns, governmental regulations, and shifts in work and social dynamics have influenced the worldwide transformation of lifestyle. Therefore, the preceding chapters will explore the evolution of lifestyles at home, residential halls, and university in the aftermath of the pandemic.

The global health crisis has resulted in significant transformations in work patterns, lifestyle choices, and consumer behaviours, impacting travel and tourism, social interactions, health consciousness, sustainability, and entertainment consumption. The imposition of international travel restrictions has redirected attention towards domestic and nature-based tourism, while measures such as social distancing have affected social gatherings and interactions. Moreover, there has been a heightened emphasis on mental health support and an increased focus on health and hygiene practices, such as frequent handwashing and mask-wearing in crowded settings. The pandemic has also prompted a re-evaluation of sustainability and eco-consciousness, leading to initiatives to reduce waste and embrace more sustainable practices. Furthermore, there has been a notable shift towards online entertainment and media consumption due to limited access to traditional venues. One of the most notable lifestyle changes has been the widespread adoption of remote work and hybrid work models. Many employees and employers have realized that remote work is viable and often more effective. This shift has resulted in alterations to daily routines, work environments, and blurred boundaries between work and personal life.

Digital Transformation and Online Services

The COVID-19 outbreak has expedited the digital transformation of diverse sectors, assimilating online shopping, telemedicine, virtual fitness classes, and remote learning into everyday life. This transition has led to a greater dependence on digital platforms for work, education, entertainment, and healthcare consultations. A study conducted in Italy from April 5th to 24th, 2020, sought to examine the immediate effects of the pandemic on dietary habits and lifestyle changes among 4500 individuals aged 12 years and older. The study employed a structured questionnaire to collect demographic information, anthropometric data, dietary and lifestyle habits, and other pertinent data.

Social restrictions and lockdowns have also influenced alterations in consumer spending patterns, with prior research indicating that crises can impact individuals' willingness to purchase both essential and non-essential items. To investigate these changes further, an online survey was administered to 3,833 participants aged 18–64 during the initial peak of the pandemic in Italy (Di Crosta et al. 2021). The study revealed that anxiety and COVID-related fear were linked to consumer behaviour regarding essential items, while depression was predictive of spending on non-essential items. Additionally, personality traits, perceived economic stability, and self-justifications for purchasing influenced consumer behaviour towards essential and non-essential items.

These findings offer a deeper understanding of the shifts in consumer behaviour during the pandemic. They can inform the development of marketing strategies that consider psychological factors to meet consumers' changing needs and emotions. The study highlighted the significant impact of the COVID-19 pandemic on consumer behaviour, leading to increased spending and a heightened psychological impulse to buy essential and non-essential items. Moreover, Di Crosta et al. (2021) study identified various psychological factors as predictors of these changes in consumer behaviour, with distinct predictors for essential and non-essential items. These pandemic-induced changes in spending habits could have long-term effects on consumer behaviour.

It's Important to note that Di Crosta et al. (2021) examined consumer behaviour from a broad perspective using a non-clinical sample, thereby excluding dysfunctional aspects of consumer behaviour such as impulsivity, compulsive buying, and hoarding behaviour, which may be triggered during a crisis. As such, it would be advantageous to combine the results of this study with investigations into the dysfunctional aspects of consumer behaviour in the context of the COVID-19 pandemic. While the study employed an integrative approach to assess the impact of various psychological factors concurrently, this could have resulted in an aggregation bias, potentially obscuring the specific roles of individual factors in influencing consumer behaviour. Future research should adopt a more detailed approach to unravel the role of each factor. Despite these limitations, this study is one of the first to explore changes in consumer behaviour during the COVID-19 pandemic from a behavioural economic perspective. It offers a thorough analysis of the psychological factors driving changes in consumer behaviour. It enhances our understanding of the precursors to changes in consumer behaviour during the ongoing health crisis.

Lifestyles at Work and Learning

During periods of closure and remote work or study, many young individuals have experienced disruptions in their sleep patterns. A study by Zheng et al. (2020) examined the lifestyle behaviours of 631 young adults before and during the pandemic, focusing on physical activity, sedentary behaviour, and sleep. The study revealed a notable decline in physical activity and an increased sedentary behaviour and sleep duration during the pandemic compared to pre-pandemic times. This was attributed to the absence of a structured daily routine and reduced social interaction, leading to irregular sleep patterns. Some young individuals adjusted their sleep schedules to accommodate remote work and online learning, appreciating its flexibility. As they spent more time at home, they engaged in domestic activities and hobbies such as cooking, gardening, and do-it-yourself projects and reconnected with family and loved ones. Increased screen time for remote work, online learning, and entertainment was also identified as contributing to sleep disturbances due to exposure to blue light. The study's findings on the sedentary lifestyle of young adults during the pandemic may inform the development of targeted health education and behaviour interventions for this population during current and future similar events.

Learning Mode for Students During the Pandemic

Young People Defined

The shift from adolescence to adulthood has been described as "emerging adulthood" in numerous scholarly works. It typically refers to the period following adolescence and preceding the assumption of young adult responsibilities. During this phase, individuals transition from school to work, undergo changes in identity and responsibilities, and experience a heightened need for life planning. This pivotal transitional period is also called the volitional years, offering significant opportunities for exploring identity in the realms of relationships, career, and worldviews (Wood et al. 2017). Emerging adulthood is generally recognized as the phase between adolescence and full adulthood, typically occurring between 18 and 25, during which young adults learn social roles and undergo maturation (Hochberg and Konner 2020) (Figs. 1.4 and 1.5).

The suggested age bands by the Association for Young People's Health encompass individuals between 10 and 24 (Rigby et al. 2018). These age groupings align with the definitions provided by the United Nations General Assembly, Unicef, and the World Health Organization (Unicef, 2011; World Health Organization, 2017; United

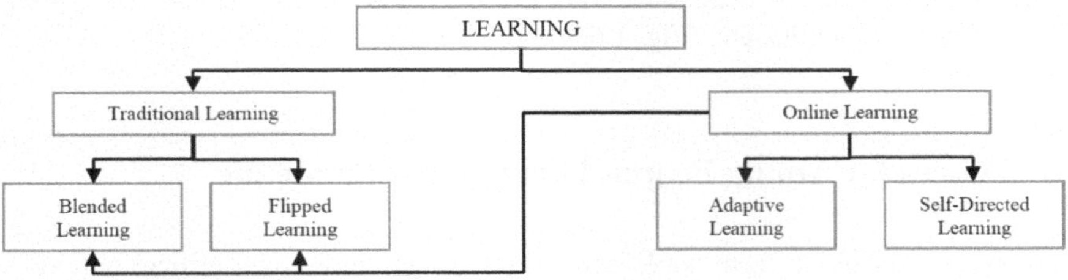

Fig. 1.4 Learning strategies—influence the learners through traditional learning, online learning or hybrid learning environments (obtained from Lalitha and Sreeja 2020)

Entity/Instrument/ Organization	Age	Reference
UN Secretariat/UNESCO/ILO	Youth: 15-24	UN Instruments, Statistics
UN Habitat (Youth Fund)	Youth 15-32	Agenda 21[7]
UNICEF/WHO/UNFPA	Adolescent: 10-19, Young People: 10-24, Youth: 15-24	UNFPA[8]
UNICEF /The Convention on Rights of the Child	Child until 18	UNICEF[9]
The African Youth Charter	Youth: 15-35	African Union, 2006[10]

Fig. 1.5 Several UN entities, instruments and regional organizations have somewhat different definitions of youth, which the United Nations secretariat recognizes (Image obtained from https://www.un.org/esa/socdev/documents/youth/fact-sheets/youth-definition.pdf)

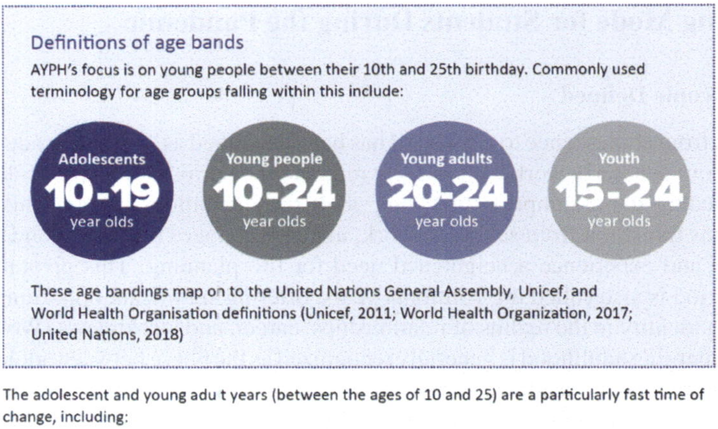

Fig. 1.6 Definition of age bands

Nations, 2018), which categorize individuals as follows: adolescents (10–19 years old), young people (10–24 years old), young adults (20–24 years old), and youth (15–24 years old). Throughout this book we will use different terms to resemble youth to generalize the specific age range we want to cover. This includes adolescents, young people, emerging adults, etc. (Fig. 1.6).

Challenges for Young People Through the Pandemic

The transitional phase from adolescence to early adulthood is a critical period in a child's development as they progress to the next stage of their life. The shift to university and the subsequent personal growth experienced by young adults during their academic pursuits have been extensively studied. For instance, many adolescents undergo significant life changes as they transition to adulthood during their university years, leading to increased independence, self-awareness, and cognitive development (Pittman and Richmond 2008). Research on teenagers and young adults in higher education is particularly pertinent, given the record enrolment of over 2.66 million students in UK universities and higher education institutions in 2020/2021, despite the challenges posed by the COVID-19 pandemic (House of Commons Library 2022). Even before the onset of the pandemic, young adults were identified as a vulnerable demographic for depression (Owens et al. 2022). During the COVID-19 crisis, a study of young adults (aged 18 to 25 years) in the UK revealed heightened levels of psychological distress, anxiety, and depression compared to other age groups, particularly those aged 25 and older (Smith et al. 2020). The increased psychological distress may be attributed to the abrupt changes brought about by the pandemic, including lockdowns and school closures, which necessitated a rapid adaptation to online learning. These changes exacerbated significant stress, particularly academic stress, and placed young adult students at a heightened risk of developing depression (Versteeg and Kappe 2021).

The maturation of the brain and an Individual's environment Interact complexly to influence the development of cognitive, emotional, and social skills during young adulthood (Wood et al. 2017). This interaction becomes even more intricate when considering vulnerable populations, such as adolescents with mental health disorders, which can significantly alter their developmental trajectory at this life stage. Various conditions impacting physical, cognitive, or emotional functioning can obstruct the assumption of adult roles, academic success, workforce transition, and independent living. These conditions are common among young individuals with autism spectrum disorders, those in foster care, those involved in juvenile justice systems, those receiving special education services, and those with severe mental disorders (Courtney 2009; Hendricks and Wehman 2009; Osgood et al. 2005).

The onset of numerous mental health disorders, such as depression and anxiety, often aligns with the transition from adolescence to adulthood, increasing the likelihood of these conditions persisting into adulthood. Moreover, adolescents with severe mental illness may struggle with impulse control and self-regulation (Ong and Thompson 2018; Walker and Gowen 2011), potentially delaying their social and emotional development and impeding their progress in education, relationships, and health management. Young adults with a history of mental health disorders may also experience poorer developmental outcomes, including lower rates of school completion, unemployment or truancy, involvement in criminal activities, substance abuse, and unplanned pregnancies (Wood et al. 2017). This life stage is also a period of increased experimentation with various substances (Schulenberg et al. 2004).

Cigarette smoking rates—12.2% in adolescence increased to 40.2% in young adulthood.
Binge drinking—10.7% to 41.9% in young adulthood.
Illicit drug use from 11.2 to 20.3% in young adulthood.
Heavy alcohol use from 2.6 to 14.9% in young adulthood.

Changes During Adolescence

Adolescence is a pivotal stage in human development, marked by significant physical and Social transformations that signify the transition from childhood to adulthood. These changes profoundly impact an individual's physical, emotional, and social well-being. From a biological standpoint, Hochberg and Konner (2020) characterize emerging adulthood as a period of brain maturation, learning intimacy and support, fortifying existing friendships, engaging in family-oriented socialization, and developing social skills for relationships and reproduction. Žukauskienė et al. (2020)

further note that this transition encompasses subjective criteria such as family capability, relationship maturity, norm conformity, and objective criteria like role changes, biological changes, and legal transitions.

Biological Changes on Adolescents

During the critical phase of adolescence, significant physical and behavioural changes occur. Physical changes typically commence between the ages of 11–12 and may encompass alterations in body shape, height, and the growth of pubic, body, and facial hair. Concurrently, the adolescent brain undergoes substantial development, enhancing self-control, planning, problem-solving, and decision-making skills. This developmental process extends into the mid-20s. The transition from childhood to adulthood, particularly during adolescence (10–19 years), is linked with a significant restructuring of brain networks, as evidenced by longitudinal brain imaging studies (Mills et al. 2016).

Puberty, a crucial biological event in adolescence, generally occurs between the ages of 10 and 14 and involves hormonal changes that stimulate the development of secondary sexual characteristics. These changes include the deepening of the voice and the growth of facial hair in boys, the development of breasts, and the onset of menstruation in girls (Piekarski et al. 2023). Adolescents also undergo rapid physical growth, including increases in height and weight, accompanied by heightened nutritional needs. Hormonal fluctuations, particularly of testosterone and estrogen, play a pivotal role in sexual development and drive changes in mood and behaviour during adolescence. Additionally, differences associated with psychopathology in adolescence are observed in grey and white matter volumes, rates of change, and the interconnectedness of different brain regions. In postnatal brain development, the primary sensorimotor cortex is the first to reach maximum grey matter density, while the prefrontal cortex is the last to mature, and these brain regions are essential for various cognitive functions (Fig. 1.7).

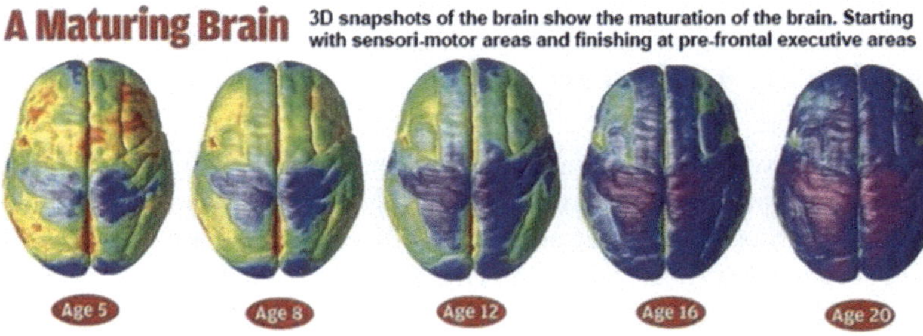

Fig. 1.7 Diagram of a developing youth brain obtained from https://www.quora.com/Is-the-brain-of-a-teenager-of-age-15-completely-developed-like-an-adult

During adolescence, the subcortical regions of the brain, particularly the limbic and reward systems, mature earlier than the prefrontal areas, leading to an imbalance (Frere et al. 2020). This imbalance may account for the characteristic emotional reactivity and propensity for risk-taking behaviours among adolescents, including violence, self-harm, substance abuse, and unprotected sexual activity. The heightened malleability of the adolescent brain allows external influences to significantly impact cortical circuits, fostering both intellectual and emotional development but also rendering adolescents susceptible to detrimental influences and risky behaviours. This biological imbalance between seeking sensation and underdeveloped self-regulatory behaviours contributes to risky conduct. While most adolescents successfully navigate the transition to independence, this period is also associated with an increased prevalence of psychiatric disorders such as psychosis, mood disorders, and substance abuse, believed to stem from disruptions in normal brain maturation. The typical onset age of various mental disorders indicates sensitive developmental stages during which specific processes react strongly and sensitively to environmental influences. Puberty serves as an example of a sensitive period for social learning and the emergence of mental disorders linked to social-cognitive symptoms due to reproductive system maturation and hormonal changes. These hormonal changes impact the brain's neuronal networks, rendering them highly sensitive to biological changes and influencing stress susceptibility and resilience. Studies utilizing diffusion tensor imaging have demonstrated that pubertal hormones influence white matter development and the functional connectivity of the brain (Piekarski et al. 2023), elucidating the immaturity of executive behavioural control during adolescence. The interplay between these factors and individual differences, such as genetic variations, in the onset or moderation of psychopathology is intricate. While neurodevelopment during adolescence represents a vulnerable period for mental illness, the transition from mental health to illness is heavily influenced by social and cultural contexts. The interactions of this context are likely to be intricate, reciprocal, and potentially influenced by age, necessitating a multilevel approach to identify the primary factors contributing to the onset of mental illness in young individuals.

It Is Imperative to develop mental health models that can anticipate the emergence of mental disorders during adolescence, a period marked by significant neurological development, to facilitate early detection. The prefrontal cortex, responsible for decision-making and impulse control, continues to mature. At the same time, the limbic system, associated with emotions and reward processing, develops more rapidly, resulting in heightened emotional reactivity and susceptibility to peer influence (Frere et al. 2020). Recent research has demonstrated substantial reorganization and refinement of the adolescent brain, leading to increased efficiency and adaptability. The "social brain," responsible for comprehending and engaging with others, undergoes constant change. Magnetic resonance imaging studies showed that brain development persists until age 25 (Giedd et al. 2014). Importantly, Chung and Hudziak (2017) delineate various changes in the maturation of the "transitional age brain" and underscore the interplay between mature subcortical areas and immature regulatory areas, with the more developed areas responsible for risk-taking overlapping with the still-developing areas for executive functions. Other studies on brain development revealed the early plasticity of the brain, with observed patterns influenced by enrichment through experience or thinning in deprived states, such as adverse childhood experiences and trauma. Cortical grey and white matter degradation occurs between 0 and 3 years, with a second critical period between 13 and 25 years of age. In addition, white matter maturation continues until the age of 30 in pathways involved in executive functions Piekarski et al. (2023) proposed a "mismatch hypothesis" between three primary brain regions in adolescents to elucidate this behaviour. The nucleus accumbens, the center of motivation and pleasure, and the amygdala, which integrates positive and unpleasant emotional responses, may develop before the prefrontal areas that regulate attention and mood. The difference in time for the brain regions to become fully develop may in part explain how emotion regulation evolves continuously through life experiences. This plasticity also led Chung and Hudziak to advocate for the positive shaping of brain structures and intervention through treatments and therapies, including during the transitional age phase of adolescence.

Sociological Changes on Adolescents

During adolescence, peer groups gain significant importance and exert a strong influence, while families continue to play a crucial role (Morris et al. 2021). Young individuals start to form their sexual identity and seek connections beyond their family. The transition to adulthood has become more extended and varied than in the past (Henkens et al. 2022), and numerous social changes occur in the early 20s (Office for National Statistics 2019). During their late teens and early 20s, young people reassess their relationships with their parents and caregivers, establish their peer network, and strive for financial independence.

The social transition from youth to adulthood Is critical as It has long-term implications, such as job satisfaction, marriage, and family life. In terms of the social aspect of transitioning from youth to adulthood, adolescents undergo role transformation, which can negatively impact their self-esteem (Yang et al. 2020). During this period, they rapidly learn about intimacy and mutual support, intensify existing friendships, engage in family-oriented socialization, become politically aware, form new relationships, and develop their identity as they prepare to become adults. Identity development occurs in multiple dimensions: psychological, personal, and social. These dimensions emerge during the stage of identity formation and stabilization. Once the identity is considered stable, individuals develop a firm ego identity, stabilize their behaviour and character, and acquire community-sanctioned roles. While identity formation during adolescence was traditionally seen as a critical milestone, some adolescents may struggle with multiple new identities due to personal experimentation and exploration.

During intense self-exploration and identity formation, young people explore different aspects of themselves, such as their values, beliefs, and interests, and often experiment with various roles to find their place in society. Key tasks during this period include establishing a sense of personal identity and self-worth, gaining independence, and learning how to cope with life events and challenges (Arain et al. 2013). Adolescents seek independence and responsibility, and everyone in their lives their emotional health and well-being. This includes their peers, who become increasingly important as young people seek acceptance and form close friendships. Peer pressure can significantly impact behaviour, including decisions related to substance use, risk-taking, and conformity. Exploring relationships, including understanding romantic relationships, sexual education, and developing healthy relationships, are crucial aspects of this stage. Adolescents are more likely to engage in risky behaviour, such as experimenting with drugs, alcohol, and risky sexual behaviours. This tendency is linked to the developing brain's heightened reward system and susceptibility to peer influence. Young people become better at weighing risks, learning from experience, and controlling impulses as they mature. They start to question authority and societal standards, debate ideas and opinions, form their code of ethics, and consider their future goals and plans (Romer 2010).

While adolescents seek autonomy, the influence of family relationships remains significant. Disputes with parents may emerge as teenagers navigate new boundaries and obligations, and the nature of family connections can significantly affect a teenager's emotional health. Teenagers encounter decisions regarding their academic pursuits and future professions, including choices related to subjects, extracurricular activities, and higher education, which can impact their long-term prospects. Societal and cultural elements, such as media, technology, and cultural standards, shape teenagers' attitudes and actions, influencing their self-perception, body image, and principles.

Mental Health of Young People

Adolescence represents a distinct and transitional phase characterized by physical and psychological development (Arain et al. 2013; Romer 2010). According to the World Health Organization (2021), approximately 14% of adolescents aged 10–19 globally experience mental health challenges. In China, a study found that 22.2% of children and adolescents exhibited symptoms of depression, with the prevalence of depressive symptoms increasing from 24.5% in the first year of junior secondary school to 40.1% in the third year of senior secondary school (Li et al. 2019; Tang et al. 2019). Many mental health issues in adulthood originate during adolescence and early adulthood, impacting a young person's ability to achieve their full potential in areas such as relationships, family dynamics, and educational and occupational attainment. The adolescent brain's ongoing development helps explain the emotional instability, diminished impulse control, and propensity for risk-taking often observed during this phase (Frere et al. 2020). The adolescent brain is likely to support the specific challenges of this life stage, where novelty-seeking, reward-seeking, and risk-taking behaviours may be adaptive in facilitating the transition from the family environment to increased independence. Understanding the normal and abnormal development of the brain during this period also provides insight into the onset of mental disorders. Mental health issues, particularly anxiety and depression, have become a significant global concern during the COVID-19 pandemic and subsequent lockdowns. A longitudinal study involving 1958 adults in the UK revealed that at least two-thirds of adults experienced persistent mental health symptoms for over 12 weeks, with approximately 8% of adults diagnosed with long-term mental health conditions (McPherson et al. 2021).

Similarly, a study from India indicated that adolescents who contracted COVID-19 were at a heightened risk of developing depression (Daniel et al. 2022). The fear, stress, and uncertainties surrounding COVID-19 may have contributed to the deterioration of mental health. McPherson et al. (2021) suggested that COVID-19-related stress had a detrimental impact on mental health, as individuals were concerned about their health, future, and family during the pandemic. Their heightened concerns were associated with increased levels of anxiety and depression during the pandemic (Haque et al. 2022). This underscores the imperative to enhance mental health interventions to mitigate the psychological crisis among populations at higher risk in the post-COVID era. The wellbeing of young people is pivotal to their overall health and lays the foundation for good health in later life.

Approximately 75% of individuals with mental, emotional, and behavioural disorders experience the onset of these conditions during early adolescence (Emerging Adulthood as a Critical Stage in the Life Course—Handbook of Life Course Health Development—NCBI Bookshelf (nih.gov). Around 50% of those diagnosed with a lifetime mental health disorder first exhibit symptoms before the age of 15, and 75% before the age of 18. In Chap. 4, we will examine and analyze recent evidence, including findings from a qualitative study conducted post-COVID-19 Era (Fig. 1.8).

- The first signs of many serious long-term conditions emerge at this age, including three quarters of lifetime mental health disorders
- Adolescence is a time when risk taking behaviours begin and life-long health behaviours are set in place
- Young people's health is not improving enough compared to other age groups
- Young people are not getting the health services or information they require, and their accounts are often less positive than those of other age groups
- Health inequalities are widespread by the time of transition to adulthood, and some are widening
- Positive trends in young people's health behaviour, such as falls in teenage pregnancy, must be supported in order to continue
- Ignoring chronic adolescent disease costs money, and investing in adolescent wellbeing has benefits beyond just health outcomes
- Effects of poor healthcare in adolescence can last a lifetime
- Investment in adolescence maintains and reinforces successful health interventions delivered in early childhood

Fig. 1.8 There are several compelling reasons to invest in the mental health of young people, including

Sharp Rise in Mental Health Cases (Problem)

In 2023, NHS Digital (England 2023) reported a notable increase in the prevalence of mental health disorders among children and young people in England. This data, collected from 9,117 individuals aged 11–19 between January and October 2017, followed previous surveys conducted in 1999 and 2004. The participants and their parents utilized standardized tools to assess mental disorders based on the International Classification of Disease (ICD-10) diagnostic criteria. The survey revealed that 14.4% of 11–16-year-olds and 16.9% of 17–19-year-olds met the criteria for a mental disorder at the time of the survey, with variations by gender and age. Additionally, it was found that 75% of mental and substance use disorders emerge before the age of 25, with behaviour problems being more common in boys and emotional problems more prevalent in girls, particularly in older age groups. Furthermore, the survey highlighted that a quarter of 11–19 year olds with a mental disorder also had a life-limiting long-term illness, compared to 4.2% of those without a mental disorder. It is important to note that similar prevalence studies are not conducted in other UK countries. However, the Scottish Schools Adolescent Lifestyle and Substance Use Survey (SALSUS) regularly reports on emotional and behavioural problems in Scottish schoolchildren aged 13 and 15.

Depression, which affects around 4.5% of adults in the UK, is marked by persistent feelings of sadness and low mood, as well as a reduced interest or enjoyment in activities and social interactions (American Psychiatric Association, 2013; WHO, 2018). Extensive empirical research has concentrated on depression in university students, consistently finding that an average of 30.6% of students meet the clinical threshold for diagnosis (Ibrahim et al. 2013). This prevalence has been linked to the transitional nature of adolescence and university life, as young adults leave home, gain independence, and take on increased responsibilities.

Anxiety and depression are prevalent emotional disorders among adolescents (World Health Organization 2021). Anxiety is characterized by heightened nervousness, apprehensive thoughts, and physical changes such as elevated blood pressure, while major depressive disorder significantly impacts emotions, cognition, and behaviour (American Psychological Association). The research primarily focused on anxiety and depression to assess the mental health of adolescents (World Health Organization 2021).

The implementation of lockdown measures in the UK has been linked to potential adverse effects on mental health, such as disruptions to sleep and dietary patterns. A longitudinal study conducted by Evans et al. (2021) compared self-reported data from 254 UK undergraduate university students, focusing on their sleep behaviour, general well-being, symptoms of depression and anxiety, and alcohol consumption. The study revealed a notable increase in the percentage of participants meeting the clinical threshold for depression, rising from 15% before the COVID-19 pandemic to 34% during the initial UK lockdown in April and May of 2020. This suggests a significant surge in depression among university students during the lockdown, possibly attributed to concerns about contracting COVID-19, reduced social interaction, and substantial alterations to daily routines and life experiences. Additionally, further research by Owens et al. (2022) examined the impact of the pandemic on mental health and well-being, and the influence of lockdown severity. The study, which involved 389 university students aged 18–25, assessed their sleep quality, well-being, mental health, and rumination. The findings indicated that over 50% of students met the threshold for probable depression at both testing points. Moreover, participants residing in areas with stricter lockdown measures reported significantly higher levels of self-reported mental well-being, suggesting that the severity of lockdown measures has a detrimental impact on mental health. Furthermore, females reported higher levels of depression at both testing points, indicating that they may have encountered more significant challenges with mental health concerning COVID-19.

Recent research conducted by Meda et al. (2021) revealed that the symptoms of depression among university students in Italy worsened significantly during the lockdown period. However, subsequent analysis post-lockdown indicated a return of depression levels in these students to pre-pandemic levels. This discovery underscores the need for further research to comprehensively comprehend the impact of the COVID-19 pandemic on the mental health of students. While the prevalence of depression among university populations is concerning, studies indicate that students engaging in maladaptive coping behaviours exhibit notably higher levels of depression, anxiety, and reduced life satisfaction (Mahmoud et al. 2012). The Office for National Statistics (ONS) does not routinely collect data on cases of depression or anxiety that have been clinically diagnosed. However, it does gather information on symptoms of depression, self-reported anxiety, and other related indicators. In England, data on the prevalence of psychiatric conditions among individuals aged 11–19 can be found in the ONS survey on children's mental health.

Additionally, SALSUS and the Scottish Health Survey provide some data on similar age groups in Scotland (Scottish Government 2017a,b), although these data are not based on clinical diagnoses. Other population surveys also include measures indicating symptoms of depression or anxiety for this age group, even if they do not provide a formal diagnosis. Overall, it appears that a significant proportion of young people aged 10–24 may experience symptoms of depression or anxiety at some point during these years, with young women being more likely to report or experience these symptoms than young men. However, estimates of emotional problems can vary depending on the sample's age and the types of measurements used.

The Most Common Mental Disorders Among Young People

Stress

Stress encompasses the psychological and physical demands placed on an organism by various events, and prolonged exposure to stress can have adverse effects on mental health. The term can refer to the stress response, stimuli, or an ongoing interaction. From a biological perspective, cortisol regulates the stress response based on detecting external and/or internal stimuli. This book will specifically focus on chronic stress and defines stress as an ongoing interaction between an individual and their environment.

Stress is an inherent aspect of daily life, as all organisms encounter challenges from their external surroundings and internal environment (related to personal needs and demands such as hydration, hunger, and happiness). These challenges can range from significant life events like natural disasters, grief, or pandemics to everyday disruptions of routines and minor irritations. Therefore, stress is a behavioural adaptation and a mechanism of evolution, as our responses to stress aid in our survival. The "fight or flight" acute stress response activates the sympathetic nervous system, which plays a role in our innate reactions to dangers and threats in our environment (Hutmacher 2021). Stress can manifest in absolute or relative forms. Absolute stressors are concrete threats that affect all individuals similarly, while relative stresses are situations or events that trigger the stress response in only a subset of people. The intensity of the response can vary, and there are notable differences in how individuals respond to psychological stressors, which have been associated with socioeconomic factors. However, research in this area is limited due to inconsistencies in findings (Lupien et al. 2007).

While some individuals may experience positive outcomes from moderately to highly stressful events, such as improvements in self-concept, relationships, personal growth, and new priorities, the likelihood of stress leading to growth or exposure may depend on the individual's available resources to cope with the situation. Severe traumatic stressors do not have the same effect (Updegraff and Taylor 2000). Mismanaged stress can have long-term effects on an individual's functioning, and the impact of stress varies from person to person. Although the direct causal relationship between certain disorders such as depression, anxiety, and post-traumatic stress disorder and stress is not established, research consistently indicates that stress can exacerbate physiological and mental symptoms. Chronic stress has been found to elevate blood pressure, weaken the immune system, and disrupt sleep, leading to irritability or difficulties in concentration, ultimately affecting performance at work or in education and impacting quality of life (Mariotti 2015). Previous research recognizes the significance of stress and its association with negative mental health, suggesting that for vulnerable individuals, social support partially mitigates the impact of stress and mental health disorders (Gulliver et al. 2010). Findings indicate that individuals who perceive high levels of stress and negative events are more likely to have negative cognitions.

Academic Stress and Mental Health in Adolescents

Adolescents face various pressures in their daily lives, with academic stress being a significant factor (Ang and Huan 2006; Misra and McKean 2000; Qidwai et al. 2010). Studies have shown that Chinese adolescents experience higher levels of academic stress compared to their Western counterch, a trend also observed in other Asian regions such as Korea, Singapore, and Hong Kong (Ho and Yip 2003; Lee and Larson 2000). Severe academic stress in Chinese high schools has been found to negatively impact intrinsic motivation in 10th grade, while enhancing motivation by 12th grade (Liu et al. 2020). Additionally, academic stress has been identified as a risk factor for predicting depression among adolescents (Jiang et al. 2021). Furthermore, a study of 1,533 adolescents aged 14 to 19 revealed that academic stress directly predicts anxiety and depression, both of which are inversely related to physical activity and sleep duration (Zhu et al. 2021). There is a significant correlation between adolescents' academic stress and mental health. However, further investigation is needed to understand the specific impact of academic stress on mental health compared to other factors such as sleep.

Adolescents encounter many stressors in their daily lives, with academic stress emerging as a prominent concern (Ang and Huan 2006; Misra and McKean 2000; Qidwai et al. 2010). Research indicates that Chinese adolescents experience heightened levels of academic stress in comparison to their Western counterparts, a pattern also observed in other Asian regions including Korea, Singapore, and Hong Kong (Ho and Yip 2003; Lee and Larson 2000). Notably, severe academic stress in Chinese high schools has been found to have a detrimental impact on intrinsic motivation in 10th grade, while bolstering motivation by 12th grade (Liu et al. 2020). Moreover, academic stress has been identified as a risk factor for predicting depression among adolescents (Jiang et al. 2021). Additionally, a study involving 1,533 adolescents aged 14 to 19 revealed that academic stress directly predicts anxiety and depression, both of which are inversely associated with physical activity and sleep duration (Zhu et al. 2021). These findings underscore a significant correlation between adolescents' academic stress and their mental health. Nevertheless, further exploration is warranted to comprehend the specific influence of academic stress on mental health compared to other factors, such as sleep.

Depression and Loneliness

Before the COVID-19 pandemic, Wawera and McCamley (2019) noted that loneliness is a widespread issue closely linked to depression. Government-imposed lockdown measures restricted social gatherings and mandated individuals to remain at home with limited activities. The abrupt disruptions to daily routines during the

COVID-19 pandemic were found to be correlated with heightened levels of loneliness and depression (Frankeberger et al. 2022). The limitations on social interactions also led to a significant increase in loneliness among individuals (Shah et al. 2020). Previous studies have compared data from before and during the COVID-19 pandemic. In 2018, 3.9% of young adults in the United States, aged 18 to 29, self-reported experiencing psychological distress. This figure has since risen to 13.6% reporting psychological distress and 13.8% reporting feelings of loneliness (McGinty et al. 2020). This study also revealed that young adults were experiencing elevated levels of loneliness, heightened concerns related to COVID-19, and low tolerance for psychological distress. These three factors were strongly associated with meeting the clinical criteria for depression (Liu et al. 2020). During lockdown, students could only connect with their peers through virtual social platforms. While some research may argue that students can benefit from virtual social platforms and thus alleviate loneliness, previous research has shown that virtual social interaction did not significantly affect loneliness or depression among young adults during the COVID-19 pandemic (Towner et al. 2022).

Many young individuals transition from living with their families to living independently, a change that can contribute to mental health challenges. For instance, a study conducted by Kantohe and Kurnijuanto (2021) revealed that 33.3% of college students aged 18 to 28 who resided alone experienced depression, with 25% displaying severe symptoms. This phenomenon is partially attributed to the difficulties associated with establishing one's identity during the period of emerging adulthood, leading to heightened concerns and stress that contribute to psychological distress. Furthermore, a study in the United States indicated that nearly 50% of undergraduate students experienced increased psychological distress due to COVID-19-related anxieties, encompassing financial worries, social stress, and uncertainty about the future, with those reporting more concerns also reporting higher levels of depression (Liu et al. 2020). Students encountering difficulties in learning and feelings of isolation during the pandemic necessitate additional support and interventions. Concurrently, individuals begin to cultivate the attributes essential for independence, mature relationships, adult responsibilities, and education and training for their future careers. Recent societal shifts have resulted in young people dedicating more time to exploring career opportunities, pursuing further education, experiencing heightened financial reliance on their families, and postponing marriage and parenthood (Shek et al. 2019).

Suicide and Self-harm

Suicide is a relatively infrequent occurrence among young individuals, yet it remains a significant concern for public health. The reduction of suicide rates is a crucial measure of success for Public Health England, and the Scottish Government has recently established a goal to decrease suicide by 20%. Data from the Office for

National Statistics indicates that suicide rates for young men and women aged 15–19 and 20–24 in the UK are higher in the older age group and among young men compared to young women, which differs from the pattern observed for self-harm. The data also shows a peak in suicide rates in the mid-1990s, followed by a decline until around 2005. Subsequently, rates have remained relatively stable, with a slight increase in the last five years for young men and women in the 15–19 age group. In 2017, the rates for young women were 3.5 per 100,000 for 15–19 year-olds and 3.9 for 20–24 year-olds, while for young men, the rates were 7.1 for 15–19 year-olds and 11.4 for 20–24 year-olds.

Self-harm, which often involves intentional cutting or scratching and potentially deliberate overdose, is a significant issue in the field of mental health among young individuals, especially those aged 11 to 25 (Association for Young People's Health 2013). Although self-harm is not officially classified as a separate psychiatric disorder, it serves as a sign of severe mental distress. However, due to the private and sensitive nature of this behaviour, there is a scarcity of reliable data on young individuals who do not seek help from accident and emergency services or other resources. Recent efforts have aimed to estimate the prevalence of self-harm among young people. For instance, in the English Health Behaviour in School-aged Children study (Geulayov et al. 2022), 22% of the 15-year-olds surveyed reported engaging in self-harm. These rates were three times higher among 11–16-year-olds compared to 17–19-year-olds.

Most individuals who participate in self-harming behaviours have indicated that they engage in these acts at least once a month, according to Liu (2023). According to the Adult Psychiatric Morbidity Survey, 25.7% of young women aged 16–24 disclosed engaging in self-harm, in contrast to 9.7% of young men. In this age group, self-harm predominantly manifested as self-cutting. The Child and Adolescent Self-Harm in Europe (CASE) study revealed that 15.5% of adolescents aged 13–18 in England reported a history of self-harm, with the median age of onset being 13 years. Moreover, over half (54.9%) of young women aged 13–15 reported engaging in self-harm within the past year. Time trends in self-harm were assessed through face-to-face interviews in the Adult Psychiatric Morbidity Survey, indicating an overall increase in reported self-harm over time. Further insights into suicidal behaviour among older individuals can be gleaned from the Adult Psychiatric Morbidity Survey. The survey indicated that 6.7% of the population had made suicide attempts, with a higher prevalence among women (8%) compared to men (5.4%). There are also concerns about the suicide rates among university students. Data from the Office for National Statistics showed an increase in the suicide rate per 100,000 undergraduate students from 2012/13 to 2016/17, particularly among male students. However, it is important to note that during the same period, higher education students in England and Wales had a significantly lower suicide rate compared to the general population of similar age groups.

Internet Addiction

Internet addiction is defined by intense desires to use the internet and experiencing distress when these desires are not satisfied (Shaw and Black 2008). It is approximated that around 14% of internet users meet the criteria for internet addiction, with the phenomenon being identified in 1995 (Tao et al. 2010). Despite this, internet addiction has not been formally acknowledged as a disorder and has not been included in any versions of the DSM (Tateno et al. 2019). Nevertheless, several theories have been suggested to elucidate the reasons behind individuals developing an addiction to the internet.

The DSM-5 recognizes internet gaming disorder as a subject for further investigation, but it does not encompass issues related to general internet usage, online gambling, or social media and smartphone use. According to Skinner's theory of positive reinforcement, individuals may develop an addiction to the internet due to the positive emotions experienced during its use (Longstreet et al. 2019). This positive reinforcement is often linked to social media use, as it offers an accessible means for individuals to communicate and socialize without physical interaction, leading to emotional connections and social support (Demircioğlu and Köse 2018). Moreover, receiving likes and comments on social media posts can further reinforce positive emotions and promote continued use of social media platforms (Bashir and Bhat 2017). Additionally, it has been proposed that individuals who have been subjected to bullying may turn to the Internet as a means of escape, leading to dependence and potential addiction (Jia et al. 2018). Internet gaming addiction has also been identified as a type and cause of internet addiction, with users experiencing adverse effects when unable to access online gaming, such as sleep disturbances and mood swings (Jiang 2014). Furthermore, individuals who engage in online gaming are at risk of developing internet addiction and facing associated negative consequences (Jiang 2014; Baturay and Toker 2019).

The COVID-19 pandemic has had a notable impact on the sleep and dietary behaviours of young individuals. While the effects vary among individuals, several general trends and changes have emerged due to the disruptions caused by the pandemic to daily life, routines, and mental well-being. This paper will analyze young people's modified sleep patterns and eating habits in the post-pandemic period. In this section, we have explored the shift from adolescence to emerging adulthood, marked by significant physical, cognitive, emotional, and social changes. Identifying these changes is crucial for comprehending how young people have navigated the major challenges during the pandemic. The COVID-19 pandemic has significantly influenced the lives of young individuals, presenting them with distinct obstacles and uncertainties.

Current Mental Health Service

In recent years, there have been significant advancements in mental health services for young individuals in the United Kingdom, reflecting a growing recognition of the importance of addressing mental health issues within this demographic. This paper will examine the key components of the current mental health services for young people in the UK, presenting pertinent information and statistics. A significant development in the UK is introducing "Future in Mind" strategy, initiated in 2015. This strategy seeks to enhance mental health services for children and young people by advocating for early intervention, prevention, and the integration of services. It underscores the significance of collaborative efforts to provide comprehensive support across various sectors, such as education, health, and social care.

According to a 2020 report by the Education Policy Institute (EPI), there has been an increase in the funding allocated to mental health services for young people in the UK. The report notes that the government has committed £2.3 billion to mental health services for children and young people, focusing on expanding access to support and reducing waiting times. One notable advancement in providing mental health services for young individuals in the United Kingdom is the implementation of Mental Health Support Teams (MHSTs) within educational institutions. These teams are comprised of mental health professionals who operate within school environments, offering early intervention and assistance to students. The primary objective is to detect and address mental health issues at an early stage, thereby mitigating the necessity for more intensive interventions in the future. Furthermore, the UK has broadened its digital mental health services for young people alongside school-based support. Online platforms such as Kooth and Childline provide virtual counselling and support, offering accessible and confidential channels for young individuals to seek assistance. The utilization of these services has increased, indicating a growing demand for digital mental health support.

Despite the advancements in the UK's mental health services for young people, persistent challenges remain. The EPI report underscores the significant disparities in the availability and standard of services across different regions. Prolonged waiting times for specialized support and limited access to specific interventions remain areas of concern. In summary, while the UK's current mental health services for young people have shown notable progress in recent years, particularly in early intervention, service integration, and digital support, there are still issues such as regional discrepancies and waiting times, that require attention to ensure timely access to high-quality mental health care for all young individuals. One notable aspect of contemporary mental health services for adolescents is the prioritization of early intervention and prevention. These services place a strong emphasis on identifying mental health issues at an early stage to prevent their progression into more severe conditions. This approach is essential for promoting positive mental well-being and mitigating the long-term impact of mental health problems. Additionally, contemporary mental health services for adolescents emphasize the importance of accessibility and inclusivity. Efforts are being made to ensure that mental health services are easily accessible to all young individuals, regardless of their background or socioeconomic status. This includes offering services in educational institutions, community centers, and online platforms, facilitating easier access to assistance and support for young people.

In recent years, there has been an increasing recognition of the importance of a comprehensive approach to mental health. Mental health services for young people now not only focus on addressing specific mental health conditions but also on promoting overall well-being. This involves supporting physical health, social connections, and emotional resilience. These services aim to empower young individuals to lead healthy and fulfilling lives by adopting a comprehensive approach. In summary, current mental health services for young people aim to provide accessible, early intervention and holistic support. While progress has been achieved, areas still require improvement to ensure that all young individuals have access to timely and effective mental health care.

Other Factors Impacting the Mental Health of Young People

Numerous research studies have investigated the various factors that contribute to mental health challenges in adolescents, encompassing physiological, psychological, social, and cultural influences, with a specific emphasis on the role of sleep. Sleep is critical to overall health and well-being, impacting cognitive function and emotional regulation (Hirshkowitz et al. 2015; Zeek et al. 2015). Inadequate sleep can compromise these functions and potentially lead to health issues and mental health disorders, such as depression (Goldstein and Walker 2014). Despite the recommended daily sleep duration of 8 to 10 h for adolescents aged 14 to 17 in the United States, many teenagers still need to meet this guideline (Hirshkowitz et al. 2015). For example, adolescents in the United States aged 13 to 18 reported an average weekday sleep duration of 7.72 h (Zhang et al. 2017), and high school students in Virginia reported an average of 6.5 h of sleep per school night (Winsler et al. 2015). Similarly, Chinese high school students averaged 6.77 ± 0.89 h of sleep per day. In addition to sleep deprivation, adolescents frequently encounter poor sleep quality.

Several studies have shown that sleep issues can have a significant impact on attention, academic performance, behaviour, and psychosocial functioning of adolescents (Curcio et al. 2006; Fallone et al. 2001; Peltz et al. 2017). While a shorter duration of sleep does not necessarily indicate poor sleep quality, the adolescent brain can adapt to the effects of sleep restriction, potentially increasing the amount of slow-wave sleep during the available hours (Voderholzer et al. 2011). Various research works have explored the correlation between sleep, mental health, and other factors such as physical activities (Gilchrist et al. 2021), academic stress (Misra and McKean 2000), mobile phone addiction (Ma et al. 2022), internet gaming disorder (Wong et al. 2020), and parental rules (Meijer et al. 2001). However, there is limited research specifically examining the interactions among Chinese adolescents' mental health, sleep quality, academic stress, and attachment relationships collectively, indicating a need for further investigation in the existing literature.

Attachment Relationships and Mental Health in Adolescents

Attachment relationships, defined as emotional bonds that develop between individuals over time and distance (Ainsworth and Bell 1970), are primarily observed within the framework of parent–child relationships. This bond is considered a fundamental element of socialization and significantly impacts on future interpersonal connections. The quality of parent–child relationships is closely associated with various outcomes in children, including emotional challenges such as depression, anxiety, and withdrawal (Pinquart 2017; Pinquart and Kauser 2018). As adolescents seek greater independence, they tend to transition their reliance from parents to peers (Allen 2008). Interactions with peers become increasingly prioritized over parent–child attachment (Guarnieri et al. 2010; Kerns et al. 2007). Consequently, attachments to parents and peers become crucial in the lives of most adolescents and significantly influence their mental well-being. Adolescents who establish secure attachments with their parents and peers and foster stronger connections with their school environment tend to demonstrate better mental health outcomes (Oldfield et al. 2016). Conversely, those who form more insecure attachments with parents and peers may be at a higher risk of developing depressive symptoms (Allen et al. 2007). Peer relationships also impact adolescents' sleep patterns, but their combined influence with factors such as academic stress and sleep quality remains uncertain. Therefore, this area represents a meaningful direction for further investigation.

Conclusion

In this chapter, we have provided an overview of the current circumstances young people face in the post-pandemic era. This period is characterized by a shift from traditional to digital modes of shopping, working, and studying, due to the global population's experience with the pandemic. We have specifically focused on young people due to the complex and dynamic nature of emerging adulthood, which involves significant biological and sociological changes that contribute to developing adolescent identity and acquiring skills necessary for adulthood. Given that young people are particularly receptive to the new digital way of life, it is essential to understand how these changes may impact them, and whether the digital world is beneficial or detrimental to their well-being. This understanding is crucial for parents, educators, and society in supporting adolescents' healthy development. When examining the mental health of young adults, it is important to consider various factors such as their sleep patterns, eating habits, social support, coping strategies, and mental health status. Additionally, it is important to be inclusive of minority groups, such as international students, when considering the learning experiences of young people in emerging adulthood.

Through the studies presented in this book, we aim to evaluate the challenges and limitations of current mental health services for young people, make recommendations for addressing these issues, and improve the provision of appropriate study models and mental health care for all young individuals. One significant issue that has been discussed is the impact of the pandemic on mental health and well-being, resulting in heightened levels of stress, anxiety, and social isolation among young individuals. Empirical studies in subsequent sections will further explore these mental health challenges and the importance of providing adequate support and resources to address them. Another primary concern is the disruption to education, with the closure of schools and universities or the transition to remote learning. This has presented challenges for young individuals in adapting to online education and maintaining their academic progress. Therefore, the next chapter will examine the potential implications of this disruption on students' motivation and learning perspectives.

References

Arain M, Haque M, Johal L, Mathur P, Nel W, Rais A, Sandhu R, Sharma S (2013) Maturation of the adolescent brain. Neuropsychiatr Dis Treat 9:449–461. https://doi.org/10.2147/NDT.S39776

Arora T, Grey I (2020) Health behaviour changes during covid-19 and the potential consequences: a mini-review. J Health Psychol 25(9):1155–1163. https://doi.org/10.1177/1359105320937053

Bashir H, Bhat SA (2017) Effects of social media on mental health: a review. Int J Indian Psychol 4(3):125–131. https://doi.org/10.25215/0403.134

Baturay MH, Toker S (2019) Internet addiction among college students: some causes and effects. Educ Inf Technol 24(5):2863–2885. https://doi.org/10.1007/s10639-019-09894-3

Cao W, Fang Z, Hou G, Han M, Xu X, Dong J, Zheng J (2020) The psychological impact of the covid-19 epidemic on college students in China. Psychiatry Res 287:112934

Castells M (2010) The information age: Economy, society and culture. Rise Netw Soc I. Wiley-Blackwell, Oxford

Chang J, Yuan Y, Wang D (2020) Mental health status and it's influencing factors among college students during the epidemic of COVID-19. Nan fang yi ke da xue bao= J South Med Univ 40(2):171–176

Chung WW, Hudziak JJ (2017) The transitional age brain. Child Adolesc Psychiatry Clin N Am 26:157–175. https://doi.org/10.1016/j.chc.2016.12.017

Courtney ME (2009) The difficult transition to adulthood for foster youth in the US: Implications for the state as corporate parent and commentaries. Soc Policy Rep 23(1):1–20

Curcio G, Ferrara M, De Gennaro L (2006) Sleep loss, learning capacity and academic performance. Sleep Med Rev 10(5):323–337

Daniel M, Prashad L, Kaur A, Kallakuri S, Devarapalli S, Sagar R, Maulik PK (2022) Covid-19, adversities and depression among older adolescents in urban slums of India. Asian J Psychiatry 74:103194. https://doi.org/10.1016/j.ajp.2022.103194

Demircioğlu ZI, Köse AG (2018) Effects of attachment styles, dark triad, rejection sensitivity, and relationship satisfaction on social media addiction: a mediated model. Curr Psychol 40(1):414–428. https://doi.org/10.1007/s12144-018-9956-x

Di Crosta A, Ceccato I, Marchetti D, La Malva P, Maiella R, Cannito L, Cipi M, Mammarella N, Palumbo R, Verrocchio MC, Palumbo R, Di Domenico A (2021) Psychological factors and consumer behaviour during the covid-19 pandemic. PLoS ONE 16(8):e0256095. https://doi.org/10.1371/journal.pone.0256095

Dong H, Yang F, Lu X, Hao W (2020) Internet addiction and related psychological factors among children and adolescents in China during the coronavirus Disease 2019 (Covid-19) epidemic. Front Psychiatry:11

Ebrahim SH, Ahmed QA, Gozzer E, Schlagenhauf P, Memish ZA (2020) Covid-19 and community mitigation strategies in a pandemic. BMJ: Br Med J (Online):368

England N (2023) NHS England one in five children and young people had a probable mental disorder in 2023. https://www.england.nhs.uk/2023/11/one-in-five-children-and-young-people-had-a-probable-mental-disorder-in-2023/#:~:text=The%20Mental%20Health%20of%20Children,%2Dolds%20it%20was%2021.7%25

Evans S, Alkan E, Bhangoo JK, Tenenbaum H, Ng-Knight T (2021) Effects of the covid-19 lockdown on mental health, well-being, sleep, and alcohol use in a UK student sample. Psychiatry Res 298:113819. https://doi.org/10.1016/j.psychres.2021.113819

Fallone G, Acebo C, Arnedt JT, Seifer R, Carskadon MA (2001) Effects of acute sleep restriction on behaviour, sustained attention, and response inhibition in children. Percept Mot Skills 93(1):213–229. https://doi.org/10.2466/PMS.93.5.213-229

Frankeberger J, Sumetsky N, Friedman MR, Burke JG, Coulter RW, Mair C (2022) Changes in activity locations during the covid-19 pandemic and associations with depression, anxiety, loneliness, and alcohol use. Wellbeing Space Soc 3:100092. https://doi.org/10.1016/j.wss.2022.100092

Frere PB, Vetter NC, Artiges E, Filippi I, Miranda R, Vulser H, Paillère-Martinot ML, Ziesch V, Conrod P, Cattrell A, Walter H, Gallinat J, Bromberg U, Jurk S, Menningen E, Frouin V, Papadopoulos Orfanos D, Stringaris A (2020) Sex effects on structural maturation of the limbic system and outcomes on emotional regulation during adolescence. NeuroImage 210:116441

Geulayov G, Casey D, Bale L, Brand F, Townsend E, Ness J, Rehman M, Waters K, Clements C, Farooq B, Kapur N, Hawton K (2022) Self-harm in children 12 years and younger: characteristics and outcomes based on the multicentre study of self-harm in England. Soc Psychiatry Psychiatr Epidemiol 57(1):139–148. https://doi.org/10.1007/s00127-021-02133-6

Giedd J, Raznahan A, Alexander-Bloch A, Schmitt E, Gogtay N, Rapoport J (2014) Child psychiatry branch of the national institute of mental health longitudinal structural magnetic resonance imaging study of human brain development. Neuropsychopharmacology 40(1):43–49. https://doi.org/10.1038/npp.2014.236

Gilchrist JD, Battista K, Patte KA, Faulkner G, Carson V, Leatherdale ST (2021) Effects of reallocating physical activity, sedentary behaviours, and sleep on mental health in adolescents. Mental Health Phys Act 20:100380. https://doi.org/10.1016/j.mhpa.2020.100380

Goldstein AN, Walker MP (2014) The role of sleep in emotional brain function. Annu Rev Clin Psychol 10(1):679–708. https://doi.org/10.1146/annurev-clinpsy-032813-153716

Guarnieri S, Ponti L, Tani F (2010) The Inventory of Parent and Peer Attachment (IPPA): a study on the validity of styles of adolescent attachment to parents and peers in an Italian sample. TPM-Test Psychometrics Methodol Appl Psychol 17(3):103–130

Gulliver A, Griffiths KM, Christensen H (2010) Perceived barriers and facilitators to mental health help-seeking in young people: a systematic review. BMC Psychiatry 10(1). https://doi.org/10.1186/1471-244x-10-113

Haque MR, Ul Islam MS, Hasan MK, Hossain MS, Hossain Khan MA, Islam F (2022) Determinants of anxiety and depression among Bangladeshi adults during COVID-19 lockdown: An online survey. Heliyon 8(5):e09415. https://doi.org/10.1016/j.heliyon.2022.e09415

Hendricks DR, Wehman P (2009) Transition from school to adulthood for youth with autism spectrum disorders: review and recommendations. Focus Autism Other Dev Disabil 24(2):77–88

Henkens JHD, Kalmijn M, de Valk HAG (2022) Life satisfaction development in the transition to adulthood: differences by gender and immigrant background. J Youth Adolesc 51(2):305–319. https://doi.org/10.1007/s10964-021-01560-7

Hirshkowitz M, Whiton K, Albert SM, Alessi C, Bruni O, DonCarlos L, Hazen N, Herman J, Adams Hillard PJ, Katz ES, Kheirandish-Gozal L, Neubauer DN, O'Donnell AE, Ohayon M, Peever J, Rawding R, Sachdeva RC, Setters B, Vitiello MV, Ware JC (2015) National Sleep Foundation's updated sleep duration recommendations: final report. Sleep Health 1(4):233–243. https://doi.org/10.1016/j.sleh.2015.10.004

Ho KC, Yip J (2003) Youth.sg: The state of youth in Singapore. National Youth Council, Singapore

Hochberg Z, Konner M (2020) Emerging adulthood, a pre-adult life-history stage. Front Endocrinol 10. https://doi.org/10.3389/fendo.2019.00918

Hutmacher F (2021) Putting stress in historical context: why it is important that being stressed out was not a way to be a person 2,000 years ago. Front Psychol 12. https://doi.org/10.3389/fpsyg.2021.539799

Ibrahim AK, Kelly SJ, Adams CE, Glazebrook C (2013) A systematic review of studies of depression prevalence in university students. J Psychiatr Res 47(3):391–400. https://doi.org/10.1016/j.jpsychires.2012.11.015

Jia J, Li D, Li X, Zhou Y, Wang Y, Sun W, Zhao L (2018) Peer victimization and adolescent internet addiction: the mediating role of psychological security and the moderating role of teacher-student relationships. Comput Hum Behav 85:116–124. https://doi.org/10.1016/j.chb.2018.03.042

Jiang Q (2014) Internet addiction among young people in china: internet connectedness, online gaming, and academic performance decrement. Internet Res 24(1):2–20. https://doi.org/10.1108/IntR-01-2013-0004

Jiang S, Ren Q, Jiang C, Wang L (2021) Academic stress and depression of Chinese adolescents in junior high schools: Moderated mediation model of school burnout and self-esteem. J Affect Disord 295:384–389. https://doi.org/10.1016/j.jad.2021.08.085

Kantohe T, Kurnijuanto G (2021) Prevalence of depression among college students living alone in pandemic 2020. Eur Psychiatry 64(S1):S277–S277. https://doi.org/10.1192/j.eurpsy.2021.743

Kerns KA, Abraham MM, Schlegelmilch A, Morgan TA (2007) Mother—child attachment in later middle childhood: assessment approaches and associations with mood and emotion regulation. Attach Hum Dev 9(1):33–53. https://doi.org/10.1080/14616730601151441

Koh D (2020) COVID-19 lockdowns throughout the world. Occup Med 70(5):322–322. https://doi.org/10.1093/occmed/kqaa073

Lai A, Lee L, Wang M, Feng Y, Lai T, Ho L et al (2020) Mental health impacts of the COVID-19 pandemic on international university students, related stressors, and coping strategies. Front Psychiatry 11. https://doi.org/10.3389/fpsyt.2020.584240

Lalitha TB, Sreeja PS (2020) Personalised self-directed learning recommendation system. Proc Comput Sci 171:583–592. https://doi.org/10.1016/j.procs.2020.04.063

Lee M, Larson R (2000) The Korean 'Examination Hell': Long hours of studying, distress, and depression. J Youth Adolesc 29:249–271. https://doi.org/10.1023/A:1005160717081

Li JY, Li J, Liang JH, Qian S, Jia RX, Wang YQ, Xu Y (2019) Depressive symptoms among children and adolescents in china: A systematic review and meta-analysis. Med Sci Monit 25:7459–70. https://doi.org/10.12659/MSM.916774

Liang SW, Chen RN, Liu LL, Li X, Chen JB, Tang SY, Zhao J (2020) The psychological impact of the COVID-19 epidemic on Guangdong college students: the difference between seeking and not seeking psychological help. Front Psychol 11:2231

Liu RT (2023) The epidemiology of non-suicidal self-injury: lifetime prevalence, sociodemographic and clinical correlates, and treatment use in a nationally representative sample of adults in England. Psychol Med 53(1):274–282. https://doi.org/10.1017/S003329172100146X

Liu X, Zhao Y, Li J, Dai J, Wang X, Wang S (2020) Factor structure of the 10-item perceived stress scale and measurement invariance across genders among chinese adolescents. Front Psychol 11(537). https://doi.org/10.3389/fpsyg.2020.00537

Longstreet P, Brooks S, Gonzalez ES (2019) Internet addiction: when the positive emotions are not so positive. Technol Soc 57:76–85. https://doi.org/10.1016/j.techsoc.2018.12.004

Lupien SJ, Maheu F, Tu M, Fioccc A, Schramek TE (2007) The effects of stress and stress hormones on human cognition: implications for the field of brain and cognition. Brain Cogn 65(3):209–237. https://doi.org/10.1016/j.bandc.2007.02.007

Ma A, Yang Y, Guo S, Li X, Zhang S, Chang H (2022) Adolescent resilience and mobile phone addiction in Henan Province of China: impacts of chain mediating, coping style. PLoS ONE 17(12):e0278182. https://doi.org/10.1371/journal.pone.0278182

Mahmoud JSR, Staten RT, Hall LA, Lennie TA (2012) The relationship among young adult college students' depression, anxiety, stress, demographics, life satisfaction, and coping styles. Issues Ment Health Nurs 33(3):149–156. https://doi.org/10.3109/01612840.2011.632708

Mariotti A (2015) The effects of chronic stress on health: new insights into the molecular mechanisms of brain–body communication. Future Sci OA 1(3). https://doi.org/10.4155/fso.15.21

McGinty EE, Presskreischer R, Han H, Barry CL (2020) Psychological distress and loneliness reported by US adults in 2018 and April 2020. JAMA 324(1):93–94. https://doi.org/10.1001/jama.2020.9740

McGorry PD, Mei C, Möller-Leimkühler AM (2019) Early intervention in youth mental health: Progress and future directions.Evid-Based Ment Health 22(4):182–184

McPherson KE, McAloney-Kocaman K, McGlinchey E, Faeth P, Armour C (2021) Longitudinal analysis of the UK covid-19 psychological wellbeing study: trajectories of anxiety, depression and covid-19-related stress symptomology. Psychiatry Res 304:114138. https://doi.org/10.1016/j.psychres.2021.114138

Means B, Toyama Y, Murphy R, Bakia M, Jones K (2014) Evaluation of evidence-based practices in online learning: a meta-analysis and review of online learning studies. US Department of Education

Meda N, Pardini S, Slongo I, Bodini L, Zordan MA, Rigobello P, Visioli F, Novara C (2021) Students' mental health problems before, during, and after covid-19 lockdown in Italy. J Psychiatr Res 134:69–77. https://doi.org/10.1016/j.jpsychires.2020.12.045

Meijer AM, Habekothé RT, Van Den Wittenboer GLH (2001) Mental health, parental rules and sleep in pre-adolescents. J Sleep Res 10(4):297–302. https://doi.org/10.1046/j.1365-2869.2001.00265.x

Mills KL, Goddings AL, Herting MM, Meuwese R, Blakemore SJ, Crone EA, Dahl RE, Güroğlu B, Raznahan A, Sowell ER, Tamnes CK (2016) Structural brain development between childhood and adulthood: convergence across four longitudinal samples. Neuroimage 141:273–281. https://doi.org/10.1016/j.neuroimage.2016.07.044

Misra R, McKean M (2000) College students' academic stress and its relation to their anxiety, time management, and leisure satisfaction. Am J Health Stud 16:41

Moghe K, Kotecha D, Patil M (2020) Covid-19 and mental health: a study of its impact on students. medRxiv. https://doi.org/10.1101/2020.08.05.20160499

Morris AS, Ratliff EL, Cosgrove KT, Steinberg L (2021) We know even more things: a decade review of parenting research. J Res Adolesc off J Soc Res Adolesc 31(4):870–888. https://doi.org/10.1111/jora.12641

Oldfield J, Humphrey N, Hebron J (2016) The role of parental and peer attachment relationships and school connectedness in predicting adolescent mental health outcomes. Child Adolesc Mental Health 21(1):21–29

Ong E, Thompson C (2018) The importance of coping and emotion regulation in the occurrence of suicidal behaviour. Psychol Rep 122(4):1192–1210. https://doi.org/10.1177/0033294118781855

Osgood DW, Foster EM, Flanagan C, Ruth GR (2005) On your own without a net: the transition to adulthood for vulnerable populations. University of Chicago Press

Owens M, Townsend E, Hall E, Bhatia T, Fitzgibbon R, Miller-Lakin F (2022) Mental health and well-being of young people in the UK during lockdown (covid-19). Int J Environ Res Public Health 19(3):1132. https://doi.org/10.3390/ijerph19031132

Peltz JS, Rogge RD, Connolly H, O'Connor TG (2017) A process-oriented model linking adolescents' sleep hygiene and psychological functioning: the moderating role of school start times. Sleep Health 3:465–471. https://doi.org/10.1016/j.sleh.2017.08.003

Penttilä J, van Noort B, Imagen consortium et al (2020) Sex effects on structural maturation of the limbic system and outcomes on emotional regulation during adolescence. Neuroimage 210:116441. https://doi.org/10.1016/j.neuroimage.2019.116441

Piekarski DJ, Colich NL, Ho TC (2023) The effects of puberty and sex on adolescent white matter development: a systematic review. Dev Cogn Neurosci 60:101214. https://doi.org/10.1016/j.dcn.2023.101214

Pinquart M (2017) Associations of parenting dimensions and styles with externalizing problems of children and adolescents: an updated meta-analysis. Dev Psychol 53(5):873–932. https://doi.org/10.1037/dev0000295

Pinquart M, Kauser R (2018) Do the associations of parenting styles with behaviour problems and academic achievement vary by culture? Results from a meta-analysis. Cultur Divers Ethnic Minor Psychol 24(1):75–100. https://doi.org/10.1037/cdp0000149

Pittman LD, Richmond A (2008) University belonging, friendship quality, and psychological adjustment during the transition to college. J Exp Educ 76(4):343–362. https://doi.org/10.3200/JEXE.76.4.343-362

Qidwai W, Ishaque S, Shah S, Rahim M (2010) Adolescent lifestyle and behaviour: A survey from a developing country. PloS ONE 5(9):e12914. https://doi.org/10.1371/journal.pone.0012914

Qiu J, Shen B, Zhao M, Wang Z, Xie B, Xu Y (2020) A nationwide survey of psychological distress among Chinese people in the covid-19 epidemic: implications and policy recommendations. Gen Psychiatry 33(2):e100213

Rigby E, Hagell A, Starbuck L (2018) What do children and young people tell us about what supports their wellbeing? Evidence from existing research. https://ayph.org.uk/wp-content/uploads/2022/02/CYP-views-on-wellbeing-scoping-review.pdf

Romer D (2010) Adolescent risk taking, impulsivity, and brain development: implications for prevention. Dev Psychobiol 52(3):263–276. https://doi.org/10.1002/dev.20442

Schulenberg JE, Sameroff AJ, Cicchetti D (2004) The transition to adulthood as a critical juncture in the course of psychopathology and mental health. Dev Psychopathol 16(4):799–806

Shah SGS, Nogueras D, van Woerden HC, Kiparoglou V (2020) The covid-19 pandemic: a pandemic of lockdown loneliness and the role of digital technology. J Med Internet Res 22(11):e22287. https://doi.org/10.2196/22287

Shaw M, Black DW (2008) Internet addiction. CNS Drugs 22(5):353–365. https://doi.org/10.2165/00023210-200822050-00001

Shek DT, Dou D, Cheng MN (2019) Transition from adolescence to emerging adulthood. Encycl Child Adolesc Dev:1–10

Smith L, Jacob L, Yakkundi A, McDermott D, Armstrong NC, Barnett Y, López-Sánchez GF, Martin S, Butler L, Tully MA (2020) Correlates of symptoms of anxiety and depression and mental wellbeing associated with covid-19: a cross-sectional study of UK-based respondents. Psychiatry Res 291:113138. https://doi.org/10.1016/j.psychres.2020.113138

Tao R, Huang X, Wang J, Zhang H, Zhang Y, Mengchen L (2010) Proposed diagnostic criteria for internet addiction. Addiction 105(2):556–564. https://doi.org/10.1111/j.1360-0443.2009.02828.x

Tateno M, Teo AR, Ukai W, Kanazawa J, Katsuki R, Kubo H, Kato TA (2019) Internet addiction, smartphone addiction, and Hikikomori trait in Japanese young adult: Social isolation and social network. Front Psychiatry 10:1–11. https://doi.org/10.3389/fpsyt.2019.00455

Toulany A, Stukel TA, Kurdyak P, Fu L, Guttmann A (2019) Association of primary care continuity with outcomes following transition to adult care for adolescents with severe mental illness. JAMA Netw Open 2(8):e198415–e198415

Towner E, Tomova L, Ladensack D, Chu K, Callaghan B (2022) Virtual social interaction and loneliness among emerging adults amid the covid-19 pandemic. Curr Res Ecol Soc Psychol:100058. https://doi.org/10.1016/j.cresp.2022.100058

Turban E, Outland J, King D, Lee J K, Liang T P, Turban DC (2018) Overview of electronic commerce. In: Electronic commerce 2018: A managerial and social networks perspective. Springer International Publishing, Cham, pp 3–39

Updegraff J, Taylor S (2000) From vulnerability to growth: positive and negative effects of stressful life events. https://taylorlab.psych.ucla.edu/wp-content/uploads/sites/5/2014/11/2000_From-Vulnerability-to-Growth_Positive-and-Negative-Effects-of-Stressful-Life-Events.pdf

van der Werf ET, Busch M, Jong MC, Hoenders HJR (2021) Lifestyle changes during the first wave of the covid-19 pandemic: a cross-sectional survey in the Netherlands. BMC Public Health 21(1):1226. https://doi.org/10.1186/s12889-021-11264-z

Versteeg M, Kappe R (2021) Resilience and higher education support as protective factors for student academic stress and depression during covid-19 in the Netherlands. Front Public Health 9. https://doi.org/10.3389/fpubh.2021.737223

Voderholzer U, Piosczyk H, Holz J, Landmann N, Feige B, Loessl B, Kopasz M, Doerr JP, Riemann D, Nissen C (2011) Sleep restriction over several days does not affect long-term recall of declarative and procedural memories in adolescents. Sleep Med 12:170–178. https://doi.org/10.1016/j.sleep.2010.07.017

Walker JS, Gowen LK (2011) Community-based approaches for supporting positive development in youth and young adults with serious mental health conditions. Research and Training Center for Pathways to Positive Futures, Portland State University, Portland

Wawera AS, McCamley A (2019) Loneliness among international students in the UK. J Furth High Educ 44(9):1262–1274. https://doi.org/10.1080/0309877x.2019.1673326

Winsler A, Deutsch A, Vorona RD, Payne PA, Szklo-Coxe M (2015) Sleepless in fairfax: the difference one more hour of sleep can make for teen hopelessness, suicidal ideation, and substance use. J Youth Adolesc 44:362–378. https://doi.org/10.1007/s10964-014-0170-3

Wong HY, Mo HY, Potenza MN, Chan MNM, Lau WM, Chui TK, Pakpour AH, Lin CY (2020) Relationships between severity of internet gaming disorder, severity of problematic social media use, sleep quality and psychological distress. Int J Environ Res Public Health 17(6):1879. https://doi.org/10.3390/ijerph17061879

Wood D, Crapnell T, Lau L et al (2017) Emerging adulthood as a critical stage in the life course. In: Halfon N, Forrest CB, Lerner RM et al (eds) Handbook of life course health development [Internet]. Springer, Cham (CH). Available from: https://www.ncbi.nlm.nih.gov/books/NBK543712/; https://doi.org/10.1007/978-3-319-47143-3_7

World Health Organization (2021) Mental Health of Adolescents. [online] Retrieved from https://www.who.int/news-room/factsheets/detail/adolescent-mental-health

Yang S, Ng PYN, Chiu R, Li SS, Klassen RM, Su S (2020) Criteria for adulthood, resilience, and self-esteem among emerging adults in Hong Kong: a path analysis approach. Child Youth Serv Rev 119:105607

Youth definition 2013–1–23 (n.d.) https://www.un.org/esa/socdev/documents/youth/fact-sheets/youth-definition.pdf

Zeek ML, Savoie MJ, Song M, Kennemur LM, Qian J, Jungnickel PW, Westrick SC (2015) Sleep duration and academic performance among student pharmacists. Am J Pharm Educ 79(5):63–63. https://doi.org/10.5688/ajpe79563

Zhang J, Paksarian D, Lamers F, Hickie IB, He J, Merikangas KR (2017) Sleep patterns and mental health correlates in US adolescents. J Pediatr 182:137–143. https://doi.org/10.1016/j.jpeds.2016.11.007

Zheng C, Huang WY, Sheridan S, Sit CHP, Chen XK, Wong SHS (2020) Covid-19 pandemic brings a sedentary lifestyle in young adults: a cross-sectional and longitudinal study. In J Environ Res Public Health 17(17):6035. MDPI AG. https://doi.org/10.3390/ijerph17176035

Zhu X, Haegele JA, Liu H, Yu F (2021) Academic stress, physical activity, sleep, and mental health among Chinese adolescents. Int J Environ Res Public Health 18(14):7257

Žukauskienė R, Kaniušonytė G, Nelson LJ, Crocetti E, Malinauskienė O, Hihara S, Sugimura K (2020) Objective and subjective markers of transition to adulthood in emerging adults: their mediating role in explaining the link between parental trust and life satisfaction. J Soc Pers Relat 37(12):3006–3027

Dr. Elsie Ong is a Lecturer and a Dissertation Supervisor in UCL. She has worked in many universities in Asia and the UK for over ten years. Elsie is active in leading research that focuses on the mental health of young adults; especially those going through university transitions. Her expertise in cognitive neuroscience and psychology has also initiated further exploration on the underlying causes of mental health problems and later sparkles potentials for suicide preventions and interventions. Elsie is devoted to the study of psychological wellbeing in young adults and has published her research through internationally renowned conferences and reputed journals such as Frontiers in psychiatry. These experiences have helped to keep her most up to date on the latest development in preventions and interventions in mental health.

Chapter 2
Students' Learning During the Pandemic

Can He, Elsie Ong, and Jing Ma

Overview

Since the worldwide spread of the COVID-19 pandemic, higher education institutions had no choice but to convert traditional face-to-face teaching and learning to online learning mode. This transition was due to the policy of social distancing which was strictly applied to the spread of COVID-19 (Adedoyin and Soykan 2020; Ali 2020; Bao 2020). This unprecedented transition of learning mode has questioned whether university students' resources and facilities were well-suited for online education and whether students have enough self-regulation for efficient learning (Chiu 2022; Meeter et al. 2020). As an educator, providing students with the optimal online learning experience is an urgent and vital problem. In **this chapter**, we will elucidate the impact of the pandemic on university students. We will mainly focus on students' perceptions regarding the change in their learning and how this has impacted their engagement, motivation and other critical academic outcomes. **Study One** consisted of quantitative research to explore the relationship between university students' academic motivation and levels of engagement in online learning during the COVID-19 Era. 174 university students were recruited via some social media platforms to complete self-report questionnaires assessing motivation (intrinsic and

---

C. He (✉) · J. Ma
IOE—Psychology and Human Development, UCL Institute of Education, University College London, 24–26 Woburn Square, London, WC 1H 0AA, UK
e-mail: can.he.18@alumni.ucl.ac.uk

J. Ma
e-mail: jing.ma.21@alumni.ucl.ac.uk

E. Ong
Department of Psychology and Human Development, IOE—UCL's Faculty of Education and Society, University College London, London, WC 1E 6BT, UK
e-mail: elsie.ong@ucl.ac.uk

E. Ong (ed.), *The Emergence of the Digital World*,
https://doi.org/10.1007/978-981-97-3098-8_2

extrinsic), engagements (behavioural, cognitive, emotional and agentic), and amotivation. Results shed light on the impact of academic motivation on engagement and created significant implications for university curriculum developers, educators, and students.

International students are particularly vulnerable because of the COVID-19 pandemic. While studies have revealed the relationships between learning modes and students' mental health during this specific period, few of them have taken students' own learning preferences into account, especially in the often-overlooked minority, the international students studying in a country away from their homes. Therefore, **Study 2** investigated the effect of current learning modes during the pandemic, the learning preferences and how they impact students' mental health. 133 international students in the UK completed General Anxiety Disorder-7 (GAD-7) and the Patient Health Questionnaire-9 (PHQ-9), questionnaire to explore students current learning modes and preferences. With the review of both Chinese students studying online in Study 1 and international students studying in the UK in Study 2, considerations for future research development and practical implications were further discussed.

Keywords Learning mode, Online learning, Motivation and engagement

The Shift of Learning Mode During the Pandemic

The delivery of online courses through learning management systems, whether partial or full, constitutes online learning (Meyer 2014). In the wake of the COVID-19 pandemic, various studies have observed a decrease in university students' online learning experience, encompassing diminished learning motivation (Aguilera-Hermida 2020), reduced satisfaction with online learning (Meeter et al. 2020), and decreased engagement (Farooq et al. 2020) across diverse countries (García-Morales et al. 2021). These challenges encountered by university students have affected university retention and degree completion rates (Ferrer et al. 2020). Given the potential for online learning to become a prevalent alternative to traditional face-to-face learning in the long term, it is imperative to address the urgent and significant issue of understanding students' online learning experience (Figs. 2.1 and 2.2).

The outbreak of the COVID-19 pandemic necessitated an abrupt transition to remote learning for most higher education students, commencing in the spring of 2020. To enhance virtual classroom engagement and supplement video lectures, educators embraced various technologies that facilitated increased interactivity and hybrid approaches combining online and in-person activities. These technological advancements have significantly impacted learning, teaching, and assessment methods, potentially influencing post-pandemic educational practices.

Numerous research studies have examined students' perceptions and satisfaction with online learning compared to traditional face-to-face instruction. For example, Aguilera-Hermida (2020) conducted a study involving 270 college students, revealing a general preference for face-to-face learning over traditional online study

Fig. 2.1 Remote learning during the pandemic obtained from Hess (2021)

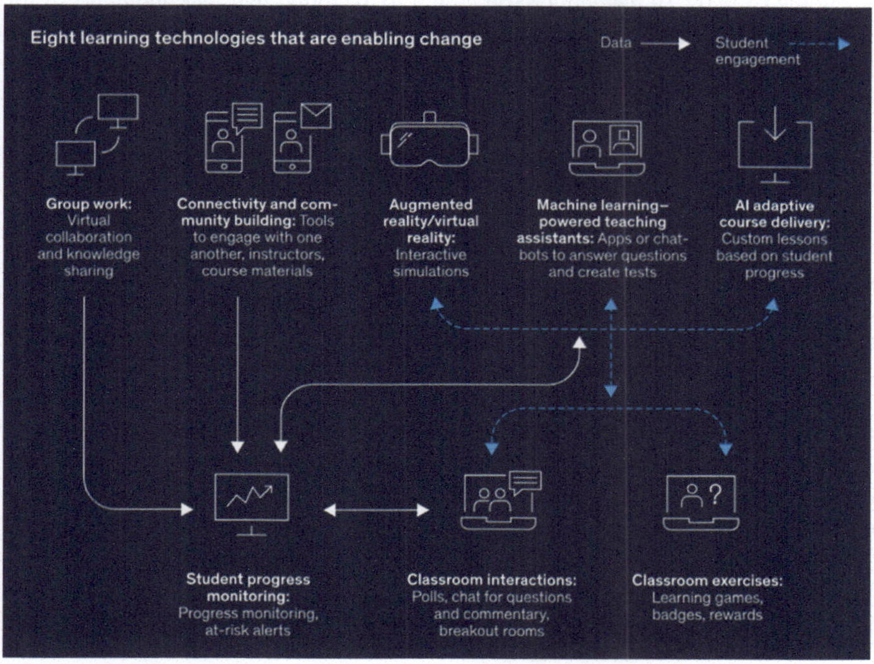

Fig. 2.2 The use of eight different classroom learning technologies public and private nonprofit colleges and universities in the United States in 2021

modes during the sudden transition to online courses. This preference is not unexpected, given the lack of preparation for both students and school staff during the abrupt transition. Moreover, this preference for face-to-face learning has been supported by studies conducted before the pandemic. Tichavsky et al. (2015) investigated whether students' perceptions and experiences of online courses influenced their learning preferences. The findings indicated that most students favored face-to-face learning, followed by blended courses, with online courses being the least preferred. However, the study also found that the preference for online courses increased from 4 to 20% among students with at least one prior online class experience, suggesting that their learning preferences may be influenced by their previous experiences and perceived stereotypes of online courses. It is important to note that certain subjects, such as music and laboratory sessions, need to be more effectively taught through online learning modes (Sahu 2020).

Several factors have been identified as influencing students' learning preferences during the COVID-19 pandemic. Son et al. (2020) found that fear and concern for personal and familial health were significant contributors to heightened mental health issues among university students. The requirement for in-person attendance in face-to-face courses and the associated risk of exposure during daily commutes may lead some students to favor online courses for safety reasons. Financial stress, particularly for international students who typically face higher tuition fees, is crucial in shaping learning preferences. The disruption of regular life due to lockdown measures has had a notable impact on social and economic aspects, with financial pressure being linked to mental health issues (Browning et al. 2021), while family income has been identified as a protective factor against anxiety (Cao et al. 2020). The shift to online learning offers potential cost savings for international students by eliminating expenses such as housing, quarantine, and travel. However, it is important to note that online courses may also entail additional costs, such as the need for well-functioning electronic devices and internet connections. Overall, these findings underscore the diverse factors influencing students' learning preferences during the pandemic, highlighting the need for a more comprehensive understanding of the relative significance of these factors, particularly among vulnerable populations such as international students.

Learning Modes and Students' Mental Health

The COVID-19 pandemic has had significant effects on individuals' lifestyles. While numerous studies have examined the pandemic's impact on mental health, Son et al. (2020) investigated the mental well-being of university students during this period. Their findings revealed that 82% of participants experienced heightened concerns regarding their academic performance, with the transition to online classes being identified as the most significant challenge. Some students reported difficulties concentrating in online courses, a factor known to detrimentally affect students' self-assurance (Martin 2010) and contribute to increased stress and mental health issues. Another study by Lai et al. (2020) compared the mental health status of international students who returned to their home countries with those who remained in their host countries during the COVID-19 outbreak. This study also supported the notion that academic stress, particularly related to adapting to new learning modes, was a contributing factor to negative mental health impacts for both returning and remaining students. It is noteworthy that academic stress will be a key factor to explore further in the next chapter, but the current chapter will focus on students learning experiences first.

Most research indicates that online learning may be perceived as causing increased stress and having a negative impact on students' mental well-being, particularly during the COVID-19 pandemic. However, Puljak et al. (2020) surveyed over 2500 college students whose instruction had shifted exclusively online due to COVID-19 and found that most participants were content with online learning and expressed a preference for its continuation. It is important to note that their study focused solely on students majoring in health sciences. Therefore, the findings may need to be more generalizable to students from other academic backgrounds. The data analysis also presented frequencies and percentages, leaving their conclusions inconclusive. Even though universities determine the mode of instruction and individual students have limited ability to change it, students still have their preferences for learning modes, which have not been adequately considered in discussions about the impact of learning modes on students' mental health during the pandemic. Consequently, Study 1 aims to investigate how the mental health of Chinese students in different learning modes and with varying learning preferences is affected by the pandemic.

Aguilera-Hermida (2020) conducted a study during the pandemic to investigate the potential impact of students' learning preferences on their mental health. The study revealed a correlation between students' preference for face-to-face learning and their challenges in adapting to online learning. It was found that students who favored in-person courses may encounter greater difficulties when transitioning to online learning. This indicates that mismatches between students' learning preferences and the prevailing modes of learning may have implications for their mental well-being.

Amid the ongoing spread and impact of the pandemic, there has been a rise in mental health concerns among students in institutions of higher education. Numerous studies examining the mental well-being of university students have indicated an increase in levels of depression and anxiety during the pandemic (Santomauro et al. 2021; Wang et al. 2020). Wang et al. (2020) conducted an online survey of over 2000 university students during the initial peak of COVID-19, revealing that 48% of participants experienced a moderate-to-severe level of depression, while 38% struggled with a moderate-to-severe level of anxiety. Furthermore, many participants reported heightened levels of anxiety and stress during the pandemic. Additionally, a longitudinal study by Charles et al. (2021) compared data from before and during the COVID-19 pandemic and also found an increase in symptoms of mood disorders among the student population, underscoring the impact of COVID-19 on individuals' mental health. To explore students' learning experience and preference in learning mode, it is important to understand factors that impact learning. These include students' engagement and motivation.

Engagement and Motivation in Online Classes

Student engagement

Student engagement refers to the active involvement of students in educational settings and their dedication to pursuing educational objectives (Christenson et al. 2012). It shows students' commitment to their cognitive development and their capacity to acquire knowledge, thereby contributing to improved learning outcomes (Britt et al. 2015). In comparison to traditional face-to-face instruction, online learning environments need more physical interaction between educators and students, presenting challenges in assessing student engagement in real time. Without active engagement, both educators and students may encounter difficulties in attaining their teaching and learning objectives. Consequently, student engagement in online learning environments is crucial in enabling educators to monitor students' learning progress and implement timely interventions. Numerous studies have demonstrated a positive correlation between student engagement and student learning, satisfaction, and academic performance online (Kuzminykh et al. 2021; Martin and Bolliger 2018; Tran and Aspiras 2022).

Various types of engagement have been identified Hu and Li (2017), with behavioural, cognitive, and emotional engagement being highlighted as the most prevalent and significant types. Behavioural engagement pertains to involvement in learning tasks, encompassing attention, effort, and persistence. Cognitive engagement involves strategically applying advanced learning strategies to complete educational activities. Emotional engagement, on the other hand, encompasses students' sense of belonging and their feelings towards the school environment, including interactions with teachers and peers (Sinatra et al. 2015). While behavioural engagement is the most readily observable, it may not fully capture students' actual participation, and does not necessarily reflect their cognitive and emotional engagement. Hu and Li (2017) further assert that a student's behavioural engagement in learning does not necessarily indicate high cognitive and emotional engagement levels. Emotional engagement is often considered a primary contributor to overall student engagement, influencing behavioural and cognitive engagement during the learning process.

Reeve and Tseng (2011) introduced a multidimensional engagement framework, which delineates three dimensions of engagement: behavioural, cognitive, and emotional. In addition to these dimensions, the framework also introduces the concept of agentic engagement, which pertains to students' proactive efforts in learning and taking initiative (Reeve 2013; Reeve and Tseng 2011). This concept is distinct from the other three types of engagement, as it emphasizes students' proactive involvement in enriching the learning process. While the traditional dimensions of engagement focus on the interaction between teachers and students in learning tasks, agentic engagement highlights students' autonomy and active participation in their academic motivation and learning experiences (Reeve 2012). Reeve (2013) underscores the significance of agentic engagement in creating a more supportive learning environment and directing and sustaining student engagement in the classroom. Furthermore, he suggests that agentic engagement accounts for aspects of student learning achievement not explained by behavioural, cognitive, and emotional engagement. In Reeve's (2013) framework, all four types of engagement are included, aligning with students' essential learning stages of thinking, acting, feeling, and communicating, respectively.

Intrinsic and Extrinsic Motivation in Student Learning

Motivation is also a core belief of teaching and learning (Mitchell and Carbone 2011). Academic motivation is characterized by students' inclination, vigor, and impetus to learn, enabling them to effectively engage in their studies and ultimately achieve their academic objectives (Martin 2007). The self-determination theory (SDT), pioneered by Ryan and Deci (2000), has delineated a spectrum of motivation, spanning from the most self-driven to the least self-driven, encompassing intrinsic, extrinsic, and amotivation. Intrinsic motivation is defined as the internal desire to participate in an activity due to its inherent satisfaction, interest, or enjoyment. In contrast, extrinsic motivation pertains to the inclination to engage in an activity as a result of external rewards or aversive consequences. In contrast, amotivation denotes a lack of intention to undertake learning actions, merely going through the motions. Research has established a strong correlation between motivation and students' learning outcomes and satisfaction in the context of online education (Baber 2020). Typically, students enrolled in online courses have been found to exhibit lower levels of motivation compared to their counterparts in traditional face-to-face settings, and their motivational factors have been closely linked to their academic performance (Stark 2019).

The relationship between motivation and engagement is clear and direct, with motivation often leading to increased engagement (Froiland and Worrell 2016; Wu 2019). According to Self-Determination Theory (Ryan and Deci 2000), individuals have three fundamental psychological needs: autonomy (a sense of control), competence (mastery), and relatedness (belonging to a group). A learning environment that fulfils these needs enhances students' intrinsic motivation and facilitates their engagement in educational settings (Reeve 2013). Saeed and Zyngier (2012) asserted that motivation is a critical factor in student academic engagement, and conversely, student engagement in learning activities is considered a reflection of academic motivation. Wu (2019) examined the relationship between students' motivation, engagement, and academic performance in a sample of 4,211 university students from three representative cohorts in the US. Various aspects of student motivation were evaluated, and engagement was measured. The findings indicated that academic motivation positively impacted academic engagement, with a moderate effect size.

Engaging in online learning presents various complexities, and it is important to recognize that theories of motivation and engagement may not directly translate to the online learning context. Online learning has provided students with increased flexibility and has catered to their needs through self-regulated learning. Compared to traditional face-to-face learning, learning autonomy has been identified as a significant intrinsic motivator for online learners, leading intrinsically motivated students to seek an autonomous online learning environment and achieve higher levels of engagement (Hsieh 2014; Law et al. 2012).

Numerous studies have explored the relationship between different types of motivation and engagement, yielding diverse findings. Crumpton and Gregory (2011) examined the relationship between motivation and engagement, focusing on their sub-constructs. They investigated academic relevancy, intrinsic motivation, and academic engagement among 44 American high school students considered low-achievers due to their poor performance in Grade 8. Intrinsic motivation was evaluated using the Intrinsic Motivation scale derived from Harter's (1981) Scale of Intrinsic and Extrinsic Motivation, while academic engagement was assessed using a scale adapted from Skinner and Belmont (1993), encompassing behavioural and emotional engagement components. The results indicated that intrinsic motivation was positively associated with a higher level of classroom engagement, with intrinsically motivated students demonstrating increased attention and participation in class. This suggests that higher levels of intrinsic learning motivation are linked to greater behavioural engagement in classroom activities. However, it is essential to note that the sample size of this study was relatively small, which may have underestimated the effects.

Based on the model proposed by Crumpton and Gregory (2011), Xiong et al. (2015) expanded the theoretical framework by incorporating extrinsic motivation as a significant variable. They discovered that it substantially influenced online engagement more than intrinsic motivation. The investigation focused on the interplay between student motivation, engagement, and retention rate within a Massive Open Online Course (MOOC) involving 17,359 participants from a public university MOOC centered on art. The study assessed student motivation across three categories: intrinsic, extrinsic, and social motivation, while engagement was evaluated behaviourally by inquiring about the frequency of video views, forum participation, quiz completion, and assignment submission. The findings indicated that intrinsic motivation positively impacted student behavioural engagement in the course, but extrinsic motivation emerged as a more influential predictor, suggesting that most students engaged in the MOOC to fulfil external incentives such as awards and certificates. Furthermore, Walker et al. (2006) explored the connection between academic identification, self-efficacy, intrinsic/extrinsic motivation, and cognitive engagement (shallow/deep) among 191 university students in the US. Motivation was gauged using the Academic Motivation Scale (AMS), while cognitive engagement was assessed using Greene and Miller's (1996) scale which comprises 10 shallow and deep engagement items. The results revealed that intrinsic motivation significantly forecasted deep cognitive engagement, while extrinsic motivation significantly predicted shallow cognitive engagement, and amotivation exhibited a negative correlation with deep cognitive engagement. Given that previous studies, such as Walker et al. (2006), did not encompass cognitive engagement comprehensively and consider other vital dimensions of engagement, such as behavioural engagement, the present study aimed to explore the associations among various motivation subconstructs (i.e., intrinsic, extrinsic, and amotivation) and diverse levels of cognitive engagement.

As the concept of agentic engagement was relatively novel when introduced by Reeve (2013), limited existing literature specifically examined the connection between different types of motivation and agentic engagement. Nevertheless, Reeve (2013) identified a positive relationship between agentic engagement and autonomous motivation, and a negative relationship with controlled motivation across behavioural, cognitive, and emotional engagement. Autonomous motivation encompassed a higher degree of self-determination along the spectrum of motivation within Self-Determination Theory (SDT), while controlled motivation represented a lower degree of self-determination. Consequently, agentic engagement was perceived to be negatively associated with extrinsic motivation and positively related to intrinsic motivation.

Study One: Motivation and Engagement of Chinese Students in Online Learning Environment During the Pandemic

Can He and Elsie Ong

Aims and objectives of the current study

Prior research has primarily focused on examining the correlation between intrinsic and extrinsic motivation and behavioural and cognitive engagement, with limited investigation into amotivation and agentic engagement. The onset of the COVID-19 pandemic has posed challenges to students' motivation and online engagement, yet there needs to be more research addressing the specific relationship between various types of motivation and engagement. To address this gap, the present study encompasses a comprehensive examination of academic motivation, including intrinsic, extrinsic, and amotivation, as well as engagement, encompassing agentic engagement. The study investigates the association between intrinsic, extrinsic, and amotivation and behavioural, cognitive, emotional, and agentic engagement among Chinese students engaged in online learning during the COVID-19 pandemic.

Hypothesis:

Individuals with a higher level of motivation (both intrinsic and extrinsic) correlates with a higher level of behavioural, cognitive, emotional and agentic engagement.
Individuals with a higher level of amotivation correlates with a lower level of behavioural, cognitive, emotional and agentic engagement.

Method

Design

A correlational research design was employed to investigate the association between the motivation and engagement of Chinese students in online learning during the COVID-19 pandemic. The study focused on the levels of intrinsic, extrinsic, and amotivation among students, and their behavioural, cognitive, emotional, and agentic engagement.

Participants

The study included university students aged 18 and above currently engaged in online learning. A total of 174 university students (24 male, 150 female) were selected through convenience sampling. The participants' ages ranged from 18 to 38 years ($M = 19.59$; $SD = 15.97$ years). The majority of respondents (81%) were enrolled in a university located in China ($n = 141$), while 12.6% were in the UK ($n = 22$), and the remaining 6.4% were in the US ($n = 5$), Thailand ($n = 2$), Canada ($n = 1$), Australia ($n = 1$), or Malaysia ($n = 1$). In terms of academic level, 66.1% were pursuing a Bachelor's degree ($n = 115$), 26.4% were pursuing a Master's degree or higher ($n = 46$), and 7.5% were pursuing an Associate degree ($n = 13$). Additionally, 60.9% of respondents were majoring in Arts and Social Science ($n = 106$), 29.3% in Business ($n = 51$), and 9.7% in Science and Engineering ($n = 17$).

Materials

This research utilized a self-administered online questionnaire consisting of three primary sections. The initial section of the questionnaire assessed demographic details, encompassing age, gender, ethnicity, the country in which the university is situated, educational attainment, and field of study. The second section gauged participants' levels of intrinsic, extrinsic, and amotivation using the Academic Motivation Scale (AMS) developed by Vallerand et al. (1992), while the final section assessed their levels of behavioural, cognitive, emotional, and agentic engagement using two scales adapted from Sun and Rueda (2012) and Reeve (2013). The questionnaire comprised 56 questions (1 completion question, seven multiple choice questions, and 48 Likert scale questions). The English version of the survey was translated into Chinese to facilitate a comprehensive understanding among Chinese participants.

Motivation

Academic motivation was assessed using the Academic Motivation Scale (AMS) developed by Vallerand et al. (1992) for students from English-speaking countries, and the Chinese version of AMS for Chinese university students, as described by Zhang et al. (2016). This 28-item instrument evaluated three motivation categories: intrinsic, extrinsic, and amotivation. Each category included four items measuring three subtypes of intrinsic motivation (i.e., intrinsic motivation to know, intrinsic motivation to stimulate, and intrinsic motivation to accomplish), three subtypes of extrinsic motivation (i.e., external regulation, introjected regulation, and identified regulation), as well as amotivation. The questionnaire presented sample questions corresponding to each motivational type.

Intrinsic Motivation: "For the pleasure that I experience in broadening my knowledge about subjects which appeal to me."

Extrinsic Motivation: "To have a better salary later on."

Amotivation: "Honestly, I don't know; I feel that I am wasting my time in school".

All survey questions were evaluated using a 7-point Likert scale, ranging from 1 (no correspondence) to 7 (exact correspondence). The levels of motivation for each of the three motivational types were determined by averaging the responses to all questions related to intrinsic motivation (including intrinsic motivation to know, to accomplish, and to experience stimulation), extrinsic motivation (external regulation, introjected regulation, and identified regulation), and amotivation. This provided an overall mean score for combined intrinsic, extrinsic, and amotivation items. The mean score for each motivational type fell within the range of 1 to 7, with a higher score indicating higher levels of intrinsic, extrinsic, and amotivation.

In the study by Zhang et al. (2016), the Chinese version of the Academic Motivation Scale (AMS) was utilized with high school students. For the current research, the term "high school" was replaced with "university" throughout the questionnaire to align with the study's specific context. For instance, the original statement "Because to get a high-paying job, I need at least a high-school degree" was modified to "Because to get a high-paying job, I need at least a university degree".

The Cronbach's alpha coefficient for the Academic Motivation Scale (AMS) among university students was reported as 0.88 by Amit-Aharon et al. (2020). Similarly, the Chinese version of the AMS demonstrated a range of 0.75 to 0.86 in Cronbach's alpha among high school students in China, as indicated by Zhang et al. (2016). These findings suggest a high level of internal consistency for the scale in both populations.

Engagement

Engagement was assessed across four sub-constructs, namely behavioural, cognitive, emotional, and agentic engagement, using two questionnaires. The questionnaire utilized to measure the first three types of engagement was adapted from Sun and Rueda (2012). This particular scale was chosen due to its prior application and validation in the context of online learning, despite the availability of numerous other engagement scales. The measurement of agentic engagement, the fourth type, was conducted using a questionnaire adapted from Reeve (2013), who is credited with coining the term (Reeve and Tseng 2011).

The revised 15-item questionnaire developed by Sun and Rueda (2012) was employed to assess behavioural (3 items), cognitive (5 items), and emotional engagement (7 items) on a 5-point Likert scale ranging from 1 (strongly disagree) to 5 (strongly agree). The mean scores for engagement items fell from 1 to 5, with higher scores indicating greater levels of student behavioural, cognitive, and emotional engagement in the online learning environment. Notably, one of the emotional engagement items, "I feel bored by the online class," was reverse-coded for scoring purposes. The Cronbach's alpha for the entire scale was 0.90, while the individual factors yielded values of 0.62 for behavioural engagement, 0.86 for cognitive engagement, and 0.90 for emotional engagement (Sun and Rueda 2012).

Reeve's (2013) questionnaire was comprised of 5 items on a 7-point Likert scale from 1 (strongly disagree) to 7 (strongly agree). Engagement item scores were calculated to mean, ranging from 1 to 7. A higher score revealed a higher level of student agentic engagement. The Cronbach's alpha showed high internal consistency, 0.84 for agentic engagement among university students (Reeve 2013).

Procedure

Participants were recruited using convenience sampling methods via online platforms. Completing all the questionnaires took approximately 15 min and was conducted between 17 April and 15 June 2022. The survey link was disseminated through various multinational applications, including Instagram, WeChat, and Weibo. Respondents provided anonymous demographic information and indicated their levels of motivation and engagement. Before participation, participants were provided with an information sheet outlining the research project's objectives and basic details. A mandatory 'opt-in' consent form was then presented to emphasize participation's voluntary nature and provide assurances regarding anonymity and confidentiality. The survey included inquiries about demographic details, such as age and gender, followed by the Academic Motivation Scale to assess academic motivation. Subsequently, two engagement scales were administered to measure participants' levels of behavioural, cognitive, emotional, and agentic engagement. Upon completion, a debrief form was included on the final page of the survey, reiterating key information about the research project's objectives.

Data Analytic Plan

IBM Statistical Package for Social Sciences (SPSS) Statistics Version 27 was used for all analyses in this study. Specifically, descriptive statistics, spearman's rho and multiple linear regression analysis were used for data analysis. The level of significance was set at 0.05 (one-tailed). Descriptive analysis was used to analyze the demographic information, including their age, gender, ethnicity, education level, location of university and major, and information about intrinsic, extrinsic, motivation, behavioural, cognitive, emotional, and agentic engagement. Spearman's rho was used to explore the association between three motivation types and four types of engagement to see their correlational relationships. In addition, multiple linear regression was used to test the prediction effects of intrinsic, extrinsic and motivation on behavioural, cognitive, emotional and agentic engagement.

Ethical Considerations

Before participant recruitment, the current study received ethical approval from the Institute of Education Research Ethics Committee in April 2022 and was permitted to carry out this research project. An information sheet was presented at the beginning of the online survey to show participants the basic information about this research project, such as the significance of their participation, the aim, and the general procedures of this study. All participants were reminded of their entitlement to withdraw from the study at any time without penalty. They were also given information about the policy of data storage and data access in the consent form. Participants could take part in the study if their consent was obtained.

Results

Descriptive data

The descriptive statistics are shown in Table 2.1. Out of the 174 participants analysed, 86.8% participants (n = 151) scored above 4 on intrinsic motivation (M = 5.03, *SD* = 0.08), and only 11.5% participants scored below 4, indicating that they are less likely to be encouraged to learn by internal motives. Similarly, 92% (n = 160) respondents scored higher than 4 on extrinsic motivation (M = 5.30, *SD* = 0.06). In contrast, for amotivation (M = 2.96, *SD* = 0.11), 70.1% of participants (n = 122) achieved a relatively low score indicating most of them learn with either internal or external motives. Regarding engagement, most people performed relatively strong behavioural engagement (89.7%, n = 156; M = 4.00, *SD* = 0.05), cognitive engagement (74.1%, n = 139; M = 3.57, *SD* = 0.06) and agentic engagement (64.4%, n = 107; M = 4.61, *SD* = 0.09), except for emotional engagement the engagement level was relatively low (49.4%, n = 86; M = 3.13, *SD* = 0.07).

Correlation between intrinsic, extrinsic, amotivation and behavioural, cognitive, emotional, and agentic engagement

The Shapiro–Wilk tests, visual inspection of histograms, and calculations of skewness and kurtosis indicated that the distributions of the three motivation variables and four engagement variables were not normal. However, this deviation from normality was deemed negligible due to the large sample size (exceeding 30 or 40; Ghasemi and Zahediasl 2012). Consequently, Spearman's correlation analysis investigated the relationship between three distinct types of motivation (intrinsic, extrinsic, amotivation) and four types of engagement (behavioural, cognitive, emotional, and agentic engagement; refer to Table 2.2). Among the three motivational types, intrinsic motivation exhibited positive associations with behavioural engagement ($r = 0.22$, $n = 174$, $p < 0.01$), cognitive engagement ($r = 0.22$, $n = 174$, $p < 0.01$), emotional engagement ($r = 0.41$, $n = 174$, $p < 0.01$), and agentic engagement ($r = 0.42$, $n = 174$, $p < 0.01$), indicating that higher levels of intrinsic motivation were linked to higher levels of all four types of engagement. Similarly, extrinsic motivation also

Table 2.1 Descriptive statistics for the study variables

	Range	*M*	*SD*	*A*	Lower level		Middle level		Higher level	
					n	%	n	%	N	%
Intrinsic motivation	1.50–7.00	5.03	0.075	0.93	20	11.5	3	1.7	151	86.8
Extrinsic motivation	2.92–7.00	5.30	0.063	0.85	13	7.5	1	0.5	160	92.0
Amotivation	1.00–7.00	2.96	0.110	0.86	122	70.1	8	4.6	44	25.3
Behavioural engagement	2.00–5.00	4.C0	0.047	0.68	6	3.4	12	6.9	156	89.7
Cognitive engagement	1.60–5.00	3.57	0.060	0.82	20	17.2	15	8.7	139	74.1
Emotional engagement	1.00–5.00	3.13	0.069	0.91	74	42.5	14	8.1	86	49.4
Agentic engagement	1.20–7.00	4.61	0.092	0.89	50	25.9	17	9.7	107	64.4

Note M = mean; SD = standard deviation; α = Cronbach's alpha

Table 2.2 Correlation between intrinsic, extrinsic, amotivation and behavioural, cognitive, emotional, and agentic engagement

Variable	1	2	3	4	5	6	7
1. Behavioural engagement	1.00						
2. Cognitive engagement	0.34^{**}	1.00					
3. Emotional engagement	0.32^{**}	0.46^{**}	1.00				
4. Agentic engagement	0.24^{**}	0.47^{**}	0.26^{**}	1.00			
5. Intrinsic motivation	0.22^{**}	0.22^{**}	0.41^{**}	0.42^{**}	1.00		
6. Extrinsic motivation	0.17^{*}	0.22^{**}	0.21^{**}	0.29^{**}	0.66^{**}	1.00	
7. Amotivation	-0.13^{*}	0.01	−0.05	−0.01	-0.21^{**}	-0.05	1.00

* $p < 0.05$, ** $p < 0.01$

displayed positive associations with behavioural engagement (r = 0.17, n = 174, p < 0.05), cognitive engagement (r = 0.22, n = 174, p < 0.01), emotional engagement (r = 0.21, n = 174, p < 0.01), and agentic engagement (r = 0.29, n = 174, p < 0.01). Conversely, amotivation exhibited a negative association with behavioural engagement (r = -0.13, n = 174, p < 0.05) and showed no significant associations with cognitive, emotional, and agentic engagement (all p > 0.05).

Prediction between intrinsic, extrinsic motivation and behavioural, cognitive, emotional, and agentic engagement

To examine the impact of intrinsic, extrinsic, and amotivation on behavioural, cognitive, emotional, and agentic engagement, a multiple linear regression analysis was conducted. In this analysis, intrinsic, extrinsic, and amotivation were treated as independent variables, while behavioural, cognitive, emotional, and agentic engagement were considered as dependent variables (refer to Table 2.3 for details).

For behavioural engagement, one outlier was excluded from the analysis due to the violation of homoscedasticity in the multiple regression. The findings indicated that intrinsic motivation, extrinsic motivation, and amotivation significantly forecasted behavioural engagement, $F(3, 169) = 4.12$, $p < 0.01$. This model accounted for 5% of the variance, although intrinsic, extrinsic, and amotivation did not make a significant contribution to the model. Another significant model was observed between intrinsic and extrinsic motivation and cognitive engagement. Intrinsic and extrinsic motivation statistically predicted cognitive engagement, $F(2, 171) = 22.45$, $p < 0.001$, explaining 20% of the variance. While intrinsic motivation significantly contributed to the model ($\beta = 0.53$, $p < 0.001$), extrinsic motivation did not ($\beta = -0.12$, $p > 0.05$). Similarly, a significant model was also found in emotional engagement, $F(2, 171) = 7.56$, $p < 0.001$. Intrinsic and extrinsic motivation accounted for 7% of the variance in emotional engagement. While intrinsic motivation significantly contributed to the model ($\beta = 0.21$, $p < 0.05$), extrinsic motivation did not ($\beta = 0.10$, $p > 0.05$). A significant model was also identified in agentic engagement. Intrinsic and extrinsic motivation significantly predicted agentic engagement, $F(2, 171) = 21.57$, $p < 0.001$, explaining 19% of the variance. While intrinsic motivation significantly contributed to the model ($\beta = 0.42$, $p < 0.001$), extrinsic motivation did not ($\beta = 0.05$, $p > 0.05$). In general, intrinsic motivation was a weak to moderate predictor for cognitive, emotional, and agentic engagement, but not for behavioural engagement. Extrinsic motivation and amotivation were not significant predictors for any of the four types of engagement, although all four prediction models were significant.

Discussion

This research aimed to investigate the relationship between the academic motivation of Chinese students and their participation in online learning during the COVID-19 pandemic. The findings indicated that higher intrinsic and extrinsic motivation levels were linked to increased engagement in all four areas studied. Robust correlations were observed between intrinsic motivation and emotional and agentic engagement. Additionally, increased amotivation was associated with lower levels of behavioural engagement, although no significant correlation was found between amotivation and cognitive, emotional, and agentic engagement. Intrinsic motivation was a modest predictor of cognitive, emotional, and agentic engagement, but unexpectedly, it did not predict behavioural engagement. Extrinsic motivation did not predict any engagement. While higher levels of intrinsic and extrinsic motivation were associated with increased behavioural engagement, they were not the strongest predictors of this type of engagement. This finding contrasts with the results of Xiong et al. (2015),

Table 2.3 Multiple linear regression to explore the extent to which intrinsic, extrinsic, amotivation predict behavioural, cognitive, emotional, and agentic engagement

Variables	Behavioural engagement					Cognitive engagement					Emotional engagement					Agentic engagement				
	b	*SE*	*β*	*t*	R^2_{adj}	*b*	*SE*	*B*	*t*	R^2_{adj}	*b*	*SE*	*β*	*t*	R^2_{adj}	*B*	*SE*	*β*	*t*	R^2_{adj}
					0.05*					0.20**					0.07**					0.19**
Intrinsic motivation	0.11	0.06	0.19	1.86		0.42	0.07	0.53**	5.81		0.20	0.09	0.21*	2.19		0.51	0.11	0.42**	4.60	
Extrinsic motivation	0.05	0.07	0.07	0.67		−0.11	0.09	−0.12	−1.32		0.11	0.11	0.10	0.98		0.07	0.13	0.05	0.50	
Amotivation	−0.03	0.03	−0.08	−1.02		–	–	–	–		–	–	–	–		–	–	–	–	

Note $R^2_{adj.}$ = Adjusted R^2; $^{*}\ p < 0.05$; $^{**}\ p < 0.001$

who found that both intrinsic and extrinsic motivation were strong predictors of behavioural engagement. It is suggested that the participants in Xiong et al.'s study enrolled in short courses and aimed to obtain a certificate in a MOOC, which may have led to their active and diverse learning motivation. Similarly, Lu et al. (2019) found that most individuals used MOOCs due to their perceived usefulness. However, the participants in this study were all university students required to take online classes due to the pandemic, so their behavioural engagement may have been influenced by other significant factors, such as their positive or negative attitudes toward online learning (Ferrer et al. 2020).

In relation to cognitive engagement, only intrinsic motivation emerged as a significant predictor of cognitive engagement, while extrinsic motivation did not show a significant association. There was no notable correlation between amotivation and cognitive engagement. These results contrast with those of Walker et al. (2006), who found that extrinsic motivation positively predicts shallow cognitive engagement and amotivation negatively predicts deep cognitive engagement. This disparity may be attributed to differences in the measurement of cognitive engagement. While Walker et al. (2006) assessed various levels of cognitive engagement, this study measured cognitive engagement, potentially underestimating the influence of extrinsic motivation on different levels of cognitive engagement.

Regarding emotional engagement, the finding that intrinsic motivation was positively linked to emotional engagement aligns with the results of Crumpton and Gregory (2011). Additionally, this study revealed that intrinsic motivation was a modest yet significant predictor of emotional engagement, indicating that intrinsically motivated students exhibited a greater sense of belonging and stronger emotional connections with school staff, teachers, and peers, making them more readily engaged in the online learning environment.

In line with the findings of Reeve (2013), a heightened level of inherent drive was linked to a greater degree of self-directed involvement. However, there was also a positive association between extrinsic motivation and self-directed engagement, contradicting Reeve's (2013) previous report. One potential explanation for this discrepancy could be the variability in the relative autonomy of extrinsic motivation. Ryan and Deci (2000) contended that extrinsic motivation exhibits significant variation in autonomy, suggesting that it may reflect genuine self-regulation rather than external regulation. This is particularly pertinent given that identified regulation, categorized as the most self-determined form of extrinsic motivation in this study, was classified as extrinsic motivation. In contrast, in Reeve's (2013) study, it was categorized as intrinsic/autonomous motivation. Consequently, the instability in autonomy or identified regulation may have contributed to the contrasting results. Furthermore, the present study revealed that intrinsic motivation only mildly predicted self-directed engagement. Consequently, students driven by intrinsic motivation were more inclined to actively participate in the online learning environment by taking proactive measures, such as seeking guidance from teachers and offering advice.

Limitations and future directions

This research has several limitations. Firstly, being a cross-sectional study, it cannot establish causal relationships based on the obtained results. Additionally, academic motivation as a personal characteristic is likely to stay mostly the same over a short period, so if a longitudinal study is to be conducted, the time interval needs to be sufficiently long. Furthermore, using convenience sampling as the sampling method in this study may introduce selection bias, thereby reducing the external validity of the results. However, using convenience sampling can be more efficient than other sampling methods. Moreover, the use of an online survey may limit the sample to internet users, thus reducing the generalizability of the findings to the broader population of Chinese students. For instance, students from rural areas may have lower participation rates in this study. However, an online survey may be preferred by a majority of the population. Another area for improvement is the need for pre-pandemic data for comparison with post-pandemic data, which makes it less likely to detect small changes associated with the pandemic, despite the current study's findings.

This study has underscored the significance of students' online engagement and has revealed the relationship between different types of academic motivation and various dimensions of student engagement. The key findings have important implications, particularly for university curriculum developers, educators (including teachers and parents), and students themselves. The study found that intrinsic motivation was a weak to moderate predictor for cognitive, emotional, and agentic engagement, suggesting that university curriculum developers should focus on factors that promote students' intrinsic motivation when designing courses, such as planning classroom activities that cater to individual interests. It is also recommended that parents and university educators emphasize the importance of internal drive for learning and promote intrinsic motivation in students' daily lives. Students should consider their interests and sources of satisfaction when choosing a major before entering university, as their intrinsic motivation plays a crucial role in enhancing or maintaining their engagement in their future university life, which may further enhance their academic performance and other academic outcomes. Future studies could delve deeper into sub-types of motivation and different levels of each type of engagement, such as subscales of intrinsic and extrinsic motivation developed in SDT, or possible mediators between academic motivation. Since agentic engagement is a relatively new concept and lacks a robust research foundation, a greater focus on it may yield more innovative and significant findings.

In summary, this research investigated the correlation between intrinsic, extrinsic, amotivation, and behavioural, cognitive, emotional, and agentic engagement. The findings indicate a positive link between intrinsic and extrinsic motivation and levels of cognitive, behavioural, emotional, and agentic engagement, as well as a negative association between amotivation and behavioural engagement. Additionally, the study revealed a significant predictive relationship between intrinsic motivation and cognitive, emotional, and agentic engagement. These results underscore the importance of different motivational types in influencing various dimensions of engagement, particularly agentic engagement. As a result, university curriculum developers, educators, and students must prioritize identifying learners' academic motivation and enhance their engagement through effective strategies. Future research should delve deeper into the relationship between academic motivation and engagement, by focusing on motivation subscales or exploring potential mediators.

Specific student population: international students

When considering learning engagement and motivation, international students are often perceived as a vulnerable group due to the significant impact of the pandemic on their educational and mental well-being. While existing research has explored the connection between learning modalities and mental health outcomes during this period, few studies have considered the individual learning preferences of international students, a minority group often overlooked. Therefore, study 2 examines the influence of international students' current learning modalities and preferences on their mental health in COVID-19. The study involved 133 international students who completed a sociodemographic questionnaire encompassing basic demographic information and inquiries regarding their current learning modalities and preferences. Additionally, the General Anxiety Disorder-7 (GAD-7) and the Patient Health Questionnaire-9 (PHQ-9) were utilized to assess participants' levels of anxiety and depression. The findings indicated that students with conflicting learning modalities and preferences tended to experience higher levels of anxiety and depression, although these differences did not reach statistical significance. Furthermore, neither learning modalities nor learning preferences alone were found to impact students' mental health significantly. Moreover, students' academic levels, annual family income, personal COVID-19 diagnosis, and frequency of exposure to COVID-19-related news were identified as significant contributors to their learning preferences. The implications of these results, and suggestions for future research and practical applications are further deliberated.

COVID-19's Influences on international Students

International students are particularly vulnerable within the student population, facing heightened susceptibility to mental health issues compared to local students due to additional stressors such as separation from home, adaptation to different cultural and educational systems, and language proficiency (Alharbi and Smith 2018; Zhang and Goodson 2011). The COVID-19 pandemic has further exacerbated their situation, placing this minority group at a greater disadvantage (Chen et al. 2020). Specific concerns of international students, such as finding a safe place to stay if the campus is evacuated, may be easily overlooked during lockdown periods (Sahu 2020). Additionally, there was a serious concern about potential hostile attitudes toward Chinese international students due to assumptions about their role in spreading the virus, which could exacerbate their perceived stress (Lowrey 2022). The Office for Students' briefing note also highlighted the challenges some international students face in returning to their home countries due to Border restrictions and financial burdens, further compounding their difficulties ("supporting international students", 2022). These issues remain significant concerns for a subset of international students in 2022. For this reason, study 2 will explore the learning experience of international students studying in the UK.

According to data released by Universities UK in 2022, the academic year 2020–2021 saw a significant influx of over 600,000 international students pursuing their studies, representing a substantial demographic. Despite their substantial numbers and financial contributions to their host countries, there is a noticeable scarcity of health-related research focused on this population (Zhang and Goodson 2011). Consequently, there is a need for more targeted research on the mental health of international students, particularly considering the current challenging circumstances. Considering these considerations, Study 2 has chosen to focus on UK international students as the targeted population, utilizing university students as a sample, specifically emphasizing their mental health in the aftermath of the pandemic.

Study Two: Learning Preferences of International Students Following the Pandemic

Elsie Ong and Jing Ma

Aims and objectives of the current Study

The present research aims to provide a more comprehensive understanding of student's mental health in the aftermath of the pandemic. It seeks to offer practical implications for educational institutions to improve their teaching methods and facilitate identifying of students at higher risk of mental health issues during the COVID-19 period. For instance, students with specific learning preferences may experience greater mental stress compared to others, making them a particularly vulnerable group requiring additional attention and support. The study focuses on international students, as previous research has recognized their heightened vulnerability to mental health challenges compared to local students (Alharbi and Smith 2018; Chen et al. 2020; Zhang and Goodson 2011).

Research questions of this study:

1. Did international students with different learning preferences differ in their mental health status following the pandemic (i.e. the endemic)?
2. Did international students with contradictive learning preferences and current learning modes suffer more mentally in terms of depression and anxiety?

3. What other factors were linked with international students' learning preferences?

Methods

Participants

Participants were recruited through online chat groups. Potential participants were informed that international students were the target population for this study. The recruitment phase lasted for over a month, starting from May till the mid of July, 2022. The recruitment phase lasted for over a month, starting from May till mid-July. In all, 133 international students (18 males, and 114 females) completed the questionnaire. The age range was from 18 to 39. One hundred and one participants were graduate students, while the other 28 were undergraduates, and the rest 4 preferred not to share this information.

Materials

Sociodemographic questionnaire

Students were asked about their age, gender, family income, learning preferences and current learning modes. There are three options for their current learning modes (currently having more online courses, currently having more face-to-face courses, currently having balanced courses) and three learning preferences (prefer to have more online courses, prefer to have more face-to-face courses, do not have any preference).

GAD-7 (Spitzer et al. 2006)

The General Anxiety Disorder-7 (GAD-7) is a seven-item questionnaire used to screen for major anxiety disorders (Wang et al. 2020). It has been found to have good reliability ($\alpha = 0.89$) and validity in the general population (Löwe et al. 2008), making it an appropriate scale for the current study to assess participants' anxiety levels. The questionnaire includes items such as excessive worrying about various things. Respondents were asked to rate their experience of anxiety-related symptoms over the past two weeks using a four-point scale, ranging from 0 "not at all" to 3 "nearly every day" for each question. The total scores range from 0 to 21, with lower scores indicating lower levels of anxiety and higher scores indicating higher anxiety levels. Scores falling within the ranges of 0–4, 5–9, 10–14, and ≥ 15 correspond to minimal or no anxiety, mild anxiety, moderate anxiety, and severe anxiety, respectively, with a clinical cut-off score of 10 (Spitzer et al. 2006).

PHQ-9 (Kroenke and Spitzer 2002)

The Patient Health Questionnaire-9 is a tool with nine items used to evaluate the severity of depression in individuals. It is based on symptoms of depression and has been tested for reliability and validity in university student populations in various studies, with a reliability coefficient (α) of around 0.85 (Adewuya et al. 2006; Dadfar et al. 2021; Zhang et al. 2013). This tool was selected for assessing depression status in the current study. For example, one of the items asks about "little interest or pleasure in doing things." Respondents were asked to rate their experiences over the past two weeks on a four-point scale, ranging from 0 "not at all" to 3 "nearly every day" for each question. The scores were then added up, resulting in a total score ranging from 0 to 27. A lower score indicates a less depressed status, while a higher score indicates the opposite. Scores falling within the ranges of 0–4, 5–9, 10–14, and ≥ 15 correspond to minimal or no depression, mild depression, moderate depression, and severe depression, respectively, with a clinical cut-off score of 10 (Kroenke et al. 2001).

Procedure

The current study has gained approval by the Psychology Department ethics committee at a university in the UK. The online information sheet and consent form were sent to potential participants via chat groups. An online link was provided to participants, and all the questionnaires were administered using 'Qualtrics' (https://www.qualtrics.com).

Participants were informed they had the right to withdraw at any given time for any reason with no undesirable outcomes. The questionnaire was displayed only after participants read the information sheet and consented to participate. After the questionnaire's completion, which took approximately 15 min, a debrief was provided for participants, and the researcher's contact information would be given for any further questions.

Data Analysis

The study utilized IBM SPSS Statistics 27 for data analysis. The independent variables included learning preferences and current learning modes, each categorized into three options. Learning preferences were categorized as preferring more online courses, preferring more face-to-face courses, or having no specific preference. Current learning modes were categorized as having more online courses, more face-to-face courses, or balanced courses. The dependent variables, anxiety, and depression levels, were assessed using validated questionnaires, totalling scores from individual questions to obtain a final score. As a result, the dependent variables were considered as continuous variables.

A MANOVA analysis was conducted to investigate research questions 1 and 2. The study examined learning preferences and current learning modes as the independent variables, each with three levels, and participants' anxiety and depression scores as the dependent variables. The third research question aimed to explore the relationship between specific learning preferences and factors such as family annual income, based on previous studies. As all variables were categorical, Chi-Square tests were used to determine the association between certain factors and international students' learning preferences in the aftermath of the pandemic (Table 2.4).

Table 2.4 Descriptive and exploratory analyses of questionnaire and test variables

Measure	N	M (SE)	Shapiro–Wilk	Mild % (n)	Moderate	Severe
GAD-7 Score	128	7.15 (3.93)	0.010	47.7 (61)	21.2 (31)	3.1 (4)
PHQ-9 Score	128	8.64 (4.50)	0.090	39.8 (51)	29.7 (38)	10.9 (14)

Results

Descriptive and Exploratory Analysis

Normality tests were conducted on the scale-level independent variables, which were the scores of the GAD-7 and PHQ-9. After excluding five outliers, 128 data points remain. The exploratory data analysis revealed that the mean scores for GAD-7 and PHQ-9 were 7.15 and 8.64, respectively (as shown in Table 4.1). Specifically, using a cut-off score of 10, 24.3% and 40.6% of participants would meet the clinical criteria for GAD and major depression, respectively. Additionally, the results of Shapiro–Wilk's test indicated that the scores of PHQ-9 were normally distributed, while those of GAD-7 were not, which impacted the subsequent MANOVA test results. Crosstab results were presented for the independent variables; learning preference and current learning mode. The sample size in each group met the minimal requirement for conducting a further MANOVA test, which should be larger than the number of dependent variables ("How to perform a two-way MANOVA in SPSS Statistics | Laerd Statistics", 2022) (Table 2.5).

Research Questions 1 and 2

Before performing the MANOVA test, additional analyses were conducted to check the assumptions for MANOVA. Firstly, the maximum Mahalanobis distance was 9.99, below the critical value of 13.82 for two dependent variables. This indicated

Table 2.5 Learning preference * Current learning mode Crosstabulation

		Currently having more online courses	Currently having more face-to-face courses	Currently having an equal number of online and offline courses	Total (n)
Learning preference	Prefer more online	18	11	4	33
	Prefer more face- to-face courses	28	28	17	73
	Do not have any specific preference	9	4	9	22
Total (n)		55	43	30	128

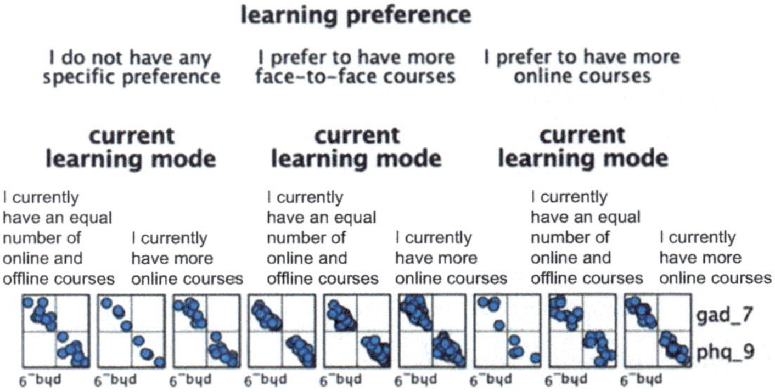

Fig. 2.3 Scatterplot result on the test of linearity

that no extreme multivariate outliers that could impact the results. Secondly, the scatterplot exhibited the expected shape, suggesting that the data followed multivariate normality (Fig. 2.3). Furthermore, the bivariate correlation indicated a significant relationship ($r(126) = 0.70$, p<0.001) between the two dependent variables, suggesting a relationship without multicollinearity. Lastly, the Box's M test for equal variance yielded a p-value of 0.08, meeting the assumption. In summary, the assumptions of normality, homogeneity of variance–covariance matrices, linearity, and multicollinearity were all satisfied. Since one of the dependent variables violated the normal distribution assumption, Pillai's trace test statistic would be utilized as it is more robust in homogeneous variance and non-normal distribution (Ateş et al. 2019; Olson 1976).

Table 2.6 presents the two-way MANOVA results. A*B was used to refer to the learning preference factor*current learning mode. For example, online*face-to-face represented participants who prefer more online courses but currently have more face-to-face courses. The results showed a non-statistically significant difference in both depression and anxiety levels yielded by both learning preferences ($F(4, 238) = 2.06$, $p = 0.09$) and by current learning modes ($F(4, 238) = 0.70$, $p = 0.60$), and the interaction effect between these two independent variables was not significant ($F(8, 238) = 1.02$, $p = 0.42$). Although none of the data provided significant results, students who preferred more online courses, but currently had more face-to-face courses did share the highest scores on both GAD-7 ($M = 10.00$, $SD = 1.18$) and PHQ-9 ($M = 11.09$, $SD = 1.35$) scales. On the contrary, students with a more face-to-face preference but currently had more online courses scaled the third highest on GAD-7 ($M = 7.43$, $SD = 0.74$) and the second highest on the PHQ-9 ($M = 9.39$, $SD = 0.85$).

The study collected and analyzed various sociodemographic data as categorical factors to determine their association with participants' learning preferences. Due to space limitations, only significant findings are presented here, with the remaining results available in the appendices. Fisher's exact test was used to assess statistical significance in cases where the expected count in at least one cell of the Chi-Square

Table 2.6 Two-way MANOVA results on mental health scales

Scale	Group	Mean (SD)	Learning preference factor	Current learning mode factor Pillai's Trace	Interaction
				F (p-value)	
			0.07	0.02	
			0.07	2.06	
			0.7	1.02	
			(0.09)	(0.6)	
			(0.42)		
			Test of between-subject effects	F (p-value)	
GAD-7	Online*online	7.33 (0.92)	1.68 (0.19)	0.13 0.88)	1.26 (0.29)
	Online*face-to face	10.00 (1.18)			
	Online*equal number	7.75 (1.96)			
	Face-to-face*online	7.43 (0.74)			
	Face-to-face*face-to-face	6.04 (0.74)			
	Face-to-face*equal no	6.41 (0.95)			
	Preference*online	7.00 (1.31)			
	No preference*face-to-face no	7.00 (1.96)			
	Preference*online	7.32 (1.31)			
PHQ-9	Online*online	8.89 (1.05)	1.52 (0.22)	0.82 (0.44)	0.97 (0.43)
	Online*face to face	11.09 (1.35)			
	Online*equal number	8.75 (2.24)			
	Face-to-face*online	9.39 (0.85)			

(continued)

Table 2.6 (continued)

	Face-to-face*face-to-face	8.14 (0.85)			
	Face-to-face*equal no	8.35 (1.08)			
	Preference*online	8.56 (1.49)			
	No preference*face-to-face	7.50 (2.24)			
	No reference*equal	5.44 (1.49)			

tests was less than 5. The results showed that factors such as study levels, annual family income, personal COVID-19 diagnosis, and frequency of following COVID-19-related news influenced the distribution of international students' learning preferences ($p = .013$, $p = .023$, $p = .034$, $p < .001$, respectively). Other factors did not reach statistical significance.

Regarding study levels, the data revealed that 48% of undergraduate students preferred online courses, while only 19.2% of graduate students shared the same preference. Conversely, 63.3% of graduate students preferred more face-to-face courses, compared to 32% of undergraduate participants. Additionally, 30% of undergraduate students had no specific preferences, unlike 17.2% of graduate students.

In terms of annual family income, it was observed that participants from the wealthiest families exhibited a strong preference for face-to-face courses, with 100% of them expressing this preference. Conversely, only 33.3% of participants from families with below-average annual income favored face-to-face courses. Online courses were more popular among students from families with well below-average, below-average, and around-average financial backgrounds, with percentages of 33.3%, 33.3%, and 35.3 respectively.

Regarding a history of COVID-19, 61.8% of participants who had been infected with the virus and 59.2% who had never been diagnosed with COVID-19 indicated a preference for face-to-face courses. Meanwhile, 52.2% of participants who needed clarification about their COVID-19 status favored online courses.

Regarding the frequency of following COVID-19-related news, the results were divided into two groups using "follow the COVID-19 news about half the time" as the midpoint. Participants who paid more attention to COVID-19 news showed percentages of 30 and 42.9 for preferring online courses as their attention deepened. Conversely, most participants who paid less attention to COVID-19 news favored face-to-face courses (Tables 2.7, 2.8, 2.9 and 2.10).

Discussion

The primary aim of this study was to investigate the correlations between the learning preferences of international students, their current modes of learning, and their mental

Table 2.7 Learning preference * study level crosstabulation

Learning preference/study level		Undergraduate	Graduate	Prefer not to say
Prefer more online courses	n	12	19	2
	%	48.0	19.2	50.0
Prefer more face-to-face	n	8	63	2
	%	32.0	63.6	50.0
Courses	n	5	17	0
	%	30.0	17.2	0
No specific preference				

Note $X^2(4, N = 128) = 11.14, p = 0.013$

Table 2.8 Annual family income * learning preference crosstabulation

Annual family income/ learning preference		Prefer more online courses	Prefer more face-to-face courses	No specific preference
Well below average	n	1	1	1
	%	33.3	33.3	33.3
Below average	n	4	8	0
	%	33.3	66.7	0
Around average	n	22	27	13
	%	35.5	43.5	21.0
Above average	n	6	33	8
	%	12.8	70.2	17.0
Well above average	n	0	4	0
	%	0	100	0

Note $X^2(8, N = 128) = 15.35, p = 0.023$

health status during the COVID-19 pandemic. The study found that 24.3% of participants experienced clinical levels of anxiety, while 40.6% experienced clinical levels of depression. When compared to the findings of Wang et al. (2020) on the mental health of the general student population during COVID-19, the prevalence of depression remained similar, while the number of students with generalized anxiety disorder (GAD) decreased by approximately 16%. This variance may be attributed to the time gap between the two studies, which aligns with recent longitudinal studies that have provided evidence supporting the stability or even improvement of mental health status as the COVID-19 pandemic persisted (Belz et al. 2021; Fancourt et al. 2021; Huckins et al. 2020). However, despite the positive outlook presented by these studies regarding the potential for mental health to not further deteriorate during the prolonged pandemic, it remains a concern for specific demographic groups. In Fancourt et al. (2021) study, it was observed that although depression and anxiety

Table 2.9 Have you been diagnosed with COVID-19 * learning preference crosstabulation

Have you been diagnosed with COVID-19/learning preference		Prefer more online courses	Prefer more face-to-face courses	No specific preference
Yes	n	7	21	6
	%	20.6	61.8	17.6
Maybe	n	12	10	1
	%	52.2	43.5	4.3
No	n	14	42	15
	%	19.7	59.2	21.1

Note $X^2(4, N = 128) = 10.18, p = 0.034$

Table 2.10 How often do you follow the COVID-19 news* learning preference crosstabulation

How often do you follow the COVID-19 news/learning preference		Prefer more online courses	Prefer more face-to-face courses	No specific preference
Never	n	2	7	3
	%	16.7	58.3	25.0
Sometimes	n	10	49	11
	%	14.3	70.0	15.7
About half the time	N	15	8	6
	%	51.7	27.6	20.7
Most of the time	N	3	7	0
	%	30.0	70.0	0
Always	N	3	2	2
	%	42.9	28.6	28.6

Note $X^2(8, N = 128) = 23.12, p < 0.001$

levels decreased over 20 weeks following the government's announcement of lockdown policies, participants aged 18 to 29, typically university attendees, still exhibited the highest mean scores for both depression (8.3) and anxiety (7.6), which closely aligns with the data obtained in the current study. This underscores the vulnerability of the university population.

The study examined the Influence of participants' learning preferences and current learning modes on the mental health of international students, specifically in terms of depression and anxiety levels. The findings revealed that neither these factors nor their interaction significantly affected the participants mental health. This was unexpected, given the timing of the data collection at the end of term 2 in 2022, three years after the onset of the COVID-19 pandemic. Previous research in this area had been conducted immediately after universities implemented measures to combat the spread of COVID-19. It is plausible that students have become accustomed to the changes in learning modes, thereby reducing the impact on their mental health. Wei (2022) longitudinal study also suggested that the influence of learning modes on university students' mental health may fluctuate over time, particularly during transition periods between online and face-to-face learning. As the current data were collected at the end of term 2, students may have already navigated through the challenging transition period, diminishing the influence of learning modes on their mental health.

The lack of significant results for the Interaction effect may be partly attributed to the uneven distribution of participants in each group, with the smallest groups consisting of only four participants. Although learning preferences did not significant affect mental health, the study corroborated previous findings that most students prefer face-to-face courses (Patricia Aguilera-Hermida 2020). It is noteworthy that, despite not reaching statistical significance, students whose learning preferences contradicted their current learning modes scored higher on both depression and anxiety scales.

The Chi-Square test results revealed that several factors were significantly associated with specific learning preferences. These factors included the participants' study levels, annual family income, whether they had been diagnosed with COVID-19, and the frequency with which they followed COVID-19-related news. More international undergraduate students expressed a greater willingness to accept online courses than international graduate students. This finding can be attributed to the fact that international graduate students, particularly those in the UK, typically spend only around one year overseas, and online courses may hinder their ability to establish connections in their new environment. In contrast, undergraduates have more time to experience life overseas. Gupta and Agrawal's (2021) qualitative analysis of university students' concerns during the COVID-19 pandemic also highlighted students' worries about the lack of interaction in online courses, indicating a need for social connections.

The present investigation identified a consistent pattern among international students from affluent family backgrounds, who tend to favor in-person courses, and those from less affluent backgrounds, who lean towards online courses. This contrasts with previous findings concerning the general undergraduate or university student population. Subashini et al. (2022) observed a positive association between the acceptance of online learning and family income among more than 600 general undergraduate participants. This was further supported by an analysis of open-ended questions from the general university student population, suggesting that high tuition fees were linked to a preference for in-person courses due to the perception that online courses did not provide sufficient value for the money paid (Behera et al. 2022). One potential explanation for this discrepancy may be that international students from lower-income families, despite their desire to maximize the value of their tuition fees, face greater living costs than local students. These costs would be even more burdensome if courses were conducted on campus.

Additionally, a higher proportion of international students who needed clarification about their COVID-19 status preferred online courses. Increased attention to COVID-19-related news was also associated with a preference for online courses. These findings align with previous research indicating that concerns about personal health and frequent consumption of COVID-19 news were linked to heightened mental health issues during the pandemic (Kellerman et al. 2022; Son et al. 2020). Consequently, it is reasonable for these students to favor online courses, as the online setting reduces contact with others and lowers the risk of infection.

Limitations and future directions

The present study employed a cross-sectional design to recruit approximately 130 international students. The sample size was relatively small for a 3 × 3 between-subjects design, and a larger study with a more evenly distributed number of participants in each group would have enhanced the study's power and yielded more representative results. Given the biased distribution of the participants' ethnicity, the study needed more capacity to accurately reflect the true proportion of international students. This limitation should be considered in future research on international students' the mental health.

Findings indicated that the percentage of participants with clinically significant depression remained consistent with previous statistics, while the percentage of Generalized Anxiety Disorder (GAD) was relatively lower in the current study. However, due to the constraints of the cross-sectional design, these differences may be influenced by other factors, such as sample variance. Therefore, future studies should gather longitudinal data to examine trends in mental health, particularly in the context of the prolonged COVID-19 pandemic. This is crucial as most studies on mental health during the pandemic have relied on data collected in the early stages, and there is a need to explore how mental health trends evolve as life with COVID-19 gradually becomes normalized.

The current research did not find a significant interaction effect on mental health between learning preferences and current learning modes. However, participants with conflicting preferences and learning modes exhibited higher scores on the PHQ-9 and GAD-7 scales across all nine groups, suggesting that these students may be more vulnerable and in need of additional support. It is recommended that future studies replicate this relationship with a larger sample size. University mental health professionals are encouraged to prioritize students whose learning modes do not align with their preferences.

While the research yielded significant findings regarding the relationship between learning preferences and various personal-level factors, incorporating a qualitative approach would be beneficial in understanding why international students with specific characteristics may have preferred a particular learning mode. This approach would provide faculties with deeper insights into specific learning modes and facilitate a better alignment between students' preferences and the delivery modes of their official courses.

Conclusion

The current study expanded upon existing research regarding the correlation between learning preferences, current learning modes, and the mental well-being of international students during the COVID-19 pandemic. Surprisingly, the study found that neither learning preferences, current learning modes, nor the interaction between these two factors significantly impacted the mental health of international students in the aftermath of the pandemic. However, students with conflicting learning preferences and current learning modes exhibited higher scores on measures of depression and anxiety, although these differences did not reach statistical significance compared to other student groups. Furthermore, the study identified several characteristics of international students' specific learning preferences. The study acknowledged certain limitations that should be considered when interpreting the results and recommended more targeted research in the future. The results and recommendations for further research have important implications for policymakers to focus on delivery modes of lessons and for mental health practitioners and educators to support vulnerable students in the post-pandemic period. The findings indicated that students with conflicting learning modes and preferences may experience greater levels of anxiety and depression, although these differences did not reach statistical significance. Additionally, students' academic levels, annual family income, personal COVID-19 diagnosis, and frequency of following COVID-19-related news significantly contributed to their specific learning preferences.

References

Adedoyin OB, Soykan E (2020) Covid-19 pandemic and online learning: the challenges and opportunities. Interact Learn Environ:1–13. https://doi.org/10.1080/10494820.2020.1813180

Adewuya A, Ola B, Afolabi O (2006) Validity of the patient health questionnaire (PHQ-9) as a screening tool for depression amongst Nigerian university students. J Affect Disord 96(1–2):89–93. https://doi.org/10.1016/j.jad.2006.05.021

Aguilera-Hermida AP (2020) College students' use and acceptance of emergency online learning due to COVID-19. Int J Educ Res Open 1:100011. https://doi.org/10.1016/j.ijedro.2020.100011

Alharbi E, Smith A (2018) Review of the literature on stress and wellbeing of international students in English-speaking countries. Int Educ Stud 11(6):22. https://doi.org/10.5539/ies.v11n6p22

Ali W (2020) Online and remote learning in higher education institutes: a necessity in light of COVID-19 pandemic. High Educ Stud 10(3):16–25. https://doi.org/10.5539/hes.v10n3p16

Amit-Aharon A, Melnikov S, Warshawski S (2020) The effect of evidence-based practice perception, information literacy self-efficacy, and academic motivation on nursing students' future implementation of evidence-based practice. J Prof Nurs 36(6):497–502. https://doi.org/10.1016/j.profnurs.2020.04.001

An B, Lim J (2017) Relationship among Korean university students' suicidal ideation, posttraumatic growth, self-efficacy, and cultural orientation. Int J Adv Nursing Educ Res 1(1):83–88. https://doi.org/10.21742/ijaner.2017.2.1.15

Ateş C, Kaymaz Ö, Kale H, Tekindal M (2019) Comparison of test statistics of nonnormal and unbalanced samples for multivariate analysis of variance in terms of type-i error rates. Comput Math Methods Med 2019:1–8. https://doi.org/10.1155/2019/2173638

Baber H (2020) Determinants of students' perceived learning outcome and satisfaction in online learning in the COVID-19 Era of COVID-19. J Educ e-learn Res 7(3):285–292. https://doi.org/10.20448/journal.509.2020.73.285.292

Bao W (2020) COVID-19 and online teaching in higher education: A case study of Peking University. Hum Behav Emerg Technol 2(2):113–115. https://doi.org/10.1002/hbe2.191

Behera A, de Sousa R, Oleksik V, Dong J, Fritzen D (2022) Student perceptions of remote learning transitions in engineering disciplines during the COVID-19 pandemic: a cross-national study. Eur J Eng Educ 1–33. https://doi.org/10.1080/03043797.2022.2080529
Belz M, Hessmann P, Vogelgsang J, Schmidt U, Ruhleder M, Signerski-Krieger J et al (2021) Evolution of psychosocial burden and psychiatric symptoms in patients with psychiatric disorders during the Covid-19 pandemic. Eur Arch Psychiatry Clin Neurosci 272(1):29–40. https://doi.org/10.1007/s00406-021-01268-6
Britt M, Goon D, Timmerman M (2015) How to better engage online students with online strategies. Coll Stud J 49(3):399–404
Browning M, Larson L, Sharaievska I, Rigolon A, McAnirlin O, Mullenbach L et al (2021) Psychological impacts from COVID-19 among university students: risk factors across seven states in the United States. PLoS ONE 16(1):e0245327. https://doi.org/10.1371/journal.pone.0245327
Cao W, Fang Z, Hou G, Han M, Xu X, Dong J, Zheng J (2020) The psychological impact of the COVID-19 epidemic on college students in China. Psychiatry Res 287:112934. https://doi.org/10.1016/j.psychres.2020.112934
Charles N, Strong S, Burns L, Bullerjahn M, Serafine K (2021) Increased mood disorder symptoms, perceived stress, and alcohol use among college students during the COVID-19 pandemic. Psychiatry Res 296:113706. https://doi.org/10.1016/j.psychres.2021.113706
Chen J, Li Y, Wu A, Tong K (2020) The overlooked minority: mental health of international students worldwide under the COVID-19 pandemic and beyond. Asian J Psychiatry 54:102333. https://doi.org/10.1016/j.ajp.2020.102333
Chiu TK (2022) Applying the self-determination theory (SDT) to explain student engagement in online learning during the COVID-19 pandemic. J Res Technol Educ 54(sup1):S14–S30. https://doi.org/10.1080/15391523.2021.1891998
Christenson S, Reschly AL, Wylie C (2012) Handbook of research on student engagement, vol 840. Springer. https://doi.org/10.1007/978-1-4614-2018-7
Crumpton HE, Gregory A (2011) "I'm not learning": The role of academic relevancy for low-achieving students. J Educ Res 104(1):42–53. https://doi.org/10.1080/00220670903567398
Dadfar M, Lester D, Hosseini A, Eslami M (2021) The patient health questionnaire-9 (PHQ-9) as a brief screening tool for depression: a study of Iranian college students. Mental Health Relig Cult 24(8):850–861. https://doi.org/10.1080/13674676.2021.1956884
Fancourt D, Steptoe A, Bu F (2021) Trajectories of anxiety and depressive symptoms during enforced isolation due to COVID-19 in England: a longitudinal observational study. The Lancet Psychiatry 8(2):141–149. https://doi.org/10.1016/s2215-0366(20)30482-x
Farooq F, Rathore FA, Mansoor SN (2020) Challenges of online medical education in Pakistan during COVID-19 pandemic. J Coll Phys Surg Pak 30(6):67–69. https://doi.org/10.29271/jcpsp.2020.Supp1.S67
Ferrer J, Ringer A, Saville K, Parris MA, Kashi K (2020) Students' motivation and engagement in higher education: the importance of attitude to online learning. High Educ:1–22. https://doi.org/10.1007/s10734-020-00657-5
Froiland JM, Worrell FC (2016) Intrinsic motivation, learning goals, engagement, and achievement in a diverse high school. Psychol Sch 53(3):321–336. https://doi.org/10.1002/pits.21901
García-Morales VJ, Garrido-Moreno A, Martín-Rojas R (2021) The transformation of higher education after the COVID disruption: Emerging challenges in an online learning scenario. Front Psychol 12:616059. https://doi.org/10.3389/fpsyg.2021.616059
Ghasemi A, Zahediasl S (2012) Normality tests for statistical analysis: a guide for non-statisticians. Int J Endocrinol Metab 10(2):486. https://doi.org/10.5812/ijem.3505
Gupta R, Agrawal R (2021) Are the concerns destroying mental health of college students?: A qualitative analysis portraying experiences amidst COVID-19 ambiguities. Anal Soc Issues Public Policy 21(1):621–639. https://doi.org/10.1111/asap.12232
Hess AJ (2021) Online learning boomed during the pandemic-but what happens when students return to classrooms? CNBC. https://www.cnbc.com/2021/03/26/online-learning-boomed-during-the-pandemic-but-soon-students-return-to-school.html

Harter S (1981) A new self-report scale of intrinsic versus extrinsic orientation in the classroom: motivational and informational components. Dev Psychol 17(3):300. https://doi.org/10.1037/0012-1649.17.3.300

Hsieh T-L (2014) Motivation matters? The relationship among different types of learning motivation, engagement behaviours and learning outcomes of undergraduate students in Taiwan. High Educ 68(3):417–433. https://doi.org/10.1007/s10734-014-9720-6

Hu M, Li H (2017) Student engagement in online learning: a review. In: International symposium on educational technology (ISET). https://doi.org/10.1109/ISET.2017.17

Huckins JF, Wang W et al (2020) Mental health and behaviour of college students during the early phases of the COVID-19 pandemic: longitudinal smartphone and ecological momentary assessment study. J Med Internet Res 22(6):e20185. https://doi.org/10.2196/20185

Kellerman J, Hamilton J, Selby E, Kleiman E (2022) The mental health impact of daily news exposure during the COVID-19 pandemic: ecological momentary assessment study. JMIR Mental Health 9(5):e36966. https://doi.org/10.2196/36966

Kroenke K, Spitzer R (2002) The PHQ-9: a new depression diagnostic and severity measure. Psychiatr Ann 32(9):509–515. https://doi.org/10.3928/0048-5713-20020901-06

Kroenke K, Spitzer R, Williams J (2001) The PHQ-9. J Gen Intern Med 16(9):606–613. https://doi.org/10.1046/j.1525-1497.2001.016009606.x

Kuzminykh I, Ghita B, Xiao H (2021) The relationship between student engagement and academic performance in online education. In: 5th International conference on e-society, e-education and e-technology. https://doi.org/10.1145/3485768.3485796

Lai A, Lee L, Wang M, Feng Y, Lai T, Ho L et al (2020) Mental Health Impacts of the COVID-19 Pandemic on international university students, related stressors, and coping strategies. Front Psych:11. https://doi.org/10.3389/fpsyt.2020.584240

Law W, Elliot AJ, Murayama K (2012) Perceived competence moderates the relation between performance-approach and performance-avoidance goals. J Educ Psychol 104(3):806. https://doi.org/10.1037/a0027179

Löwe B, Decker O, Müller S, Brähler E, Schellberg D, Herzog W, Herzberg P (2008) Validation and standardization of the generalized anxiety disorder screener (GAD-7) in the general population. Med Care 46(3):266–274. https://doi.org/10.1097/mlr.0b013e318160d093

Lowrey A (2022) Coronavirus is fueling a surge in hate crimes. Giffords. https://giffords.org/blog/2020/04/coronavirus-is-fueling-a-surge-in-hate-crimes-blog/. Accessed 26 June 2022

Lu Y, Wang B, Lu Y (2019) Understanding key drivers of MOOC satisfaction and continuance intention to use. J Electr Commer Res:20(2)

Martin AJ (2007) Examining a multidimensional model of student motivation and engagement using a construct validation approach. Br J Educ Psychol 77(2):413–440. https://doi.org/10.1348/000709906X118036

Martin F, Bolliger DU (2018) Engagement matters: student perceptions on the importance of engagement strategies in the online learning environment. Online Learn 22(1):205–222. https://doi.org/10.24059/olj.v22i1.1092

Martin J (2010) Stigma and student mental health in higher education. High Educ Res Dev 29(3):259–274. https://doi.org/10.1080/07294360903470969

Meeter M, Bele T, den Hartogh C, Bakker T, de Vries RE, Plak S (2020) College students' motivation and study results after COVID-19 stay-at-home orders

Meyer KA (2014) Student engagement online: What works and Why: ASHE higher education report, vol 40(6). John Wiley & Sons. https://doi.org/10.1002/aehe.20018

Mitchell I, Carbone A (2011) A typology of task characteristics and their effects on student engagement. Int J Educ Res 50(5–6):257–270. https://doi.org/10.1016/j.ijer.2011.05.001

Olson C (1976) On choosing a test statistic in multivariate analysis of variance. Psychol Bull 83(4):579–586. https://doi.org/10.1037/0033-2909.83.4.579

Patricia Aguilera-Hermida A (2020) College students' use and acceptance of emergency online learning due to COVID-19. Int J Educ Res Open 1:100011. https://doi.org/10.1016/j.ijedro.2020.100011

Puljak L, Čivljak M, Haramina A, Mališa S, Čavić D, Klinec D et al (2020) Attitudes and concerns of undergraduate university health sciences students in Croatia regarding complete switch to e-learning during COVID-19 pandemic: a survey. BMC Med Educ 20(1). https://doi.org/10.1186/s12909-020-02343-7

Reeve J (2012) A self-determination theory perspective on student engagement. In: Handbook of research on student engagement. Springer, pp 149–172. https://doi.org/10.1007/978-1-4614-2018-7_7

Reeve J (2013) How students create motivationally supportive learning environments for themselves: the concept of agentic engagement. J Educ Psychol 105(3):579. https://doi.org/10.1037/a0032690

Reeve J, Tseng C-M (2011) Agency as a fourth aspect of students' engagement during learning activities. Contemp Educ Psychol 36(4):257–267. https://doi.org/10.1016/j.cedpsych.2011.05.002

Ryan RM, Deci EL (2000) Self-determination theory and the facilitation of intrinsic motivation, social development, and well-being. Am Psychol 55(1):68. https://doi.org/10.1037/0003-066X.55.1.68

Saeed S, Zyngier D (2012) How motivation influences student engagement: a qualitative case study. J Educ Learn 1(2):252–267. https://doi.org/10.5539/jel.v1n2p252

Sahu P (2020) Closure of universities due to coronavirus disease 2019 (COVID-19): impact on education and mental health of students and academic staff. Cureus. https://doi.org/10.7759/cureus.7541

Santomauro D, Mantilla Herrera A, Shadid J, Zheng P, Ashbaugh C, Pigott D et al (2021) Global prevalence and burden of depressive and anxiety disorders in 204 countries and territories in 2020 due to the COVID-19 pandemic. The Lancet 398(10312):1700–1712. https://doi.org/10.1016/s0140-6736(21)02143-7

Sinatra GM, Heddy BC, Lombardi D (2015) The challenges of defining and measuring student engagement in science. Educ Psychol 50(1):1–13. https://doi.org/10.1080/00461520.2014.1002924

Skinner EA, Belmont MJ (1993) Motivation in the classroom: reciprocal effects of teacher behaviour and student engagement across the school year. J Educ Psychol 85(4):571. https://doi.org/10.1037/0022-0663.85.4.571

Son C, Hegde S, Smith A, Wang X, Sasangohar F (2020) Effects of COVID-19 on college students' mental health in the United States: interview survey study. J Med Internet Res 22(9):e21279. https://doi.org/10.2196/21279

Spitzer R, Kroenke K, Williams J, Löwe B (2006) A brief measure for assessing generalized anxiety disorder. Arch Intern Med 166(10):1092. https://doi.org/10.1001/archinte.166.10.1092

Stark E (2019) Examining the role of motivation and learning strategies in student success in online versus face-to-face courses. Online Learn 23(3):234–251. https://doi.org/10.24059/olj.v23i3.1556

Subashini N, Udayanga L, De Silva L, Edirisinghe J, Nafla M (2022) Undergraduate perceptions on transitioning into E-learning for continuation of higher education during the COVID pandemic in a developing country: a cross-sectional study from Sri Lanka. BMC Med Educ 22(1). https://doi.org/10.1186/s12909-022-03586-2, supporting international students. Dera.ioe.ac.uk. (2022). https://dera.ioe.ac.uk//35616/1/coronavirus-briefing-note-supporting-international-students.pdf. Accessed 26 June 2022

Sun JCY, Rueda R (2012) Situational interest, computer self-efficacy and self-regulation: their impact on student engagement in distance education. Br J Edu Technol 43(2):191–204. https://doi.org/10.1111/j.1467-8535.2010.01157.x

Tichavsky L, Hunt A, Driscoll A, Jicha K (2015) "It's just nice having a real teacher": student perceptions of online versus face-to-face instruction. Int J Scholarsh Teach Learn:9(2). https://doi.org/10.20429/ijsotl.2015.090202

Tran TV, Aspiras O (2022) College students' engagement and academic outcomes in online learning during the COVID-19 pandemic. Mod Psychol Stud 28(1):3. https://scholar.utc.edu/mps/vol28/iss1/3

Vallerand RJ, Pelletier LG, Blais MR, Briere NM, Senecal C, Vallieres EF (1992) The academic motivation scale: a measure of intrinsic, extrinsic, and a motivation in education. Educ Psychol Measur 52(4):1003–1017. https://doi.org/10.1177/0013164492052004025

Walker CO, Greene BA, Mansell RA (2006) Identification with academics, intrinsic/extrinsic motivation, and self-efficacy as predictors of cognitive engagement. Learn Individ Differ 16(1):1–12. https://doi.org/10.1016/j.lindif.2005.06.004

Wang X, Hegde S, Son C, Keller B, Smith A, Sasangohar F (2020) Investigating mental health of US college students during the COVID-19 pandemic: cross-sectional survey study. J Med Internet Res 22(9):e22817. https://doi.org/10.2196/22817

Wei Z (2022) Social support, psychological responses, and mental health among college students during online learning. Interact Learn Environ 1–12. https://doi.org/10.1080/10494820.2022.2078375

Wu Z (2019) Academic motivation, engagement, and achievement among college students. Coll Stud J 53(1):99–112

Xiong Y, Li H, Kornhaber ML, Suen HK, Pursel B, Goins DD (2015) Examining the relations among student motivation, engagement, and retention in a MOOC: a structural equation modelling approach. Glob Educ Rev 2(3):23–33

Zhang B, Li YM, Li J, Li Y, Zhang H (2016) The revision and validation of the academic motivation scale in China. J Psychoeduc Assess 34(1):15–27. https://doi.org/10.1177/0734282915575909

Zhang J, Goodson P (2011) Predictors of international students' psychosocial adjustment to life in the United States: a systematic review. Int J Intercult Relat 35(2):139–162. https://doi.org/10.1016/j.ijintrel.2010.11.011

Zhang Y, Liang W, Chen Z, Zhang H, Zhang J, Weng X et al (2013) Validity and reliability of patient health questionnaire-9 and patient health questionnaire-2 to screen for depression among college students in China. Asia Pac Psychiatry 5(4):268–275. https://doi.org/10.1111/appy.12103

Can He Can received her BSc and MSc in Psychology of education from University College London, and after graduation, she is committed to developing in the field of psychological counselling. Can was previously a child behavioural trainer in a private psychological institution to help train sensory integration skills of pre-school, primary and secondary school students, and has been a municipal hotline operator for years, regularly receiving supervisory training. She has participated in the Jianping Wang Cognitive Behavioural Therapy Continuous Training Program certified by Chinese Psychological Society, and in the meanwhile provide psychological counselling services for high school students in an international high school. Can currently works as a psychological consultation teacher at an international high school in Shanghai, China. She is very interested in exploring students' learning and mental health during the pandemic and is looking to further her studies in this area.

Dr. Elsie Ong is a Lecturer and a Dissertation Supervisor in UCL. She has worked in many universities in Asia and the UK for over ten years. Elsie is active in leading research that focuses on the mental health of young adults; especially those going through university transitions. Her expertise in cognitive neuroscience and psychology has also initiated further exploration on the underlying causes of mental health problems and later sparkles potentials for suicide preventions and interventions. Elsie is devoted to the study of psychological wellbeing in young adults and has published her research through internationally renowned conferences and reputed journals such as Frontiers in psychiatry. These experiences have helped to keep her most up to date on the latest development in preventions and interventions in mental health.

Chapter 3
Living in the Pandemic

Bethany Finch and Elsie Ong

Overview

In the previous chapter, we discussed individuals' challenges during the pandemic. In this chapter of this book, we will explore the global impact of COVID-19 and how people have been coping with this challenging situation. We will then focus on the specific impact of COVID-19 on young people and examine how they have been dealing with these challenges in various environments. We will present evidence from two separate studies. The **first study** will investigate coping strategies among 80 university students in the UK, using a mixed-method approach to examine the connection between coping strategies and psychological wellbeing. After identifying the significance of social interaction as an effective coping strategy for young people, we will delve into a specific group of students who have lacked these interactions with their families during the pandemic. The **second study** will qualitatively explore university students living in Hong Kong during the pandemic. We will examine the experiences of Chinese students living in residential halls and how COVID-19 impacted their lives. We will identify the stressors associated with COVID-19 and understand how students adopted different coping strategies in response to the pandemic. While various coping strategies were evident in students from both Hong Kong and the UK, very few students sought help from professional psychological resources. Therefore, the findings from both studies in this chapter highlight the

B. Finch (✉)
IOE—Psychology and Human Development, UCL Institute of Education, University College London, 24–26 Woburn Square, London, WC 1H 0AA, UK
e-mail: bethany.finch.20@ucl.ac.uk

E. Ong
Department of Psychology and Human Development, IOE—UCL's Faculty of Education and Society, University College London, London, WC 1E 6BT, UK
e-mail: Elsie.ong@ucl.ac.uk

E. Ong (ed.), *The Emergence of the Digital World*,
https://doi.org/10.1007/978-981-97-3098-8_3

urgent need for interventions and preventive strategies to address the mental health of university students, as the impacts of COVID-19 are likely to be long-lasting.

Keywords Coping strategies, Stressors, Mental health, Residential halls, Pandemic

Overview of the Impact of the COVID-19 Pandemic

The COVID-19 pandemic has had a significant global impact due to its rapid transmission and high mortality rate (Shivalkar et al. 2021). Millions of people have been diagnosed with the virus, leading to widespread social distancing measures and lockdowns to reduce its spread (Das et al. 2021, Sharma 2018). These measures have greatly affected people's daily lives and habits (Onyeaka et al. 2021). Studies have shown an increase in anxiety, depression, and stress among adolescents, survivors, and healthcare workers during this time (Chen et al. 2020; Li et al. 2019; Mazza et al. 2020).

The COVID-19 pandemic, which began in late 2019, has had a profound impact on societies worldwide, leading to a secondary crisis in mental health issues. Young people have been particularly affected, with mental health issues already on the rise before the pandemic due to factors such as academic pressures, social media, economic uncertainty, and the stigma surrounding mental health. In this chapter, we will explore the various factors contributing to the increase in mental health issues among young people following the pandemic and discuss potential strategies and solutions needed to address this issue.

What Were the Main Stressors for Young People?

In the UK, COVID-19 has been a significant source of stress for many, resulting in the loss of over 200,000 lives and impacting millions worldwide (Saltzman et al. 2020: GOV.UK 2023). The pandemic led to social isolation, temporary closures of schools and universities, loss of livelihoods, suspended medical treatment, and restricted freedom of movement (World Health Organisation 2021: Heanoy et al. 2021). Social support from family, romantic or professional relationships, or psychosocial interventions like talking therapies can help individuals cope with stress (Ozbay et al. 2007). Research by Loades et al. (2020) and Hawkley and Cacioppo (2010) has shown that social isolation and loneliness can contribute to depression and anxiety. These findings highlight the increasing relevance of studying stress, particularly concerning socioeconomic status.

Social support refers to the assistance and comfort provided through interpersonal connections and one's social circle (Dueñas et al. 2019; Olatunji et al. 2020). Studies conducted before the COVID-19 pandemic have demonstrated a strong link between social support, including support from family, friends, and significant others, and depression and suicidal thoughts in young adults (Dueñas et al. 2019; Olatunji et al. 2020). Research has also shown that individuals who received higher levels of social support during lockdowns experienced lower levels of depression compared to those with less social support (Grey et al. 2020). Furthermore, support from friends has been identified as a protective factor against depressive symptoms and stress among adolescents during the pandemic (Espinoza and Hernandez 2022). While the importance of social support among adolescents has been emphasized, it is crucial to consider the role of support from friends among young adults, especially students who have left their homes and are more focused on their relationships with peers.

Lechner et al. (2020) discovered that university students with lower levels of social support exhibited higher levels of alcohol consumption and psychological distress. These findings highlight the significance of social support among adolescents and transgender young adults and suggest an indirect connection between social support and depression among young adult students.

Social Support in University

A comprehensive study by Leal Filho et al. (2021) assessed the impact of university closures on students and staff during global lockdowns and restrictions. The study included 711 participants from 41 countries and found that 72% of respondents reported negative impacts on students' interactions with peers and academic staff and their ability to engage in teaching and learning fully. Additionally, the study highlighted accessibility challenges, particularly for students with disabilities or socioeconomic disadvantages, which could lead to feelings of exclusion and potentially affect students' mental health during the pandemic (Lazar 2021; Pokhrel and Chhetri 2021; Fawaz and Samaha 2021). However, due to the recent nature of the pandemic, conclusive research on the impact of university disruptions is still limited. Further extensive research is necessary to gain a deeper understanding of how COVID-19 has affected the mental health of students in the UK and worldwide.

Social Support and Mental Health

The significance of social support has grown in importance during the pandemic, particularly due to the enforced self-isolation measures, which have posed challenges for individuals and potentially impacted their mental well-being (Szkody et al. 2021). Szkody and colleagues (2021) conducted a study examining the role of social support during COVID-19 among 344 university students in the USA, utilizing online surveys recruited through snowball sampling. The findings revealed that participants who engaged in self-isolation received less social support, leading to adverse effects on their mental health. Specifically, those reporting lower levels of social support experienced heightened feelings of loneliness (Szkody et al. 2021). Consequently, these individuals also reported increased depressive symptoms and anxiety, indicating an association between social support and maladaptive emotional regulation. This study offers valuable insights into the impact of community disconnection on the mental health of university students.

Research has established a connection between social isolation and social support (Amit et al. 2020). The prevalence of social support and loneliness has increased during the pandemic, potentially contributing to heightened social isolation as individuals feel disconnected from their communities due to changes in communication and a general lack of connectedness (Saltzman et al. 2020). Zhou and colleagues (2021) investigated social isolation, social support, depressive symptoms, and anxiety in 11,133 Chinese university students through an online survey. Respondents reporting high levels of social support exhibited lower levels of social isolation, suggesting that social support may be a protective factor against social isolation (Zhou et al. 2021). Furthermore, using questionnaires, Bibi and colleagues (2021) conducted a longitudinal study on social support and social isolation in 355 university students. Their findings were consistent with previous research, indicating the critical role of social support in reducing anxiety symptoms and overall mental well-being (Bibi et al. 2021). Given the longitudinal nature of this study, it can be inferred that consistent social support is effective in mitigating the risk of suicidal thoughts, as the participants' thoughts and feelings were documented over an extended period (Caruana et al. 2015). These studies underscore the importance of social support in promoting positive mental health among students and highlight how the pandemic may have heightened levels of social isolation due to changes in connectedness.

Bostan et al. (2020) found that university students were particularly affected during the COVID-19 lockdown, experiencing anxiety, stress, frustration, and depressive disorders due to changes in academic structures and examinations. Assessing students' perspectives, responses, and progress during the pandemic is crucial. Boden et al. identified stressors of the COVID-19 pandemic, such as infection, economic hardship, layoffs, stigmatization, or quarantine restrictions, which may have adverse effects on mental health. Han et al. (2021) categorized stressors related to infectious diseases into six groups and developed a checklist to assess participants' experiences of COVID-19-related stressors associated with contagious diseases.

Examples of the Stressors in the Six Categories:

(1) **Self-related events**—You have the experience of contacting with a confirmed COVID-19 case;
(2) **Family-related events**—A member of your family was a confirmed COVID-19 case
(3) **Friend-related events**—A close friend of yours was diagnosed with COVID-19

(4) **Acquaintance-related events**—Someone you know (not including your family members or close friends) had COVID-19-like symptoms (fever, coughing)
(5) **Information-related events**—You heard others talking about the severity and contagiousness of COVID-19
(6) **Other COVID-19-related events**—Your family members had to be in contact with others because of work.

How Did Young People Cope During the Pandemic?

During the COVID-19 pandemic, many individuals found themselves spending more time indoors and experiencing reduced social interaction, which contributed to worsening mental health issues (Cao et al. 2020). Young people faced significant challenges adjusting to the shift from traditional in-person learning to remote education (Onyeaka et al. 2021). The varying coping mechanisms employed during this stressful lockdown period may account for individual psychological well-being differences, there needs to be more research on how young people have adapted to cope with these unprecedented circumstances.

The term "coping" refers to the cognitive and behavioural efforts employed in response to negative or adverse situations, such as the ongoing pandemic (Ray et al. 1982). Individuals with adaptive coping strategies can mitigate the detrimental effects of such events (Leipold & Greve, 2009). There exists variability in individuals' perspectives on what constitutes an adaptive coping strategy, and even within the same individual, opinions on adaptive coping strategies may differ across different stages of life. For instance, during the initial phase of adolescence (ages 11–13), emphasis is placed on strategies such as planning, positive reframing, and acceptance (Bourduge et al. 2022). This emphasis may be linked to the development of metacognitive abilities, which facilitate the adaptation of coping efforts to stressors by enhancing the range and flexibility of available coping responses.

In contrast, the latter phase of adolescence (ages 14–17 years) sees an increased utilization of coping strategies associated with emotional and instrumental support (Bourduge et al. 2022). Generally, the most adaptive coping strategies encompass active coping, planning, positive reframing, and acceptance, while denial, behavioural withdrawal, and substance use are considered maladaptive (Ong and Thompson 2018).

Coping is a dynamic behaviour that evolves based on individual experiences, with people employing various coping strategies in response to stressful events. Childhood experiences contribute to the development and abandonment of coping strategies that are deemed ineffective (Ong and Thompson 2018). Dawson and Golijani-Moghaddam (2020) discovered in the UK that individuals utilizing adaptive coping strategies tend to have higher levels of psychological well-being. Furthermore, in a cross-sectional study conducted in the Philippines, Labrague et al. (2021) investigated the impact of coping strategies on loneliness among university students. They found that students employing problem-oriented coping strategies experienced fewer physical and mental health issues, although their resilience levels were low. Similar findings were reported in international studies, indicating a significant decline in resilience levels among students in Italy, Spain, and Poland during the pandemic (Forycka et al. 2022; Morales-Rodríguez, 2021; Quintiliani et al. 2022). Given the often-correlated nature of coping and resilience, this suggests a need for further research to comprehend the interplay of coping strategies, resilience, and depression within the context of higher education.

Study One: Exploring Psychological Wellbeing and Coping Strategies Among University Students During the Pandemic

Bethany Finch and Elsie Ong

Keywords University students, Depression, Coping, Resilience, Anxiety

Aims and objectives of the current study

Considering the nature of the COVID-19 pandemic, research explicitly focusing on coping strategies and depression in university students is still emerging. Research has indicated that mental health has been adversely affected in students. However, much of the current research is predominately on quantitative research methods. Therefore, the current study proposed a mixed methodology to explore using different Coping strategies in university students. This could add depth to the existing knowledge on the links between psychological well-being and coping of individuals during the pandemic. The current research investigates how university students adopt different coping strategies through the pandemic era.

Methodology

Design

A correlational and qualitative design was used in this study. Participants completed two questionnaires to assess their perceived coping strategies and psychological well-being states. Through thematic analysis, the current study aims to explore insight into how mental health was affected and how Coping strategies have evolved throughout the pandemic. Open-ended questions were used to explore how students have accessed online support and if their tendencies towards adaptive or maladaptive coping strategies have changed. Based on their responses, participants were grouped into either a minimal, mild, moderate, or severe depression group, and a low, medium, or high Coping strategies group.

Participants

Participants were university students aged 18 to 25 who responded to a post requesting the participation of students in an online questionnaire posted within a university forum and participants recruiting online platforms. All current participants had also been students during the initial March 2020 UK lockdown at the beginning of the pandemic. This study consisted of 80 participants recruited via convenience sampling, of which 61 were female, 14 were male and five identified as non-binary or third gender. Participants ranged in age from 20 to 25 ($M = 23.76$, $SD = 1.43$) however, two participants preferred not to disclose their age.

Materials

The study utilized the **Beck Depression Inventory-II (BDI-II)** to assess depressive symptoms and attitudes. This self-reporting 21-item questionnaire, developed by Beck et al. (1996), employs a 4-point scale to measure participants' feelings over the preceding two weeks. The BDI-II encompasses various topics such as guilt, sadness, and changes in appetite and sleep, as Warmenhoven et al. (2012) noted. Scores on the BDI-II range from 0 to 63, with different score ranges indicating varying levels of depression severity: 0–13 for minimal depression, 14–19 for mild depression, 20–28 for moderate depression, and 29–63 for severe depression. The BDI-II has demonstrated high reliability and effectiveness within university and college populations ($\alpha = 0.93$), and has been found suitable for use with university students of diverse ethnic backgrounds, as ethnicity did not significantly impact response to items (Carmody, 2005).

Coping strategies were assessed using **The Brief Resilient Coping Scale (BRCS)** developed by Sinclair and Wallston (2004). This 4-item scale measures individuals' inclination to employ positive, adaptive coping skills when confronted with stressful or challenging life events or circumstances. Participants rate the extent to which the items describe their behaviour on a 5-point scale, with scores ranging from 4 to 20. Scores of 4–13 indicate low resilient coping, 14–16 suggest medium resilient coping, and 17–20 indicate high resilient coping behaviour. Despite its small number of items, the BRCS has been found to possess adequate reliability and effectiveness in capturing coping strategies ($\alpha = 0.76$), and is effective when used in young adults and student populations (Limonero et al. 2014).

Open-ended Questions

The current study allowed participants to answer five open questions relating to their experiences of mental health and Coping strategies during the COVID-19 pandemic. The questions included were:

1. "Do you feel as if the COVID-19 pandemic has affected you? If so, in what ways?"
2. "During the pandemic, did you access any form of online support for mental health? (For example, online therapy, online GP appointments, etc.)"
3. "What coping strategies did you use before the pandemic?"

4. "Did you change the strategies you used to cope with stressful situations due to the pandemic?"
5. "If relevant, which coping strategies have helped you best deal with depression or other mental health issues?"

These questions were optional, and deliberately open to allow participants to include as much or as little data as they felt comfortable. Qualitative data were collected online rather than in-person interviews due to ongoing COVID-19 restrictions but also allowed participants to be honest and open about potentially challenging topics surrounding the pandemic and mental health.

Procedure

The research study received ethical approval from the university. Participants were provided a brief overview of the research and informed that their involvement was voluntary, and their data would remain anonymous. They were also assured they could skip any questions they were uncomfortable with. Following this, participants were asked to provide demographic information and complete three questionnaires. Subsequently, they were requested to respond to open-ended questions regarding coping mechanisms and experiences with depression during the COVID-19 pandemic. A debrief was then provided to the participants. The qualitative data was imported into Nvivo and analyzed using a six-step reflexive thematic analysis method (Braun and Clarke 2006; Braun and Clarke 2019). The data was reviewed multiple times to identify recurring themes, and codes were assigned to repeated information and topics across participant responses. These codes were then used to extract overarching themes related to participants' experiences during the pandemic and their reflections on life before the pandemic. These themes were carefully assessed to ensure their relevance to the research and to avoid any significant overlap. Subsequently, the main themes were further defined and expanded to include sub-themes and relationships within the qualitative data, following the guidelines outlined by Braun and Clarke (2019).

Results

Reliability of Scales

Cronbach's alpha was calculated for each scale to assess the internal reliability of the scale items. The Beck Depression Inventory-II (BDI) consisted of 21 items ($\alpha = 0.93$), indicating a high level of reliability. The Brief Resilient Coping Scale consisted of 4 items ($\alpha = 0.73$), indicating an acceptable level of reliability (Table 3.1).

Table 3.1 Means and standard deviations of participants' scores for each scale

Scale	M	SD
Beck depression inventory-II	14.39	10.95
Brief resilient coping scale	13.27	3.49

Depression and Coping Strategies Scores

The prevalence of students who met the threshold for depression was 41.2%. 47 participants had minimal depression (58.8%), 13 participants had mild depression (16.3%), 10 participants had moderate depression (12.5%), and 9 participants had severe depression (11.3%). One participant did not complete the questionnaire. While depression in the sample was relatively high, previous research indicated that levels of depression would be significantly more prevalent in student populations than the current study indicated.

Results indicated that many participants had low Coping strategies, with 40 participants categorized as low resilient copers (50.6%), 21 as medium resilient copers (26.6%), and 18 participants as high resilient copers (22.8%). One participant did not complete the questionnaire.

The Relationship between Depression and Coping strategies

A Pearson correlation coefficient was conducted and revealed that depression and Coping strategies were strongly correlated, $r(77) = -0.514$, $p < 0.001$ (Fig. 3.1).

Qualitative Research Findings

Of the 80 participants who participated in the research questionnaire, 73 answered the optional open-ended questions after completing the previous questionnaires (Figs. 3.2 and 3.3).

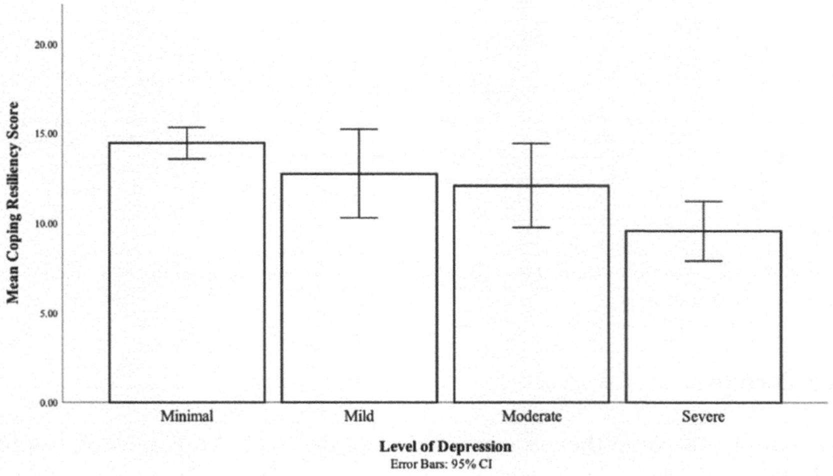

Fig. 3.1 A bar chart to show the relationship between levels of depression and coping strategies

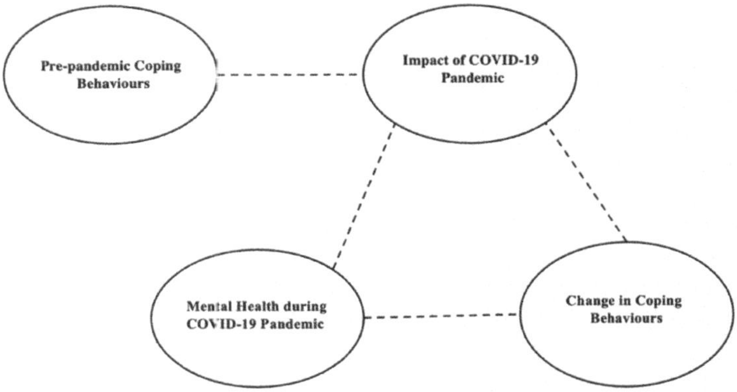

Fig. 3.2 A thematic map to show the main themes of the qualitative analysis and their relationship to one another

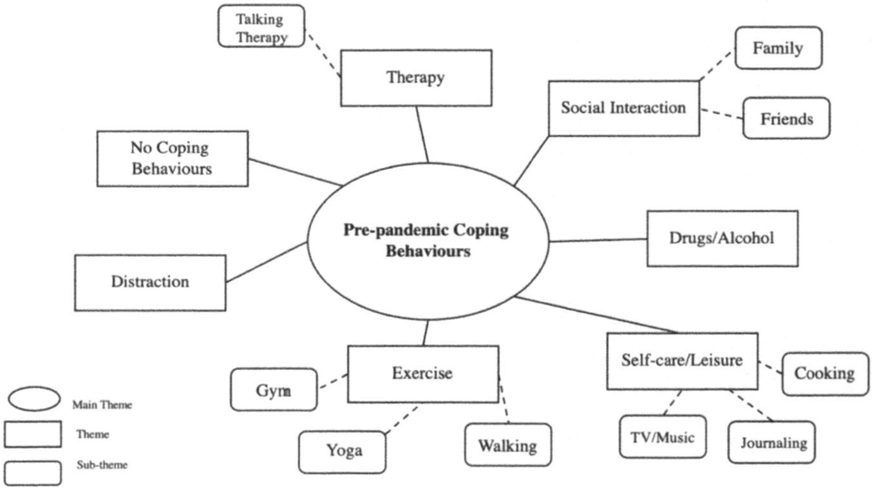

Fig. 3.3 A thematic map to show the themes and sub-themes derived from the main theme pre-pandemic coping strategies

Main Themes

The main overarching themes extracted from the data Pre-Pandemic Coping strategies

This theme was defined by the discussion surrounding experiences when the students were asked to think back and retrospectively report if and how they used to utilise Coping strategies before the start of the pandemic.

In response to the question "What coping strategies were employed before the pandemic?", participants retrospectively discussed various themes related to their utilization of coping strategies before the onset of the COVID-19 pandemic, as presented in Table 3.2. The responses indicated a diverse array of coping strategies that were favored before the pandemic. Many participants mentioned themes related to social interactions with friends and family, engaging in exercise and attending the gym to alleviate stress. Self-care and leisure activities such as watching TV, reading, listening to music, journaling, and cooking were also cited. Distraction and "keeping busy" were frequently mentioned, although there were limited elaboration on how participants diverted themselves from stressful situations. Six participants mentioned therapy as a coping mechanism they had previously utilized. A small number of responses indicated the use of drugs and alcohol as coping mechanisms, although this did not appear to be prevalent across the sample. Most responses indicated that no coping strategies were recalled, suggesting a narrative that coping strategies were not necessarily deemed necessary before the pandemic, as many participants felt their mental health was not particularly concerning.

Impact of COVID-19 Pandemic

Responses concerning the impact of the COVID-19 pandemic on the lived experiences of participants throughout the qualitative responses defined this theme (Fig. 3.4).

Throughout the answers given to the range of questions asked, several key themes emerged from the data due to repetition in participant's responses, as shown in Table 3.3. One of the most reoccurring ideas that surfaced from the participants' answers was surrounding the change in mental health during the pandemic and especially during the lockdown. Many students reiterated feelings of depression and

Table 3.2 Pre-pandemic coping strategies themes and example quotes

Themes	Example quotes
Social interaction	*"I used to surround myself with positive people, family, and friends"* *"Friends and socialising, doing fun things, laughing together"*
Exercise	*"Going to the gym"* *"Exercise, gym classes in nice gyms and running"*
Self-care/leisure	*"Listening to music…self-care activities (e.g., film, face masks)"* *"…Cooking, art"*
Distraction	*"Try and keep myself busy"* *"Distraction—staying busy"*
Therapy	*"I had antidepressants and a small amount of therapy"* *"Talking therapy"*
Alcohol/drugs	*"Video games and cannabis"* *"Drugs and alcohol"*
No coping strategies	*"I haven't felt I've needed any [coping strategies]"* *"Didn't feel necessary before the pandemic"*

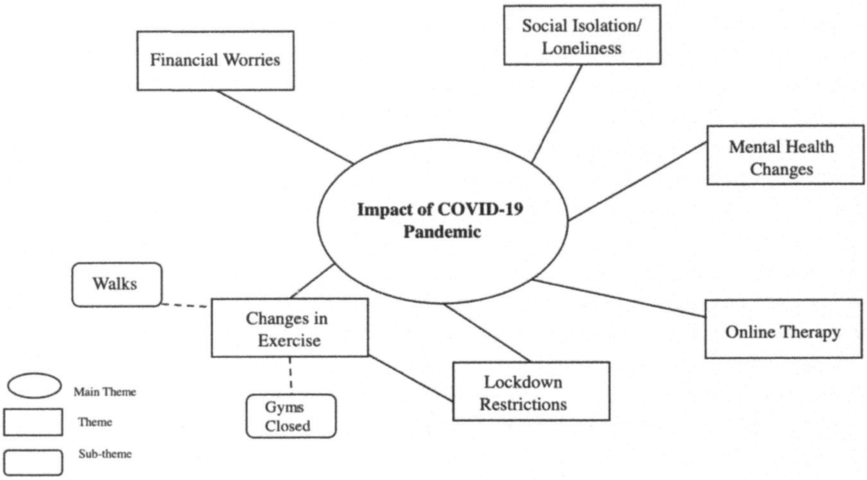

Fig. 3.4 A thematic map to show the themes and sub-themes derived from the main theme, the impact of the COVID-19 Pandemic

anxiety. Social isolation and loneliness were also heavily mentioned, as the lockdown changed how they could interact with their friends and families. Changes in exercise were frequent in the sample as gyms were closed, and walks became more frequent to break up the monotony of being at home. Elements of lockdown restrictions were also mentioned, with jobs and universities moving online. Several participants discussed accessing ongoing therapy online. However, financial worries did impact some students and interfere with their access to therapy during the pandemic.

Mental Health During COVID-19 Pandemic

This theme was defined by the significant impact of COVID-19 on students' mental health (Fig. 3.5).

These themes explored several crucial ideas discussed by participants concerning how they felt the pandemic had impacted their mental health, as shown in Table 3.4. Depression was expected to be the most common concern of students during COVID-19. However, the theme of anxiety was significantly more prominent in the sample. Participants often described feelings of anxiety surrounding catching the virus, social interactions, their lives, and the state of the world going forward after the pandemic. While several participants mentioned depression, anxiety appeared to have been the most common mental health concern. Interestingly, the idea that mental health was worsened during the height of lockdown and the pandemic. However, these concerns had eased or returned to normal as restrictions were lifted, as mentioned throughout the answers on several occasions.

Conversely, a smaller group of participants indicated that they felt that the pandemic and lockdown had improved their mental health. Some students discussed how it had given them time to reflect, take a step back from responsibilities and allow

Table 3.3 Impact of COVID-19 pandemic themes and example quotes

Themes	Example quotes
Social isolation/loneliness	*"Feelings of isolation due to lack of social contact"* *"I couldn't see my friends in the same way"*
Mental health changes	*"...I'm always anxious and less trusting of people"* *"It made me want to kill myself because I had no way of making new friends"*
Lockdown restrictions	*"...Work from home in a new job and limited social contact"* *"More time meant you had to focus on other things and compare yourself to everyone"*
Changes in exercise	*"I couldn't go to the gym, [I] felt like I had lost a lot of the hard work I had put in before Covid"* *"...An aimless walk had to suffice"*
Online therapy	*"Online talking therapy"* *"[I accessed] online GP appointments, online CBT from NHS mental health services, online therapy (private)"*
Financial worries	*"Due to financial hardship, I had to stop therapy"* *"I had to stop therapy as the company I worked for was 2 months behind on the payroll and I couldn't afford it anymore"*

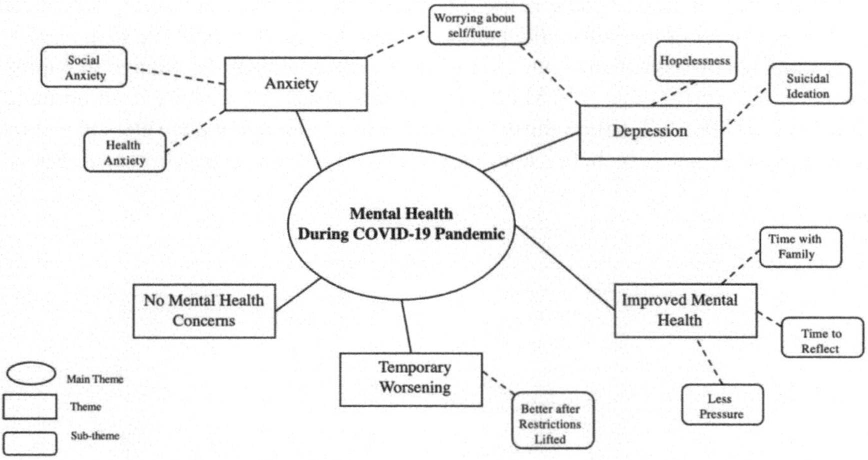

Fig. 3.5 A thematic map to show the themes and sub-themes derived from the main theme of mental health during the Covid-19 pandemic

them to access the help they needed for any mental health concerns. A few participants suggested they believed the pandemic had not impacted their mental health at all.

Table 3.4 Mental Health during COVID-19 Pandemic Themes and Example Quotes

Themes	Example quotes
Depression	*"I worry more about what people think about my life progresses. I think I might be depressed"* *"I became more depressed during the pandemic"*
Anxiety	*"I feel a lot more anxious about interacting with people and going out"* *"It's amplified my pre-existing anxiety and panic attacks"*
Temporary worsening	*"I felt lonely during lockdown but fine now"* *"It depends at which stage; my well-being has fluctuated over the last two years"*
Improved mental health	*"I feel I'm stronger for it. I'm more used to being alone with my thoughts"* *"I found it much easier to cope in lockdown"*
No mental health concerns	*"I was working throughout the pandemic, so everything was quite normal and not so much of a change"* *[Do you feel the pandemic has affected your mental health?] "No"*

Change in coping strategies

This theme was defined by the responses indicating changes in Coping strategies when comparing coping before the pandemic and during the pandemic (Fig. 3.6).

Participants discussed an extensive range of experiences of the change in coping strategies, shown in Table 3.5. Many participants discussed starting or continuing talking therapy or CBT online during the lockdown, with some answers suggesting this helped students cope better and learn more effective coping strategies. Social

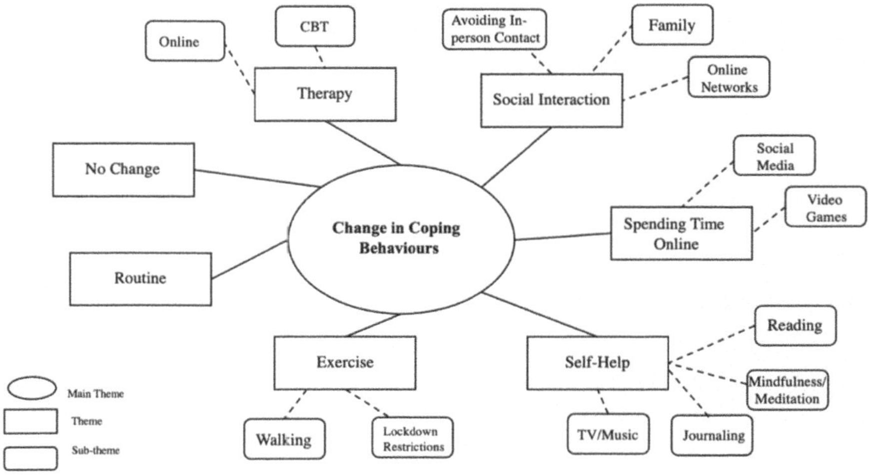

Fig. 3.6 A thematic map to show the themes and sub-themes that derive from the main theme change in coping strategies

Table 3.5 Change in coping strategies themes and example quotes

Themes	Example quotes
Social interaction	*"Speaking to my support network"* *"Communicating with friends/family"*
Spending time online	*"More time online"* *"...Play video games on my Nintendo Switch"*
Therapy	*"Online talking therapy"* *"Through starting therapy I've learnt more effective ways [of coping]"*
Exercise	*"I had to [change strategies] because I couldn't go to the gym, but I tried to walk, run and exercise"* *"Go out for walks more frequently"*
Self-help	*"A lot more mindfulness focused/introspection as opposed to social"* *"I began listening to podcasts regularly and audiobooks to gain a greater understanding of what my feelings were"*
Routine	*"Keeping a routine"* *"I was forced to pause my busy lifestyle"*
No change	*"No, my [coping] strategies stayed the same"* *"Not as in that time I knew I wasn't the only one at home"*

interaction was a key theme to emerge from the data, with frequent mention of talking with family and friends, which was also indicated as a common coping behaviour before COVID-19. Despite this, there was a move to online communication and relying on support networks outside of physically meeting in person due to restrictions, as well as spending more time with family than before. There was also a strong theme of self-help behaviours, with many participants discussing using mindfulness techniques, gratitude journaling and listening to podcasts as well as reading self-help books. Further, participants discussed a change in exercise due to the lockdown however it was still a popular coping behaviour. Some students discussed spending more time online, and the importance of keeping a routine.

Despite many themes relating to the change in coping strategies, most participants indicated they had not changed their coping strategies because of the pandemic. This could be due to the quantitative findings from the BRCS which indicated the sample was predominantly low resilient copers. Many suggested they did not use any coping strategies before the pandemic, and this did not change despite the impact of lockdown restrictions.

Discussion

The research findings revealed that individuals with greater levels of coping strategies had experienced notably lower levels of depression. The study's student sample exhibited low coping strategies, aligning with recent research indicating a decrease in coping resiliency among UK students due to the pandemic. Participants shared diverse experiences during the pandemic, and there was an observable shift in coping strategies post-COVID, with many emphasizing the significance of exercise, self-care, and distraction techniques before the lockdown. While exercise remained a common coping strategy both before and after the lockdown, changes in exercise patterns were frequent due to the closure of gyms and a shift to daily walks. Additionally, there was a substantial increase in the utilization of online therapy, cognitive-behavioural therapy (CBT), mindfulness, and gratitude journaling. Furthermore, 41.2% of participants met the threshold for depression, with 58.8% of these individuals experiencing only mild depressive symptoms. These findings suggest that depression was not as prevalent as anticipated; qualitative analysis indicated that participants were facing higher levels of anxiety and social isolation rather than depression being the primary mental health concern. Future research could replicate the current study using an anxiety measure instead of a depression measure to explore whether quantitative data would support these qualitative findings. These findings underscore the need for early intervention and increased demand for mental health resources within universities.

Given the current high levels of depression and anxiety, universities play a critical role in raising awareness and providing support for students. Although higher education institutions may perceive the pandemic as less relevant now, current, and incoming students have significantly impacted their academic journeys. A recent report by the SERU Consortium at the University of California and the University of Minnesota recommended increased funding for student Counselling services, outreach programs, and well-being education for all staff, which could effectively prevent students from experiencing clinically significant levels of depression and anxiety (Chrikov et al. 2020). Additionally, the current research indicates that coping strategies could serve as a protective factor against depression and potentially anxiety in individuals. Introducing coping and resilience workshops in primary and secondary education from an early age may help enhance resilience in children, providing them with a strong foundation for coping as they transition into university and encounter significant periods of change and stress. Prior studies have shown that implementing resilience programs in UK schools led to a short-term decrease in depression symptoms, suggesting that a long-term mandatory implementation of resilience workshops and integration of psychoeducation into the school and higher education curriculum could have a positive and preventive impact at an early intervention level (Challen et al. 2014). This could also help mitigate the negative effects of future events; if students had been taught ways to enhance their coping resilience before the pandemic, the impact of COVID-19 on mental health might have been less significant.

One of the key themes identified in the data was the shifts in social support and how young people accessed it. Before the pandemic, students emphasized the importance of social support from friends and family. Many participants mentioned that their primary coping mechanism was spending time with their extended support network, including parents, siblings, friends, and peers they socialized with during their free time at university and beyond. This is consistent with previous pre-COVID research, which has shown that positive social interactions can improve coping skills, build resilience, and lead to more positive mental health outcomes during times of stress (Camara et al. 2017; Southwick et al. 2016; Thoits, 1995). However, due to the pandemic, the way participants accessed social support changed significantly because of lockdown restrictions and social anxiety. While social support had previously been obtained from family and friends, and in some cases mainly from peers and friends, as in-person socialization was limited, participants reported spending more time with family. This was a positive outcome for some, but others experienced tension within their family unit, leading to stress or negative interactions.

While some respondents discussed experiencing social isolation during the lockdown period, many young individuals reported utilizing online support networks as a substitute for in-person social interaction. These online interactions included virtual video and phone calls with friends, engaging in online gaming, and using social media platforms. While many participants viewed these interactions as positive coping mechanisms that helped maintain relationships, some highlighted challenges associated with the shift to online communication. Specifically, some individuals mentioned increased reliance on social media due to limited daily activities, which positively and negatively affected their mental well-being. This observation aligns with previous research indicating that social media usage can enhance feelings of closeness, particularly among adolescents (Nesi et al. 2018). However, conflicting research has suggested that social media can lead to social comparison, jealousy, and privacy concerns (Fox and Moreland 2015). Further investigation is necessary to understand the impact of COVID-19 on online behaviour and the potential long-term effects of changes in socialization patterns among young people.

Limitations

The current research considered the format of open questions presented to participants. While many participants responded, providing a large qualitative data set, a significant portion of the responses were brief and needed more detail. To improve the findings, future research could conduct in-person semi-structured interviews to allow participants to share more comprehensive information about their experiences without being restricted by predetermined questions. This approach could lead to a deeper exploration of coping strategies and depression before and during the pandemic, providing greater insight into the main issues faced by students.

One limitation of the current research is the gender imbalance, with 76.25% of respondents being female. Previous research has shown that the mental health of females was significantly more affected by the pandemic than that of males, suggesting that the current findings may not be easily generalized to the broader student population. Future studies could aim to recruit more male and non-binary participants to determine if these findings hold on a larger scale. Additionally, the research focused on UK students but did not gather data on the ethnic backgrounds of the participants. Analyzing the ethnic information could help generalize the findings or identify potential differences within the sample.

Furthermore, the research did not consider the participants' university courses. Previous studies (e.g. Ajinjya et al. 2016) have suggested that there may be differences in depression rates based on the chosen courses, with Arts and Humanities students being more susceptible to major depression in some cases. However, this aspect should have been explored in the current research, and it could be a valuable area for investigation in future studies, particularly in the context of experiences during the pandemic.

Future directions

Despite these results, many of the responses indicated that participants could not recall utilizing any coping strategies. This led to a narrative suggesting that coping strategies were not deemed necessary before the pandemic, as many participants believed their mental health was in better condition. This retrospective bias may be more representative, as psychological theory suggests that individuals employ coping mechanisms in response to stress, often unconsciously, making them difficult to identify (Cramer 2001). Therefore, these findings do not necessarily imply that participants did not use coping strategies, but rather that they may have needed to be made aware of the strategies they were potentially employing to alleviate mental stress.

To further enhance these findings, future research could present participants with various coping techniques, including mental heuristics and physical activities, and inquire whether they have previously utilized these techniques. Additionally, further qualitative analysis suggested that levels of depression were not as severe due to the transient effect of the pandemic on mental health, with some participants reporting a temporary worsening of mental health during the lockdown that eased when restrictions were lifted. This suggests that the severity of mental health issues during the pandemic may not be permanent. To investigate this further, future research could employ repeated measures techniques to compare levels of depression and anxiety now and in several years to determine whether these findings are temporary or enduring.

In conclusion, the current findings suggest that the COVID-19 pandemic has significantly impacted the mental health of university students. This could serve to inform parents and universities about the potential risks of heightened anxiety and depression, to better support students who may be struggling with mental health concerns at a higher rate than before the pandemic. Increasing the availability of support services offered by universities could help mitigate this potential increase and ensure that students are adequately supported throughout their studies, particularly during this critical development period into adulthood. This research provides a solid foundation for future exploration into the impact of COVID-19 on mental health and coping strategies, which could strengthen the current findings and offer future directions for effectively supporting students during this unprecedented time. In this study, since coping strategies in the form of social interaction have been identified as critical in impacting students' psychological wellbeing, we will further explore this aspect in a specific student population who lack this social connection with their families in an educational setting. Specifically, we will examine the lived experience of university students living in residential halls during the pandemic and further investigate their coping strategies.

Study Two: How University Students Living in Residential Halls Coped During the Pandemic

Elsie Ong

Aims and objectives of the current study

The current study can show how COVID-19 has impacted a specific population such as students living away from their families. This qualitative research aimed to explore the experience of university students living in residential halls and how they were affected by COVID-19. Using a Focus group interview, numerous stressors associated with COVID-19 were identified, and how students adopted different coping strategies in response was also investigated.

Study design

A qualitative design was used to examine the alignment of the educational aims of residence halls at the four participating local universities. Focus group interviews were conducted with all participants in which four open-ended questions were asked. In the present study, Colaizzi's (1978) phenomenological method was applied to qualitatively analyse the psychological experiences of students living in halls of residence under the influence of COVID-19. Colaizzi's phenomenological method focuses on the experiences and feelings of the participants and finds common patterns rather than individual characteristics in the research subjects. This scientific approach guarantees the authenticity of the participants' collected experiences to meet scientific standards.

Although English is the language of instruction at the university, some focus groups were conducted in Chinese (Cantonese or Mandarin) to create a more relaxed atmosphere if interviewees wished. In those cases, focus groups were transcribed verbatim in English. Possible errors in translation from Chinese into English were eliminated through careful comparison between the transcripts and the notes taken at the focus groups.

Methodology

Participants

A total of 20 participants from a public university in Hong Kong attended the focus group interviews of this study. Four participants were male (20.00%) and 16 were female (80.00%). Regarding cultural background, half were local ($n = 10$, 50.00%), and another half were non-local ($n = 10$, 50.00%). Most participants were undergraduates ($N = 11$, 55.00%). All interviews were conducted about 1 month after the stay-at-home order (between March 2020 and May 2020). The inclusion criteria included: (a) participants must be enrolled as full-time students in the university at the time of the interviews; (b) must be residents in one of the residential halls on campus; (c) must not have left the hall to return to their own home during the pandemic. The number of required interviewees requested was determined by the total number of participants who met the inclusion criteria until the data were saturated, and no new topics were generated.

Procedures

The participants were recruited through mass emails sent to the current hall residents by the warden and hall manager. After the participants agreed to join, written informed consent was gathered. Then, a demographic information questionnaire was given, including information such as university, gender, faculty of study, cultural background, and residence hall residence. After gathering the demographic information, participants were informed that the following focus group interview would be recorded. It was clear that the study participants were allowed to withdraw at any time.

The questions aimed to understand students' living experiences in residence halls under COVID-19. Two open-ended questions asked were (1) How long did you stay in your hall during this academic year 2019/20 (including the virus outbreak)? (2) How did the virus outbreak period draw impact your hall life? In the end, participants were debriefed and dismissed. The whole interview for each participant took approximately 45 min.

Data analysis

All interview recordings were transcribed and translated into English (if they were not conducted in English). An independent transcription checker checked all transcriptions to confirm all followed the same format and that the content was accurate with what the participants said. The interview transcriptions were read and reread to increase familiarity with the data and identify general themes. The data were analysed using Nvivo 11 to examine how the living experiences in residence halls influence the hall residents learning developments. Researchers made explicit presuppositions (personal views, background knowledge and ideas gained from reviewing the literature regarding the phenomenon to be bracketed. All elements and perspectives were treated with equal weight and arranged the data into meaningful clusters, invariant themes within the data were identified by viewing the data from varied perspectives. Lastly, each theme was described based on invariant themes and the essence and structure of the experiences. An overview grid was used to facilitate the process of extracting themes, which summarized the main similarities and differences of data from different focus groups.

Ethical review

This study was reviewed and approved by the Ethics Committee. All participants have signed informed consent.

Results

This study explored the psychological experience of university students living in residential halls and how they were affected by COVID-19. The findings were summarised using phenomenological methods into three main themes: loneliness, anxiety, and coping methods.

(1) ***Loss of connection***

Feeling lonely is the most common psychological experience reported by the participating students (12 out of 20). The decreased numbers of both hall activities and hall residents mainly brought it.

Decreased number of hall activities

Hall activity is an important platform for students to meet people, build relationships in the hall community, and cultivate a sense of belonging. However, the majority of hall activities planned for the semester were cancelled due to the pandemic, resulting in fewer opportunities for students to have face-to-face interaction with others:

> *I think being a sports team player in the hall is quite important to me because I can play sports with my friends to build up some friendships. I have been practising for two years for the Inter-Hall Competition, but it was cancelled. I feel quite disappointed.*—H5

> *All hall activities were cancelled. I didn't get what I was expecting from residential halls. I was just studying and staying in my room.*—H12

Regarding the hall life without hall activities, one participant commented:

> *I would think that lacking social interaction would be the greatest impact of the situation on hall life. I would say it's quite meaningless to live in a hall without social interaction.*—H4

Decreased number of hall residents

Another direct impact of the pandemic in the hall context was the decrease in student residents. With the concern of sharing living space and facilities with others, some students decided to quit when the university offered a full refund of the hall fee in February. Similarly, chances for the remaining residents to interact with others decreased significantly:

> *A lot of people were not in the halls. Local and international students both went back home. -H15*

This perspective was also supported by two other students (H3 and H17) who agreed that there are not many residents left in the hall because many mainland students went home which creates an odd atmosphere in the hall.

> *It's just like a building with no people there.—H3*

(2) ***Anxiety***

Feeling anxious was another frequently reported psychological status by the participants (7 out of 20). It was mainly caused by three reasons, which include the worries about the infection, hall tutor duties, and hall policies.

Anxious about the infection

Participants expressed their genuine concern about the potential risk of getting infected by students who came back to the hall after the Spring Festival in February from other cities or countries:

The only concern is what if the people coming back from abroad do not comply with the 14-day rule of quarantine. The majority of locals stayed in Hong Kong; non-locals went elsewhere and came back. Local people are scared that they may have COVID-19.—H8

Some were nervous about the maintenance of the hygiene condition in the hall:

We used to have regular cleaning services provided by the house. Due to COVID-19, they stopped the service. The cleaning of the shared toilet is a little bit…It is a bit of a burden to live in the hall now.—H13

As a result, students tended to become paranoia about protection measures and stressed by the usage of common areas in the hall:

I cannot be as sociable as before. I tend to stay in my room to avoid the chance of transmission.—H19

Anxious about the hall tutor duties

Since the COVID-19 outbreak, hall tutors as a special group of student residents have been facing some additional challenges than their hallmates. One mentioned that:

Our hall population has to remain low-density and we have to encourage students not to come back to the hall, and yeah that causes us a lot of time and energy to communicate with them one by one.—H1

As the situation continued to evolve with the pandemic, hall tutors would constantly receive ad hoc tasks, which required their prompt response. Another tutor added:

I guess we probably know what to expect for our duties but there are always upcoming new tasks for you to handle…We need to be very flexible and adaptive, I think.—H2

Consequently, this kind of disruption and changes in their daily operation system increased their level of anxiety.

Anxious about the hall policies

As mentioned by hall tutors, another main stressor brought by COVID-19 was the uncertainty in hall policies:

The situation has kept changing all the time, so the policies are changing as well. You have to respond very quickly and that's quite stressful.—H1

Today we don't know what to expect for tomorrow and don't know what it will be like tomorrow.—H2

Some students felt unsatisfied with the policy regarding the return of hall residents from outside of Hong Kong:

I am not happy with how the school arranges things because most halls allow students to complete their quarantine in halls. It has caused a lot of trouble because quarantine is supposed to be staying in the room and not coming out at all, but they still come out without a mask and go to common areas. It is not quite proper…even though they have tightened the rules that they are not allowed to exit the room unless their food delivery arrives but it is still not satisfying. -H20

The discrepancy between the policy and the extent to which it was carried out also resulted in the build-up of participants' stress.

(3) ***Coping Strategies***

Nevertheless, some students (11 out of 20) developed various coping strategies that helped them to keep focus and perspective when dealing with negative emotions and overcoming difficult situations.

Strengthen the connection with one's existing support system

Although it was challenging for student residents to expand their social circles in the hall during the pandemic, some chose to proactively reach their existing support system when they felt anxious or lonely. The system may consist of family members and friends who live remotely from the hall. Some participants shared that they would use phone calls and digital communication to overcome the geological distance:

> *Though I have to keep a distance from my friends, I communicate with them on WhatsApp or through some social media.*—H5

Students may also recognize the remaining hallmates as a part of their support system. And sometimes, the support is not a one-way street. One participant expressed her appreciation of the strengthened relationship with her hallmates:

> *We kind of share our academic stress together and we hang around. Sometimes we cook together as we can't get food outside. I feel like the bonding is quite strong and I am happy living here.*—H14

Some participants realised that their hallmates who had left Hong Kong might also suffer from uncertainty about the future. By reaching out to them, participants constituted a part of others' support systems, which in turn brought them stronger connections with others:

> *We decided to keep in contact through WhatsApp group. As some of them are still interested in coming back to the hall next year, we try to keep everyone updated with the latest information online.*—H7

Focus on things one can control

To reduce stress and avoid a lack of structure, some participants chose to direct their attention to things that they could control. For example, one resident brought her computer to the hall to focus more on her research work:

> *I made the hall my office. The hall is big and the living area is comfortable as well. There is a canteen in the hall building. It is very convenient to have food.*—H10

Another student agreed and added her decision making of living in the hall during the pandemic:

> *I can have more concentration on my study. The library service is more accessible if I stay in the hall.*—H11

Coping with acceptance

To adapt to uncontrollable stressors, such as the decrease in the numbers of hallmates and hall activities, some students used another coping strategy—acceptance—to empower themselves to focus on things they could do:

> *As those who left have already made up their mind, I cannot do much about it.—H7*

A majority of students coped with the change in their living atmosphere by accepting the fact that this is not something they could change and therefore they have to adapt to this.

Discussion

This study explored the experience of university students living in residential halls and how they were affected by the global pandemic: COVID-19. Using phenomenological methods, the findings were summarised into three themes: experiencing loss of connection; anxiety; and coping strategies adopted during the pandemic.

Loss of connection

In this study, more than half of the participants (n = 12) living in residential halls under COVID-19 reported that they felt a loss of connection due to fewer hall activities and a reduction of hall residents. This could be especially prominent given that peer interaction was their major form of social interaction. These students were living away from home, and the countermeasures against COVID-19, such as social distancing practices, have underpinned significant changes in their lives. The limited physical interactions with their families and friends may lead to negative emotions such as loneliness and helplessness.

The current study's findings align with previous research on the potential impact of the pandemic on the mental well-being of students residing in university dormitories (Cao et al. 2020). Previous studies have shown that Chinese college students experienced various stressors related to the COVID-19 outbreak, such as academic, social, and family disruptions, leading to boredom, frustration, and isolation (Liang et al. 2020; Brooks et al. 2020). These disruptions have been linked to distress among college students.

Anxiety

The study also revealed that many participants (N = 8) reported experiencing stress and anxiety during the pandemic. Most (6 out of 8) expressed direct concerns about contracting COVID-19, while others were anxious about fulfilling their hall tutor duties and uncertain policies related to hall administration and quarantine arrangements. The unfamiliar and unpredictable nature of their living environment contributed to their anxiety, consistent with previous research indicating that the pandemic has led to heightened concerns about personal and familial health among university students (Son et al. 2020). Furthermore, national survey results indicated that most college students experienced excessive fear, worry, and nervousness, perceiving the epidemic as a serious threat (Chen et al. 2020). Similarly, Cao et al.

(2020) found that a substantial proportion of college students reported varying levels of anxiety, with economic effects, disruptions to daily life, and academic delays positively associated with anxiety symptoms, while social support was negatively correlated with anxiety levels. These findings underscore the importance of monitoring the mental health of university students during epidemics.

Coping strategies

The stress induced by the pandemic may lead students to utilize their academic knowledge and experience to employ various coping mechanisms. The current investigation demonstrates that students employed a variety of collective, engagement, and avoidance coping strategies during the COVID-19 outbreak. Webster et al. (2006) define collective coping as seeking guidance and strategies directed towards groups that are culturally valued. This is typically achieved through family or other group support, considering cultural norms and group needs. Engagement coping refers to direct actions and personal adjustments in response to a stressor, while avoidance coping involves handling the stressor through behavioural or emotional avoidance.

Webster et al. (2006) explored how cultural influences may impact the use of collective coping compared to engagement and avoidance coping in 179 Chinese Canadian adolescents. The results indicated that Chinese individuals tend to employ collective coping to a greater extent than engagement or avoidance, suggesting a preference for seeking assistance from others. Similarly, Liang et al. (2020) also found that seeking help is a common characteristic of collectivist cultures such as traditional Chinese culture. Consistent with these findings, one of the primary coping strategies utilized by residents in the current study was strengthening connections with hallmates and friends, through digital or face-to-face communication. However, most participants in this study adopted engagement coping strategies, either confronting the reality even if it does not align with their expectations or actively directing their attention to controllable aspects, such as studying and research. Both approaches represent active adaptations to COVID-19, an unpredictable and unchangeable negative event. According to Carver et al. (1993), such measures enable individuals to "make every effort to stay engaged with the important goals that give structure to their lives."

In a separate study, Main et al. (2011) examined the relationship between stressors and coping strategies in the context of a COVID-19 related pandemic, severe acute respiratory syndrome (SARS). The psychological adjustment of Chinese college students was assessed by psychological symptoms, perceived general health and life satisfaction. The results showed that active coping positively predicted life satisfaction when controlling for stressors, which could explain the unexpectedly positive statements of some participants in the current study. In addition to collective and engaging coping strategies, some dormitory residents used avoidance strategies to adapt psychologically to the situation by isolating themselves in their rooms and minimizing interaction with peers.

Although Main et al. (2011) found that the use of avoidant coping strategies positively predicted psychological symptoms, they emphasized that all types of coping serve as a buffer against the negative effects of stressors on perceived overall health.

Main et al. (2011) concluded that different coping interventions during the pandemic can alleviate stress and promote mental health. Furthermore, Ding et al. (2021) argued that avoidant coping can be considered more adaptive during uncontrollable events such as the SARS-related stressors. It is thought that people who use avoidance strategies tend to ignore or avoid the source of stress. They can reduce the emotional stress that a problematic situation triggers by leaving the situation unchanged.

Another notable finding was that students often seek help from friends and family or cope with the situation and rarely seek professional psychological help. Many reasons have been proposed to explain why they do not seek professional help for common psychological health problems (Zhang and Hao 2019). Similarly, Son et al. (2020) found that students' coping behaviours are essential to planning and designing support systems. Participatory models of intervention development can be used in this context, where the engagement of researchers and psychologists with the target group to adapt intervention programmes to their specific context has shown promise (Cappella et al. 2011).

Conclusion

The chapter emphasises the importance of social connections and community engagement for young people. The pandemic has limited their opportunities to socialise, participate in extracurricular activities and get involved in community initiatives. The potential impact on their personal development, social skills and sense of belonging is discussed. In conclusion, the chapter emphasises the many challenges young people face after the pandemic. It underscores the need for comprehensive support systems, including educational assistance, mental health resources, economic opportunities, and community engagement, to help them overcome these challenges and thrive in a post-pandemic world.

References

Ajinkya S, Schaus JF, Deichen M (2016) The relationship of undergraduate major and housing with depression in undergraduate students. Cureus 8(9):e786. https://doi.org/10.7759/cureus.786

Beck AT, Steer RA, Brown G (1996) Beck depression inventory–II (BDI-II)[Database record]. APA PsycTests. https://doi.org/10.1037/t00742-000

Bibi A, Blackwell SE, Margraf J (2021) Mental health, suicidal ideation, and experience of bullying among university students in Pakistan. J Health Psychol 26(8):1185–1196

Bostan S, Erdem R, Öztürk YE, Kılıç T, Yılmaz A (2020) The effect of COVID-19 pandemic on the Turkish society. Electr J Gen Med:17(6)

Bourduge C, Teissedre F, Morel F, Flaudias V, Izaute M, Brousse G (2022) Lockdown impact on stress, coping strategies, and substance use in teenagers. Front Psych 12. https://doi.org/10.3389/fpsyt.2021.790704

Braun V, Clarke V (2006) Using thematic analysis in psychology. Qual Res Psychol 3:77–101. https://doi.org/10.1191/1478088706qp063oa

Braun V, Clarke V (2019) Reflecting on reflexive thematic analysis. Qual Res Sport Exercise Health 11:589–597. https://doi.org/10.1080/2159676X.2019.1628806

Brooks SK, Webster RK, Smith LE, Woodland L, Wessely S, Greenberg N, Rubin GJ (2020) The psychological impact of quarantine and how to reduce it: a rapid review of the evidence. The Lancet 395(10227):912–920
Camara M, Bacigalupe G, Padilla P (2017) The role of social support in adolescents: are you helping me or stressing me out? Int J Adolesc Youth 22(2):123–136. https://doi.org/10.1080/02673843.2013.875480
Cao W, Fang Z, Hou G, Han M, Xu X, Dong J, Zheng J (2020) The psychological impact of the COVID-19 epidemic on college students in China. Psychiatry Res 287:112934. https://doi.org/10.1016/j.psychres.2020.112934
Cappella E, Jackson DR, Bilal C, Hamre BK, Soulé C (2011) Bridging mental health and education in urban elementary schools: Participatory research to inform intervention development. Sch Psychol Rev 40(4):486–508
Carmody DP (2005) Psychometric characteristics of the beck depression inventory-II with college students of diverse ethnicity. Int J Psychiatry Clin Pract 9(1):22–28. https://doi.org/10.1080/13651500510014800
Caruana EJ, Roman M, Hernández-Sánchez J, Solli P (2015) Longitudinal studies. J Thorac Dis 7(11):E537
Challen AR, Machin SJ, Gillham JE (2014) The UK resilience programme: a school-based universal nonrandomized pragmatic controlled trial. J Consult Clin Psychol 82(1):75–89. https://doi.org/10.1037/a0034854
Chen J, Shi J, Zhao X (2020) Consideration of effective psychological aid in the epidemic of COVID-19. J Tongji Univ 41:1–4
Chrikov I, Soria KM, Horgos B, Jones-White D (2020). Undergraduate and graduate students' mental health during the COVID-19 pandemic. SERU Consortium, University of California–Berkeley and University of Minnesota.. Retrieved from the University of Minnesota Digital Conservancy, https://hdl.handle.net/11299/215271.
Colaizzi PF (1978) Psychological research as the phenomenologist views it. In: Valle RS, King M (eds) Existential-phenomenological alternatives for psychology. Oxford University Press, p6
Cramer P (2001) The unconscious status of defence mechanisms. Am Psychol 56(9):762–763. https://doi.org/10.1037/0003-066X.56.9.762
Das AK, Islam MN, Billah MM, Sarker A (2021) COVID-19 pandemic and healthcare solid waste management strategy—a mini-review. Sci Total Environ 778:146220. https://doi.org/10.1016/j.scitotenv.2021.146220
Dawson DL, Golijani-Moghaddam N (2020) COVID-19: psychological flexibility, coping, mental health, and wellbeing in the UK during the pandemic. J Contextual Behav Sci 17:126–134. https://doi.org/10.1016/j.jcbs.2020.07.010
Ding Y, Fu X, Liu R, Hwang J, Hong W, Wang J (2021) The impact of different coping styles on psychological distress during the COVID-19: the mediating role of perceived stress. Int J Environ Res Public Health 18(20):10947. https://doi.org/10.3390/ijerph182010947
Dueñas JM, Fernández M, Morales-Vives F (2019) What is the protective role of perceived social support and religiosity in suicidal ideation in young adults? J Gen Psychol 147(4):432–447. https://doi.org/10.1080/00221309.2019.1697638
Espinoza G, Hernandez HL (2022) Adolescent loneliness, stress and depressive symptoms during the COVID-19 pandemic: the protective role of friends. Infant Child Develop 31(3). https://doi.org/10.1002/icd.2305
Forycka J, Pawłowicz-Szlarska E, Burczyńska A, Cegielska N, Harendarz K, Nowicki M (2022) Polish medical students facing the pandemic—assessment of resilience, well-being and burnout in the COVID-19 era. PLoS ONE 17(1):e0261652. https://doi.org/10.1371/journal.pone.0261652
Fox J, Moreland JJ (2015) The dark side of social networking sites: an exploration of the relational and psychological stressors associated with Facebook use and affordances. Comput Hum Behav 45:168–176. https://doi.org/10.1016/j.chb.2014.11.083

Grey I, Arora T, Thomas J, Saneh A, Tohme P, Abi-Habib R (2020) The role of perceived social support on depression and sleep during the COVID-19 pandemic. Psychiatry Res 293:113452. https://doi.org/10.1016/j.psychres.2020.113452

Han Z, Tang X, Li X, Shen Y, Li L, Wang J, Chen X, Hu Z (2021) Covid-19-related stressors and mental health among Chinese college students: a moderated mediation model. Front Public Health 9. https://doi.org/10.3389/fpubh.2021.586062

Hawkley LC, Cacioppo JT (2010) Loneliness matters: a theoretical and empirical review of consequences and mechanisms. Ann Behav Med 40(2):218–227. https://doi.org/10.1007/s12160-010-9210-8

Heanoy EZ, Nadler EH, Lorrain D, Brown NR (2021) Exploring people's reaction and perceived issues of the COVID-19 pandemic at its onset. Int J Environ Res Public Health 18(20):10796. https://doi.org/10.3390/ijerph182010796

Labrague LJ, De Los Santos JAA, Falguera CC (2021) Social and emotional loneliness among college students during the COVID-19 pandemic: the predictive role of coping behaviours, social support, and personal resilience. Perspect Psychiatr Care 57(4):1578–1584. https://doi.org/10.1111/ppc.12721

Lazar J (2021) Managing digital accessibility at universities during the COVID-19 pandemic. Univers Access Inf Soc 1–17. https://doi.org/10.1007/s10209-021-00792-5

Leal Filho W, Wall T, Rayman-Bacchus L, Mifsud M, Pritchard DJ, Lovren VO, Farinha C, Petrovic DS, Balogun AL (2021) Impacts of COVID-19 and social isolation on academic staff and students at universities: A cross-sectional study. BMC Public Health 21(1):1–19. https://doi.org/10.1186/s12889-021-11040-z

Lechner WV, Laurene KR, Patel S, Anderson M, Grega C, Kenne DR (2020) Changes in alcohol use as a function of psychological distress and social support following COVID-19 related university closings. Addict Behav 110:106527. https://doi.org/10.1016/j.addbeh.2020.106527

Leipold B, Greve W (2009) Resilience: a conceptual bridge between coping and development. Eur Psychol 14(1):40. https://doi.org/10.1027/1016-9040.14.1.40

Liang SW, Chen RN, Liu LL, Li X, Chen JB, Tang SY, Zhao J (2020) The psychological impact of the COVID-19 epidemic on Guangdong college students: The difference between seeking and not seeking psychological help. Front Psychol 11:2231

Limonero JT, Tomás-Sábado J, Gómez-Romero MJ, Maté-Méndez J, Sinclair VG, Wallston KA, Gómez-Benito J (2014) Evidence for the validity of the brief resilient coping scale in a young Spanish sample. Span J Psychol:17. https://doi.org/10.1017/sjp.2014.35

Li JY, Li J, Liang JH, Qian S, Jia RX, Wang YQ, Xu Y (2019) Depressive symptoms among children and adolescents in china: A systematic review and meta-analysis. Med Sci Monitor 25:7459–70. https://doi.org/10.12659/MSM.916774

Loades ME, Chatburn E, Higson-Sweeney N, Reynolds S, Shafran R, Brigden A, Linney C, McManus MN, Borwick C, Crawley E (2020) Rapid systematic review: the impact of social isolation and loneliness on the mental health of children and adolescents in the context of COVID-19. J Am Acad Child Adolesc Psychiatry 59(11):1218–1239. https://doi.org/10.1016/j.jaac.2020.05.009

Main A, Zhou Q, Ma Y, Luecken LJ, Liu X (2011) Relations of SARS-related stressors and coping to Chinese college students' psychological adjustment during the 2003 Beijing SARS epidemic. J Counsel Psychol 58(3):410

Mazza MG, de Lorenzo R, Conte C, Poletti S, Vai B, Bollettini I, Melloni EMT, Furlan R, Ciceri F, Rovere-Querini P, Benedetti F (2020) Anxiety and depression in COVID-19 survivors: role of inflammatory and clinical predictors. Brain Behav Immun 89:594–600. https://doi.org/10.1016/j.bbi.2020.07.037

Morales-Rodríguez FM (2021) Fear, stress, resilience and coping strategies during COVID-19 in Spanish university students. Sustainability 13(11):5824. https://doi.org/10.3390/su13115824

Nesi J, Choukas-Bradley S, Prinstein MJ (2018) Transformation of adolescent peer relations in the social media context: chapter 1—a theoretical framework and application to dyadic peer

relationships. Clin Child Family Psychol Rev 21:267–294. https://doi.org/10.1007/s10567-018-0261-x
Olatunji OA, Idemudia ES, Olawa BD (2020) Family support, self-efficacy and suicidal ideation at emerging adulthood: a mediation analysis. Int J Adolesc Youth 25(1):920–931. https://doi.org/10.1080/02673843.2020.1779762
Ong E, Thompson C (2018) The importance of coping and emotion regulation in the occurrence of suicidal behaviour. Psychol Rep 122(4):1192–1210. https://doi.org/10.1177/0033294118781855
Onyeaka H, Anumudu CK, Al-Sharify ZT, Egele-Godswill E, Mbaegbu P (2021) COVID-19 pandemic: a review of the global lockdown and its far-reaching effects. Sci Prog 104(2):003685042110198. https://doi.org/10.1177/00368504211019854
Ozbay F, Johnson DC, Dimoulas E, Morgan CA, Charney D, Southwick S (2007) Social support and resilience to stress: from neurobiology to clinical practice. Psychiatry 4(5):35–40. https://www.ncbi.nlm.nih.gov/pmc/articles/PMC2921311/pdf/PE_4_5_35.pdf
Quintiliani L, Sisto A, Vicinanza F, Curcio G, Tambone V (2022) Resilience and psychological impact on Italian university students during COVID-19 pandemic: distance learning and health. Psychol Health Med 27(1):69–80. https://doi.org/10.1080/13548506.2021.1891266
Ray C, Lindop J, Gibson S (1982) The concept of coping. Psychol Med 12(2):385–395. https://doi.org/10.1017/S0033291700046729
Saltzman LY, Hansel TC, Bordnick PS (2020) Loneliness, isolation, and social support factors in post-COVID-19 mental health. Psychol Trauma Theory Res Pract Policy 12(S1):S55–S57. https://doi.org/10.1037/tra0000703
Sharma S (2018) Perceived academic stress among students. Res Rev Int J Of Multidiscip 3(8):421–425. https://doi.org/10.5281/zenodo.1401248
Shivalkar S, Pingali MS, Verma A, Singh A, Singh V, Paital B, Das D, Varadwaj PK, Samanta SK (2021) Outbreak of COVID-19: a detailed overview and its consequences. In: Coronavirus therapeutics, vol II, pp 23–45. https://doi.org/10.1007/978-3-030-85113-2_2
Sinclair VG, Wallston KA (2004) The development and psychometric evaluation of the brief resilient coping scale. Assessment 11(1):94–101. https://doi.org/10.1177/1073191103258144
Son C, Hegde S, Smith A, Wang X, Sasangohar F (2020) Effects of COVID-19 on college students' mental health in the United States: interview survey study. J Med Internet Res 22(9):e21279
Southwick SM, Sippel L, Krystal J, Charney D, Mayes L, Pietrzak R (2016) Why are some individuals more resilient than others: the role of social support. World Psychiatry 15(1):77. https://doi.org/10.1002/wps.20282
Szkody E, Stearns M, Stanhope L, McKinney C (2021) Stress-buffering role of social support during COVID-19. Fam Process 60(3):1002–1015
Thoits PA (1995) Stress, coping, and social support processes: Where are we? What next? J Health Soc Behav:53–79. https://doi.org/10.2307/2626957
Warmenhoven F, van Rijswijk E, Engels Y, Kan C, Prins J, van Weel C, Vissers K (2012) The Beck Depression Inventory (BDI-II) and a single screening question as screening tools for depressive disorder in Dutch advanced cancer patients. Support Care Cancer 20(2):319–324. https://doi.org/10.1007/s00520-010-1082-8
Webster S, Kuo B, Vogel D (2006) Multicultural coping: Chinese Canadian adolescents, male gender role conflict, and psychological distress. Psychol Men Masculinity 7(2):83–100. https://doi.org/10.1037/1524-9220.7.2.83
Zhang JW, Hao ZH (2019) Influence of public stigma on attitude toward psychological help in college students: the chain mediating effect of self-compassion and self-stigma. Chin J Clin Psychol 27:1227–1231
Zhou SJ, Wang LL, Qi M, Yang XJ, Gao L, Zhang SY, ... Chen JX (2021) Depression, anxiety, and suicidal ideation in Chinese university students during the COVID-19 pandemic. Front Psychol 12:669833

Bethany Finch is working as a Child and Adolescent Mental Health and Wellbeing Practitioner, having completed a PGDip qualification in Child Wellbeing Practice at the Anna Freud Centre in 2023. She has previously gained an MSc in Child Development from UCL after completing an Undergraduate degree in Psychology from the University of Warwick. She has been interested in young people's mental health, particularly in schools and university settings, since running Warwick Nightline whilst studying. Nightline is a student-led, non-judgemental peer-to-peer listening service created to improve the mental wellbeing of students, where she completed over 600 hours of volunteering.

Dr. Elsie Ong is a Lecturer and a Dissertation Supervisor in UCL. She has worked in many universities in Asia and the UK for over ten years. Elsie is active in leading research that focuses on the mental health of young adults; especially those going through university transitions. Her expertise in cognitive neuroscience and psychology has also initiated further exploration on the underlying causes of mental health problems and later sparkles potentials for suicide preventions and interventions. Elsie is devoted to the study of psychological wellbeing in young adults and has published her research through internationally renowned conferences and reputed journals such as Frontiers in psychiatry. These experiences have helped to keep her most up to date on the latest development in preventions and interventions in mental health.

Chapter 4
Students' Mental Health in the Post-COVID Era

Yuefei Jiang, Carol Zheng, Taran Dale, and Elsie Ong

Overview

In the previous chapter, we delved into the experiences of university students during the pandemic. In this chapter, we will shift our focus to the experiences of high school and university students in the post-pandemic context. Drawing on previous research that has established a connection between academic pressure, sleep quality, and mental health, we aim to explore the interplay of these variables and their respective influences. Our initial study (**Study 1**) will examine the impact of Depression, Anxiety, and Stress on the mental health of adolescents in China. 328 Chinese high school students participated in this study, completing questionnaires to assess their mental health, sleep quality, academic stress, and attachment relationships. The data analysis revealed the significant importance of good sleep for Chinese adolescents in high schools, underscoring the urgency of addressing sleep habits in educational settings as an effective intervention to enhance their psychological well-being.

The original version of the chapter has been revised: Author name has been updated. A correction to this chapter can be found at
https://doi.org/10.1007/978-981-97-3098-8_8

Y. Jiang (✉) · C. Zheng · T. Dale
IOE—Psychology and Human Development, UCL Institute of Education, University College London, 24–26 Woburn Square, London, WC 1H 0AA, UK
e-mail: yuefei.jiang.21@ucl.ac.uk

C. Zheng
e-mail: yintong.zheng.21@alumni.ucl.ac.uk

T. Dale
e-mail: tarandeep.dale.22@alumni.ucl.ac.uk

E. Ong
Department of Psychology and Human Development, IOE—UCL's Faculty of Education and Society, University College London, London, WC 1E 6BT, UK

E. Ong (ed.), *The Emergence of the Digital World*,
https://doi.org/10.1007/978-981-97-3098-8_4

Research has indicated that young adults are particularly vulnerable to mental health challenges during COVID-19, yet few studies have specifically focused on these issues and potential predictors. Therefore, our second study (**Study 2**) examined the academic experiences of students and their levels of depression post-COVID-19, as well as related factors such as psychological well-being, loneliness, self-efficacy, interpersonal support, and social support. The findings revealed that loneliness and self-efficacy were significant predictors of depression among students in the post-COVID-19 era, highlighting their importance as students adapt to new learning environments.

While previous studies have explored the relationship between suicidal ideation (SI) and emotion regulation (ER), there has been limited research on contributing factors such as social support. In conjunction with Study 2, **Study 3** was conducted to investigate further the role of social support in a post-pandemic setting. This study aimed to explore the moderating effect of social support on the relationship between ER and SI. The findings indicated that reappraisal is associated with lower levels of SI, and while there was no direct correlation between suppression and SI, higher levels of suppression were linked to increased SI. However, social support alone did not moderate the relationship between ER and SI, emphasising the significance of combining social support with effective ER. In conclusion, these studies underscore the importance of implementing appropriate interventions in educational settings to equip students with the necessary skills to enhance their psychological well-being and reduce levels of SI.

Academic Life in the Post-COVID-19 Era

The British government announced its intention to revert to plan A on January 27th, 2022, with reduced restrictions and regulations governing social activities (Department of Health and Social Care 2022), and this day marked the onset of the Post-COVID-19 Era in England, as individuals seek to return to their pre-pandemic routines. Many countries have cautiously lifted COVID-19 restrictions as citizens gradually adapt to a new normal amidst numerous uncertainties (Misra et al. 2022). Most university students shifted to a hybrid learning mode during this period before fully returning to face-to-face instruction. Consequently, examining students' psychological well-being as they transition back to face-to-face classes after two years of remote or hybrid learning is imperative. A comprehensive understanding of students' mental health from both intrapersonal and interpersonal perspectives is essential for universities to offer improved support resources to students (Fig. 4.1).

The ongoing lockdowns have significantly impacted universities and other institutions of higher education globally. In the UK, the initial lockdown began to ease in July 2020, prompting schools and universities to adopt various strategies to address teaching during the pandemic. As the pandemic progressed, the UK Government implemented varying levels of lockdown and social distancing measures throughout

Fig. 4.1 Obtained from https://www.bbc.co.uk/news/education-56285701

2020 and 2021, which affected in-person teaching. While some universities transitioned to fully online instruction, many UK universities employed a combination of small in-person groups and predominantly online teaching (Watermeyer et al. 2021). Numerous students faced disruptions as they were required to leave campuses and return home to isolate from their peers.

Self-Efficacy

As Bandura (1977) conceptualized, self-efficacy refers to an individual's belief in the ability to perform the behaviours necessary to produce specific outcomes. In the context of mental health, strong self-efficacy enables young people to cope effectively with stressors and adversity (Muris 2002). The development of self-efficacy is associated with a sense of control over one's situation, promoting positive attitudes and adaptive coping mechanisms. Self-efficacy is an indicator of self-confidence and an inhibitor of depression (An and Lim 2017).

Emotional Regulation (ER)

Self-efficacy and ER play a central role in young people's mental health. They shape their ability to overcome challenges and build resilience. Emotion regulation involves modulating and controlling emotional reactions to different situations (Gross 1998). Emotion regulation is similar to the coping strategies covered in the previous chapters in that effective ER enables young people to cope with stressors without becoming overwhelmed, thus reducing the risk of mental health problems (Aldao et al. 2010). It includes strategies such as cognitive reappraisal, expressive suppression, and mindfulness and provides a toolkit for individuals to manage the complexity of their emotional experiences.

Numerous studies have shown the link between self-efficacy and ER and young people's mental health. Adolescents with higher self-efficacy are more likely to have positive mental health and lower levels of mental health problems (Luszczynska et al. 2005). Similarly, effective ER has been linked to lower levels of anxiety and depression symptoms in adolescents (Aldao et al. 2010). These findings underline the importance of promoting these psychological characteristics for young people's well-being.

Adolescence's transitional nature, characterized by the exploration of one's identity and increasing autonomy, underlines the importance of self-efficacy and ER. Young people face a variety of stressors ranging from academic pressures to social challenges, so cultivating self-confidence and emotional competence is paramount (Compas et al. 2017). A strong sense of self-efficacy empowers adolescents to set and achieve goals and promotes a positive mental attitude. At the same time, effective ER enables them to cope with the emotional turbulence often accompanying this developmental phase.

Educational and therapeutic interventions aimed at improving self-efficacy and ER have shown promise in promoting young people's mental health. School-based programs that integrate elements of cognitive behavioural therapy and mindfulness effectively improve self-efficacy and ER skills (Werner-Seidler et al. 2017). By equipping young people with these psychological tools, the interventions help them to overcome challenges and maintain their psychological well-being.

In summary, self-efficacy and ER are integral to young people's mental health. Cultivating self-confidence and effective ER empowers young people to manage the complexities of their lives, promoting resilience and positive mental health outcomes. In our quest to promote the psychological well-being of young people, interventions and educational programs that target these psychological constructs can play a transformative role in shaping theirodellingies.

Study One: Exploring the Relationships Between Mental Health, Sleep Quality, Academic Stress and Attachment Relationships in Adolescents from Chinese High Schools

Yuefei Jiang

Aims and objectives of the current study

Adolescence presents unique obstacles for individuals aged 16–18 as they grapple with significant lifestyle changes (Qidwai et al. 2010). In Chinese high schools, senior students (Grade 3, 17–18 years old) and sophomore students (Grade 2, 16–17 years old) constitute a distinct group due to their preparation for *Gaokao* (i.e.

the competitive college entrance exams in China). These students often experience decreased sleep, strained attachment relationships, and various mental disorders, such as anxiety, depression, and stress, due to intense academic pressure. Expanding on existing literature, this study focuses on four specific dimensions within this population: mental health, sleep quality, academic stress, and attachment relationships.

While numerous studies have examined adolescents' mental health, sleep, academic stress, and attachment relationships, few have concentrated explicitly on Chinese adolescents, particularly those preparing for Gaokao. This limited focus may be attributed to challenges in accessing this demographic due to societal protections. Furthermore, despite many studies exploring mental health, academic stress, sleep quality, and attachment relationships individually or in pairs, no research has investigated their collective interactions and relative influences. Drawing from insights in previous literature, this study centers on this distinct population with three primary objectives.

The primary objective is to evaluate the psychological well-being of participants, focusing on anxiety, depression, and sleep patterns. Additionally, the study aims to analyze and contrast the mental health, sleep behaviours, and academic stress levels of Chinese high school senior and sophomore students. It seeks to determine if senior students exhibit higher negative emotional symptoms, shorter sleep duration, poorer sleep quality, and increased academic stress. Furthermore, the research aims to investigate the interconnectedness and relative significance of the relationships between participants' mental health, sleep quality, academic stress, and attachment relationships. It focuses on identifying the variable that most significantly influences their psychological well-being.

Method

Design

The present study employed a quantitative, cross-sectional research design, in which questionnaires were distributed to all participants. Four specific scales were utilized: the Depression, Anxiety and Stress Scale-21 Items (DASS-21), Pittsburgh Sleep Quality Index (PSQI), Perceptions of Academic Stress Scale (PASS), and Inventory of Parent and Peer Attachment (IPPA). These scales were utilized to explore the students' mental health, sleep quality, academic stress, and attachment relationships, which were this study's primary variables of interest. Additionally, the DASS-21 provided sub-variables for depression, anxiety, and stress, each categorized into five levels ranging from normal to extremely severe. The PSQI yielded two sub-variables: sleep duration and quality (PSQI score). However, as sleep duration is a component of sleep quality, the PSQI score was used to represent overall sleep quality. Furthermore, the IPPA collectively assessed mother–child, father-child, and peer relationships as unified entities.

In addition to the overall dataset, a subset was created based on student grade levels, dividing them into senior and sophomore students. This differentiation investigated whether senior students experience more negative emotional symptoms, shorter sleep durations, poorer sleep quality, and heightened academic stress.

Participants

Three hundred twenty-eight students from three high schools in East China participated in this research using convenience and stratified sampling. Three schools represented three different academic performance levels in either urban or rural areas. The participants from Schools A and B were senior high school students who would take the college entrance exam two months after the survey, with ages ranging from 17 to 18 years. The participants from School C were sophomore students who would take the college entrance exams one year later, and their ages ranged from 16 to 17 years. The detailed distribution of the total number and gender across each school can be found in Table 4.1. The approximate gender ratio is 54.27% (female) to 43.90% (male). All participants were Chinese.

Measures

The study utilized four Chinese version scales, including the DASS-21 (Wang et al. 2016), PSQI (Liu et al. 1996), PASS (Jiang et al. 2023), and IPPA (Yu and Zhou 2002), to ensure clear understanding among Chinese participants. Some items were modified to reflect the participants' current reality better.

The Depression, Anxiety and Stress Scale-21 Items (**DASS-21**) scale, developed by Lovibond and Lovibond (1995a) as a condensed version of the original 42-item scale, is a self-reported measure commonly used to assess depression, anxiety, and stress over the past week. Various studies have confirmed its reliability (Brown et al. 1997; Lovibond and Lovibond, 1995b; Lovibond, 1998; Page et al. 2007). The scale has been validated for cross-cultural applicability, particularly among college students (Ahmad et al. 2018; Antúnez and Vinet 2012; Beiter et al. 2015; Camacho et al. 2016; Lee and Kim, 2022; Tonsing, 2014) and adolescents (Szabo 2010). In China, Wang et al. (2016) found internal consistency indices of 0.83, 0.80, and 0.82 for the Depression, Anxiety, and Stress subscales, respectively, and 0.92 for the total

Table 4.1 Participants' gender, age and categorisation

	N	Male	Female	Blank	Age range	N (cleaned)	Seniors	Sophomores
School A	133	50	83	0	17–18	117	117	0
School B	96	48	42	6	17–18	88	88	0
School C	99	46	53	0	16–17	94	0	94
Total	328	144	178	6		299	205	94

DASS-21 score. It has been frequently validated in evaluating Chinese mental health (Cao et al. 2023; Ma et al. 2022; Zhang et al. 2016).

Each category in the DASS-21 consists of seven items. The depression scale assesses feelings of dysphoria, unhappiness, devaluation of life, self-criticism, lack of enthusiasm or engagement, anhedonia, and inertia. The anxiety scale evaluates physiological arousal, skeletal muscle effects, situational anxiety triggers, and subjective anxiety experiences. The stress scale gauges difficulties in relaxation, nervous arousal, and a tendency towards agitation, overreaction, and impatience. Each item is scored from 0 (did not apply to me at all) to 3 (applied to me very much or most of the time). The scores calculated for three classifications are categorized into five severity levels—normal, mild, moderate, severe, and extremely severe.

Pittsburgh Sleep Quality Index

The PSQI is a 19-item self-administered questionnaire to assess sleep quality and disturbances over one-month. While the scale comprises ten primary items, the 10th item, consisting of five questions rated by a roommate or bed partner, is primarily utilized for clinical purposes, and not scoring (Buysse et al. 1989). Consequently, it should have been incorporated in the present study. The remaining nine items were categorized into seven component scores: subjective sleep quality, sleep latency, sleep duration, sleep efficiency, sleep disturbance, use of sleep medication, and daytime dysfunction. Each component score ranges from 0 (indicating no difficulty) to 3 (indicating severe difficulty). The summation of the seven component scores results in a PSQI score ranging from 0 to 21. Buysse et al. (1989) identified a PSQI score >5 as the threshold for distinguishing good from poor sleepers, with a diagnostic sensitivity of 89.6% and specificity of 86.5%.

The PSQI was Introduced In China a"d va'Idated for use with Chinese adults over twenty years ago (Liu et al. 1996). It is now widely employed in various populations, including children (Ho et al. 2021). However, there is ongoing debate regarding the optimal cutoff for the PSQI in adolescent populations. Setyowati and Chung (2021) assessed the sleep quality of 528 adolescents (aged 13–16 years). They suggested that a score of 6.5 may offer the optimal balance of sensitivity and specificity in evaluating adolescents' sleep quality. This finding was supported by Guo (2022), who investigated the sleep quality of 5399 Chinese students and proposed that 6.5 is the optimal cutoff for diagnosing sleep disturbance in Chinese nonclinical adolescents. Nevertheless, some studies (Chehri et al. 2020; Ju et al. 2019; Larche et al. 2021; Passos et al. 2017) have indicated that the factor structure of the PSQI remains unclear in adolescent populations based on factor model analyses. Given that the participant characteristics align with those of Setyowati & Chung (2021) and Guo (2022), this study adopted 6.5 as the cutoff for sleep quality.

Perceptions of the Academic Stress Scale

The Personal Academic Stress Scale (PASS) is an 18-item self-administered tool Bedewy and Gabriel (2015) created to assess students' academic stress and its origins. The items are categorized into four factors: performance pressures, illustrated by statements such as "The unrealistic expectations of my parents stress me out"; workload perceptions, embodied by sentiments like "I perceive the volume of assigned work to be excessive"; academic self-concepts, demonstrated by declarations like "I am confident in my potential for academic success"; and time constraints, expressed by comments such as "I have sufficient relaxation time post-work". Each item was rated on a 5-point Likert scale, ranging from "Strongly Disagree" to "Strongly Agree."

The reliability of PASS was examined with a sample of 100 university students in Egypt (Bedewy and Gabriel 2015). The overall internal consistency reliability (Cronbach's alpha) was 0.70, and the internal consistency reliability of the individual subscales ranged from 0.50 to 0.60. Despite these coefficient alphas being relatively low, they are still considered acceptable. PASS has been employed in various studies across countries, including the United States, Nigeria, India, Brazil, and China. França and Dias (2021) validated the Brazilian version of PASS and obtained acceptable reliability results (Cronbach's $\alpha = 0.83$ and McDonald's $\omega t = 0.86$). Jiang et al. (2023) also evaluated academic stress among Chinese and American college students, finding similar internal consistency among three subscales for both cohorts. Although the PASS has not been widely used, it is currently the most suitable scale for assessing academic stress.

The PASS is an 18-item self-administered questionnaire created by Bedewy and Gabriel (2015) to assess students' academic stress and its origins. The items are categorized into four dimensions: performance pressures, exemplified by statements such as "I feel stressed due to the unrealistic expectations of my parents"; workload perceptions, represented by sentiments like "I consider the amount of assigned work to be excessive"; academic self-concepts, indicated by assertions such as "I am confident in my academic potential"; and time constraints, conveyed through comments like "I have adequate relaxation time after completing my work". Each item is rated on a 5-point Likert scale, with one indicating "Strongly Disagree" and five indicating "Strongly Agree".

The reliability of the PASS was assessed in a study involving 100 university students in Egypt (Bedewy and Gabriel 2015). The overall internal consistency reliability, as measured by Cronbach's alpha, was found to be 0.70. In contrast, the internal consistency reliability of the individual subscales ranged from 0.50 to 0.60. Despite these coefficient alphas being relatively low, they are still considered to fall within an acceptable range. The PASS has been employed in various studies conducted in different countries to evaluate students' academic stress, including the United States (Johnson 2021), Nigeria (Aihie and Ohanaka 2019), India (Sharma 2018), Brazil (França and Dias 2021), and China (Jiang et al. 2023). França and Dias (2021) validated the Brazilian version of PASS using two reliability measures and obtained results (Cronbach's $\alpha = 0.83$ and McDonald's $\omega t = 0.86$) that indicated acceptable and sufficient reliability. Additionally, Jiang et al. (2023) assessed academic stress among Chinese and American college students and found similar internal consistency among three subscales for both cohorts. Despite its relatively limited usage, the PASS is currently considered the most appropriate scale for assessing academic stress.

Given that the participants in this study are high school students rather than undergraduates, two questions related to jobs/careers were adapted to reference college entry exams, which are more relevant to the current survey. Specifically, Item No. 2, "I am confident that I will be successful in my future career," was adjusted to "I am confident that I will be successful in my college entry exams." Similarly, the final item, "Even if I pass my exams, I am worried about getting a job," was revised to "Even if I pass my exams, I am worried about college entrance exams."

Inventory of Parent and Peer Attachment (IPPA)

The IPPA is a self-report questionnaire developed to assess the emotional and cognitive aspects of adolescents' interactions with their parents and peers, contributing to their psychological security (Armsden and Greenberg 1987). This instrument is rooted in Bowlby's attachment theory. The present study utilizes its revised version, consisting of 25 items for each subscale: mother, father, and peer. These items measure three overarching dimensions—trust, communication, and alienation—using a five-point Likert scale (1 = rarely or never true, 5 = almost always or always true). Following reverse scoring, higher scores indicate better attachment quality. In the peer attachment section, adolescents evaluate their level of trust (e.g., "My friends accept me as I am"), communication (e.g., "I can tell my friends about my problems and troubles"), and alienation (e.g., "I feel angry with my friends"). Numerous studies conducted in diverse countries have affirmed the reliability and validity of the IPPA (Greenberg 2009). Furthermore, it has been successfully utilized among Chinese adolescents (Chen et al. 2016, 2019; Zhang et al. 2011), demonstrating strong reliability and validity.

Ethical Considerations

The research adhered to the ethical guidelines outlined by the British Psychological Society Code of Ethics and Conduct (British Psychological Society 2021) and the Ethics Policy of the Institute of Education at University College London (UCL). Approval for the study was obtained from the university Research Ethics Committee. Participants were duly informed of the voluntary nature of their participation, the confidentiality of their responses, and their right to withdraw their data without providing a reason. All personal data were handled following the General Data Protection Registration and University Code of Conduct for Research, ensuring that only the researchers had access to them.

Pilot Study and Adjustments

Due to differences in languages and cultures and to ensure the accuracy and feasibility of the survey, three Chinese high school students and two high school teachers conducted the survey first as pilot subjects. Based on their feedback, specific alterations were made:

(1) A few items deemed unsuitable for current participants were identified and rectified., such as some items on the PASS mentioned above.

(2) The procedure was streamlined to better align with the participants' typical habits when completing psychological scales. Initially, written consent forms were planned to be collected. However, the pilot participants expressed that needed to become more familiar with signing such forms. Hence, all participants retained consent forms instead of returning them. The submission of completed scales implied agreement to participate in the study. Participants who did not wish to participate were advised to refrain from submitting the scales.
(3) The time required to complete all scales was confirmed to be 15–20 min.

Procedure

Due to inconvenient access to the internet and computer, all participants completed the written questionnaires using pens in the regular classroom setting.

Before the survey, the written scales were provided to the teachers responsible for the survey in three high schools. The teachers were personally briefed about the survey process and given step-by-step instructions in advance by the researcher, particularly emphasising participants' voluntariness, and anonymity. During the survey, Chinese version information sheets and consent forms were distributed to the students. The participants finished the questionnaire immediately in the class. They could include their names or remain anonymous and were free to submit or withhold their responses based on their preference.

Data analysis

All written data were collected and processed with IBM SPSS Statistics Version 29. Analytical procedures were implemented to test the proposed questions, including Cronbach's alpha, a single-factor confirmatory factor analysis, descriptive statistics, one-way ANOVA, Pearson correlation, and multiple regression analysis.

Results

This study aimed to odelling the collective interplay and relative strength of associations among mental health, sleep quality, academic stress, and attachment relationships of Chinese high school students, investigating the most influential predictor of students' mental health. It also aimed to contrast the mental health, sleep duration, sleep quality and academic stress between the senior and sophomore students.

Reliability Tests

In the current investigation, all information was obtained through a self-administered survey, which may lead to potential bias. A single-factor confirmatory factor analysis was performed as part of the statistical procedures to address this concern. The results revealed that the first factor accounted for 21.39% of the variance, falling below the 50% threshold commonly associated with significant standard method variance (Eichhorn 2014). This outcome indicates that the method did not substantially influence the measurement of underlying constructs, suggesting an absence of notable common method bias.

Furthermore, the 328 participants were provided with four sets of scales, and their reliability was initially evaluated using Cronbach's alpha. The DASS-21 scale, comprising 21 items, demonstrated high internal consistency ($\alpha = 0.91$), while the PSQI scale with 18 items showed acceptable reliability ($\alpha = 0.78$), and the PASS scale, also with 18 items, exhibited good internal consistency ($\alpha = 0.82$). The IPPA scale, consisting of 75 items, demonstrated sound reliability ($\alpha = 0.85$). These findings collectively indicate that all scales utilized in the study were reliable, and the overall assessment demonstrated internal consistency.

Data Cleaning

Among 328 respondents, thirteen questionnaire sets were found to be missing data. Five participants identified themselves as belonging to single-parent households on the scale, thus only completing either the father-child or mother-child scale in the IPPA. Two sets were left entirely IPPA uncompleted, and four were partially completed, needing more information in the peer relationship scale. Furthermore, in two questionnaire sets, several questions in the PSQI were left blank. As a result of the research requirements for complete responses, these thirteen questionnaire sets were excluded. Moreover, an additional 16 sets of questionnaires were excluded as outliers based on the box plots. In total, 299 valid sets of questionnaires were distributed across School A (117), School B (88), and School C (94). The ratio of senior students (205) to sophomore students (94) was 68.56% to 31.44% (see Table 4.1).

Primary Information on Participants' Mental Health and Sleep Quality

The basic information regarding participants' mental health and sleep quality was documented and analysed using Microsoft Excel and Descriptive Statistics in SPSS (see Table 4.2).

According to the predetermined threshold of the DASS-21 (Lovibond and Lovibond 1995a), it was determined that 26.80% of the student population demonstrated stress levels surpassing the moderate range, 65.90% exhibited anxiety levels exceeding the moderate range, and 34.80% displayed depression levels higher than

Table 4.2 Descriptive statistics for main variables

Variables	Mean	SD	Minimum	Maximum	N
Sleepdura	6.51	0.90	4	9	299
PSQI	6.19	2.83	0	14	299
Stress	14.80	7.05	0	36	299
Anxiety	12.30	6.78	0	34	299
Depression	10.83	7.33	0	36	299
Dass-21	37.93	18.58	2	86	299
PASS	52.25	8.91	30	73	299
IPPA	253.81	40.48	151	351	299

moderate. Notably, 28.40% of the students were found to have severe to extremely severe anxiety (Table 4.3).

Based on the established cutoff score of the DASS-21 scale (Lovibond and Lovibond 1995a).

Concerning sleep patterns, the participants' average sleep duration was 6.51 h per day. Specifically, 41.47% of the students reported sleeping six hours or less per day in the preceding month, while only 10.70% reported sleeping eight hours or more daily. During the same period, 47.83% of students reported sleep durations ranging between six to eight hours. Regarding sleep quality, as measured by the PSQI scores, 55.18% of students had scores exceeding 5, a threshold distinguishing 88.5% of patients and controls (Buysse et al. 1989). When employing 6.5 as the threshold (Setyowati and Chung 2021), the findings revealed that 38.13% of participants experienced suboptimal sleep conditions (Table 4.4).

Influence of Student Grade Levels

Initial exploratory data analyses revealed that the scores for DASS-21, sleep duration, and PSQI of senior and sophomore students were not normally distributed, as indicated by the Kolmogorov–Smirnov test results ($p < 0.001$). By contrast, the Kolmogorov–Smirnov test showed that the scores for PASS and IPPA of senior and sophomore students were normally distributed ($p > .05$). A key point was that the sample size ($N = 299$) was large. Moreover, Levene's Test of five scores indicated that groups have similar variance ($p > 0.05$), and the assumption of Equality of Variances across groups was also met. Therefore, parametric analyses could be implemented according to the Central Limit Theorem.

A One-way ANOVA was conducted to investigate whether the DASS-21, sleep durations, PSQI, PASS, and IPPA scores differed with student grade levels. The

Table 4.3 Information on stress, anxiety and depression

	Stress %	Anxiety %	Depression %
Normal	57.20	25.10	47.20
Mild	16.10	9.00	18.10
Moderate	17.40	37.50	26.40
Severe	8.40	10.00	4.70
Extremely severe	1.00	18.40	3.70
Moderate+	26.80	65.90	34.80
Severe+	9.40	28.40	8.40

Table 4.4 The frequency of sleep duration and general PSQI score

Sleep duration (h)	Frequency	%	PSQI	Frequency	%
<=6	124	41.47	>5	165	55.18
>6 & <8	143	47.83	>6.5	114	38.13
>= 8	32	10.70	<= 6.5	185	61.87

results revealed significant main effects for student category on the following metrics (Table 4.5). A Tukey post hoc test further detailed these effects. Senior students showed significantly lower mean DASS-21 scores (M = 35.93, SD = 1.29) than sophomore students (M = 42.30, SD = 1.89, p = 0.006). Meanwhile, senior students exhibited shorter mean sleep durations (M = 6.18, SD = 0.06) than sophomore students (M = 7.23, SD = 0.07, $p < 0.001$), and lower on the PSQI (M = 5.88, SD = 0.19) compared to sophomore students (M = 6.87, SD = 0.31, p = 0.005). Additionally, senior students achieved lower PASS scores (M = 51.05, SD = 0.63) relative to sophomore students (M = 54.87, SD = 0.84, $p < 0.001$). On the IPPA, senior students (M = 259.16, SD = 2.80) outscored sophomore odellin (M = 242.15, SD = 4.02, $p < 0.001$).

Correlation Analysis

A Pearson correlation analysis was conducted to explore the complex relationships among DASS-21, PSQI, PASS, and IPPA scores in Table 4.6.

The results indicated: a significantly positive relationship between DASS-21and PSQI scores, [r (299) = 0.49, $p < 0.001$]; a significantly positive relationship between DASS-21 and PASS scores, [r (299) = 0.47, $p < 0.001$]; a significantly negative relationship between DASS-21 and IPPA scores, [r (299) = −0.39, $p < 0.001$]; a significantly positive relationship between PSQI and PASS scores, [r (299) = 0.31, $p < 0.001$]; a significantly negative relationship between PSQI and IPPA scores, [r (299) = −0.29, $p < 0.001$]; and a significantly negative relationship between PASS and IPPA scores, [r (299) = −0.28, $p < 0.001$] (Fig. 4.2).

Table 4.5 One-way analyses of variance in senior and sophomore students

Measure	Seniors		Sophomores		F(1, 297)	η^2
	M	SD	M	SD		
DASS-21	35.93	1.29	42.30	1.89	7.74**	0.03
Sleep duration	6.18	0.06	7.23	0.07	123.36***	0.29
PSQI	5.88	0.19	6.87	0.31	8.15**	0.03
PASS	51.05	0.63	54.87	0.84	12.27***	0.04
IPPA	259.16	2.80	242.15	4.02	11.80***	0.04

** $p < 0.01$, *** $p < 0.001$

Table 4.6 Descriptive statistics and correlations for main variables

Variable	N	M	SD	1	2	3	4
1. Dass-21	299	37.93	18.58	–			
2. PSQI	299	6.19	2.83	0.49**	–		
3. PASS	299	52.25	8.92	0.47**	0.31**	–	
4. IPPA	299	253.81	40.48	−0.39**	−0.29**	−0.28*	–

** $p < 0.01$, 2-tailed

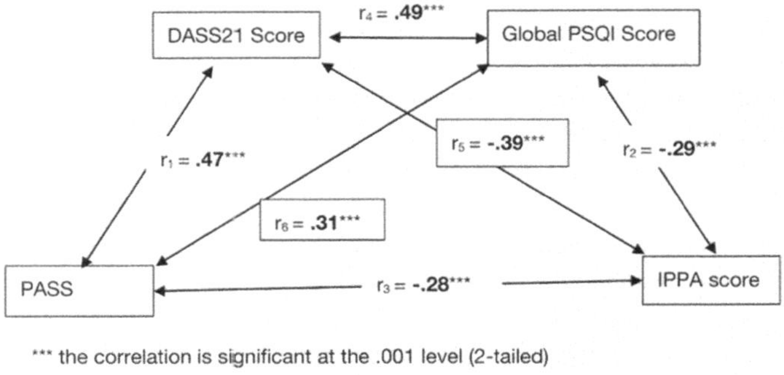

Fig. 4.2 Correlation between DASS-21, PSQI, PASS, and IPPA Scores

Multiple Regression

A multiple regression analysis was conducted to assess whether the PSQI, PASS, and IPPA scores significantly predicted the DASS-21 scores. The complete model, including PSQI, PASS, and IPPA scores, was statistically significant: [adjusted $R^2 = 0.39$, $F(3, 295) = 63.10$, $p < 0.001$].

(1) An adjusted R2 greater than 0.3 indicates that the research results reliably reflect the influence of PSQI, PASS, and IPPA scores on DASS-21 scores.
(2) The regression equation was significant [$F(3, 295) = 63.10$, $p < 0.001$], suggesting that at least one of the three independent variables significantly influences DASS-21 scores.
(3) All variance inflation factor (VIF) values ranged between 1 and 2, indicating no multicollinearity among the three independent variables. This finding suggests a moderate correlation between DASS-21 and PSQI, PASS, and IPPA scores.
(4) Upon examining the standardised coefficients, it was found that PSQI scores significantly positively affected DASS-21 scores ($\beta = 0.34$, $p < 0.001$). Similarly, PASS scores significantly positively predicted DASS-21 scores ($\beta = 0.31$, $p < 0.001$). In contrast, IPPA scores significantly negatively predicted DASS-21 scores ($\beta = -0.20$, $p < 0.001$).
(5) PSQI and PASS have standardised coefficients of 0.34 and 0.31, respectively. In contrast, IPPA has a smaller coefficient (−0.20). Therefore, PSQI appeared to be more strongly related to DASS-21 than PASS and IPPA, and IPPA was the weakest predictor of DASS-21 among them. The fitted regression model was as follows: DASS-21 Score = 14.18 + 2.22*(PSQI score) + 0.64*(PASS score)−0.09*(IPPA score). (see Table 4.7).

Discussion

The present investigation focused on Chinese high school students, specifically those preparing for college entrance examinations. It sought to analyze the disparities in psychological well-being, sleep patterns, and academic pressure between senior and sophomore students. The study delved into the intricate dynamics and comparative

Table 4.7 The coefficients of the multiple regression

Model	Unstandardised coefficients		Standardised coefficients beta	t	Sig.	VIF
	B	Std. error				
(Constant)	14.18	8.79		1.61	0.11	
PSQI	2.22	0.32	0.34	6.89	<0.001	1.17
PASS	0.64	0.10	0.31	6.32	<0.001	1.16
IPPA	−0.09	0.02	−0.20	−4.18	<0.001	1.14

Dependent Variable: DASS-21 scores

strengths of the connections among the participants' mental health, sleep quality, academic stress, and attachment relationships.

The findings revealed a significant prevalence of adverse emotional symptoms among the participants, with nearly 90% reporting sleep deprivation and 40% indicating poor sleep quality. These results are notably more severe than those documented in most prior research studies. Based on the established cutoff score of the DASS-21 (Lovibond and Lovibond 1995a), the average participants demonstrated mild levels of depression, moderate levels of anxiety, and mild levels of stress. The percentages of negative emotions, ranging from moderate to extremely severe, were 34.80% for depression, 65.90% for anxiety, and 26.80% for stress. Notably, 28.40% of the participants displayed severe to extremely severe anxiety. These findings suggest that the severity of mental health issues among the participants significantly surpasses the rates reported by the World Health Organization (2021) at 14% and the findings of Li et al. (2019) at 22.2%. However, while it approaches the results of Tang et al. (2019), it remains more severe than their reported 40.1%. Although the exact proportions may vary due to differences in sample size and measurement scales, society must acknowledge the seriousness of this issue.

There is a concerning prevalence of sleep deprivation among the study participants. The average daily sleep duration is 6.51 h, which is notably lower than the 7.72 h reported for adolescents in the United States (Zhang et al. 2017), but comparable to the 6.5 h found among high school students in Virginia (Winsler et al. 2015) and marginally less than the 6.77 h reported for Chinese high school students (Zhu et al. 2021). Only about one in ten students meet the recommended sleep duration of 8–10 h, with 41.47% of students sleeping only six or fewer hours daily. The participants' average PSQI score was 6.19, lower than the 7.25 reported by Goldstein and Walker (2014). According to Setyowati and Chung's (2021) criteria, approximately 38.13% of participants experience poor sleep quality. Existing literature suggests that sleep habits impact on the mental health of the participants (Goldstein and Walker 2014; Hirshkowitz et al. 2015; Zeek et al. 2015).

The study revealed significant differences between senior and sophomore students regarding mental health, sleep duration, sleep quality, and academic stress. Contrary to the initial hypothesis, senior students did not consistently exhibit more negative emotional symptoms, poorer sleep quality, or heightened academic stress. However, the data did support the hypothesis that seniors' average sleep duration (6.18 h) is one hour shorter than sophomores' (7.23 h). This reduction could likely be attributed to the senior students' preparations for college exams scheduled two months later, often sacrificing sleep for study to enhance academic performance. Surprisingly, despite sleep duration being a component of the overall PSQI score, senior students displayed better sleep quality. This observation aligns with Voderholzer et al.'s (2011) finding, which suggested that adolescents demonstrate resilience in sleep, potentially increasing sleep intensity under sleep restriction conditions. However, Voderholzer et al. (2011) examined the impact of sleep restriction across four successive nights, whereas our data was based on one month. Future studies could investigate how adolescents can improve sleep efficiency even when faced with sleep deprivation. Furthermore, this comparison confirmed that participants with superior sleep quality experienced fewer negative emotions and reduced academic stress, despite sleeping less.

This study thoroughly investigates the connections between mental health, sleep quality, academic stress, and attachment relationships in Chinese high school students, significantly contributing to existing literature. While previous studies have examined individual or paired correlations among these variables, this research builds upon those findings. The study confirms that negative emotions, such as depression and anxiety, are positively linked to reduced sleep quality (e.g., Peltz et al. 2017) and increased academic stress (e.g., Jiang et al. 2021). It also validates that stronger attachment relationships are inversely related to heightened negative emotions and decreased sleep quality (e.g., De Lise et al. 2023). Furthermore, poor sleep quality is positively associated with elevated academic stress (Zhu et al. 2021). This research comprehensively explains the interconnections among mental health, sleep quality, academic stress, and attachment relationships in Chinese high school students. It also provides specific relative magnitudes for these interconnections and outlines the relative strengths of these relationships. Although all interactions were found to have statistically moderate associations based on their correlation coefficients (i.e., $0.28 < = |r| < = 0.49$), the results indicate that participants' mental health exhibits a stronger association with sleep quality and academic stress. In contrast, the connections involving attachment relationships with other variables appear relatively weaker.

The results of the multiple regres"Ion'nalysis revealed that 38.50% of the variability in Dass-21 scores can be explained by PSQI, PASS, and IPPA scores. This suggests that sleep quality, academic stress, and attachment relationships are three independent variables significantly predicting the participants' mental health. The findings indicate that sleep quality is the most influential predictor of mental health, surpassing academic stress and attachment relationships. Academic stress is the second most significant factor, while attachment relationships have the least impact. These results align with those obtained from the Pearson correlation analysis.

These findings emphasize the critical importance of sleep quality within this participant population. In addition to mental health disorders, sleep deprivation can lead to reduced attentional capacity and academic performance (Curcio et al. 2006; Fallone et al. 2001). This observation contradicts the participants' initial belief that reducing sleep duration would improve their academic performance. Instead, their unhealthy sleep habits may compromise their psychological well-being and hinder their academic achievements.

Limitations

Several limitations should be taken into account when considering this study. Firstly, the participants were drawn from a single city in East China using convenience sampling, which may limit the generalizability of the findings to students preparing for college entrance exams across China. Secondly, the reliance on self-reported questionnaires introduces potential bias and inaccuracies, as objective measures such as actigraphy could provide a more precise assessment of sleep. Thirdly, removing eight questionnaire sets due to missing data, likely due to manual completion, predominantly affects the peer relationship section, making it more susceptible to omission. The use of an online survey format could help mitigate this issue.

Additionally, the study only examined three factors influencing participants' mental health, while other confounding variables such as socioeconomic status or school timetables may also impact the results. Furthermore, the study focused on anxiety, depression, and stress to assess mental health, but mental health is a complex domain with various facets. These three symptoms are indicative of a subset of potential mental disorders, and future research should consider these limitations and employ qualitative analysis to investigate causality rather than solely focusing on the correlations identified in the current study.

Conclusion

This research comprehensively investigated the mental health, sleep patterns, academic stress, and attachment relationships of high school students in China. It confirms previous findings that reduced sleep quality, increased academic stress, and weakened attachment relationships are linked to heightened negative emotions. Additionally, the study delves into an unexplored area by examining the interactions and relative strengths of the relationships among mental health, sleep quality, academic stress, and attachment relationships. The results highlight sleep quality as the primary predictor of mental health in Chinese adolescents when considered alongside academic stress and attachment relationships. Surprisingly, senior students did not show increased anxiety, depression, or compromised sleep quality despite having shorter sleep durations compared to sophomore students. This finding supports the idea that adolescents can improve sleep efficiency even when experiencing sleep deprivation, warranting further investigation in future research.

In summary, this study presents compelling evidence that sleep quality significantly impacts adolescents' mental health more than academic stress and attachment relationships. These findings underscore the importance of educational institutions and caregivers prioritizing interventions to enhance adolescents' sleep quality, which may be the most effective approach to improving their mental health.

Emotion Regulation and Suicidal Ideation

Good mental health is crucial for humans to function appropriately, as poor mental health can hurt overall well-being and have detrimental consequences (Trompetter et al. 2017). One of the more severe consequences of poor mental health is SI, which is characterised by people having suicidal thoughts because they have difficulty healthily coping with negative emotions (Neacsiu et al. 2018). According to the World Health Organisation, alarming statistics have revealed that approximately two-thirds of the general population suffers from SI (Klonsky et al. 2021). Research into SI and mental health has found that individuals with positive mental health are more resilient to negative emotions and, therefore, less likely to experience high levels of SI (Teismann et al. 2018). Consequently, it is essential to better understand the interplay of mechanisms associated with SI.

Empirical evidence suggests that ER is essential to mental health, as appropriate regulation enables individuals to process their emotions effectively (Chervonsky and Hunt 2019). According to John and Gross (2004), there are two main ER strategies: cognitive reappraisal and expressive suppression. Cognitive reappraisal is the process by which people change their thought patterns to alter their emotional response to a situation, which generally means adopting a different perspective (Ford and Troy 2019). Expressive suppression, conversely, involves suppressing an emotional response to hide the true feelings in a situation that evokes emotion (Kelley et al. 2019). Previous literature has emphasised that individuals who engage in cognitive reappraisal strategies, which are considered adaptive, generally have more positive mental health outcomes as this ER process is associated with greater psychological resilience (Zarotti et al. 2020). In contrast, expressive suppression has been linked to poorer mental health, as this ER process is maladaptive and, therefore, associated with an increasing deterioration in the individual's well-being (Chavez-Baldini et al. 2020).

Although many studies have investigated the relationship between ER and SI, most of this literature has explicitly looked at adolescents or adults, so little research needs to be done on students. However, the literature on SI and ER in university students has gained more attention in recent years, suggesting that this subgroup has a higher risk of adopting maladaptive ER strategies due to challenges such as increasing workload and adapting to a different environment (Miller and Racine 2022). Using self-report measures, Zeifman and Colleagues (2020) investigated perfectionism, SI, and emotional dysregulation in 130 university students in a cross-sectional design. Results indicated that individuals with higher levels of self-critical thinking had more incredible difficulty regulating their emotions appropriately. As a result, these students exhibited higher levels of SI, as their ability to overcome maladaptive tendencies was lower (Zeifman et al. 2020). However, it should be noted that this study was a cross-sectional study, meaning that the researchers could not establish a cause-and-effect relationship between the variables as the data was only collected at one point in time (Setia 2016). This study could have been improved by using a longitudinal approach to collect data across multiple time points to understand the interaction between these variables better.

Study Two: Predictor of Depression Among University Students in the Post-COVID-19 Era

Carol Zheng and Elsie Ong

Keywords University students, Mental health, Loneliness, Self-efficacy, Social support

Aims and objectives of the current study

Earlier studies have emphasised the importance of depression during the pandemic. More recent research has also looked at the importance of loneliness, social support, self-efficacy, and depression during COVID-19. However, few studies have focused on students in emerging adulthood aged 18–25, who are one of the most vulnerable groups to develop mental health problems and depression during COVID-19. Direct associations between loneliness, social support, self-efficacy, and depression need to be further investigated in this age group. Another gap in the literature is the status of mental health in the post-COVID-19 period. Most countries have only started to lift restrictions this year, which explains this gap. In the post-COVID-19 era, there are fewer restrictions, and students are adjusting to a new normal—from 2 years of distance learning to more in-person classes. Their mental health and readiness needed to be assessed.

As little work has focused on the post-COVID-19 era, this study examines university students' levels of depression after COVID-19 (the return to normality) by analysing the impact of psychological well-being, loneliness, and self-efficacy, as well as interpersonal support and social support. It is hypothesised that loneliness, social support, and self-efficacy are associated with and predict the level of depression in university students.

Methods

Participants

This study examined three aspects of loneliness, social support, and self-efficacy to discover their relationships among young adults. Participants, who were university students aged 18 to 25 years, were invited to participate in the study. Using snowballing and casual methods, participants were recruited through online platforms and social media. An information sheet and consent form were handed out before the questionnaire began. 146 participants aged 18 to 25 were recruited to complete self-report questionnaires on loneliness, social support, self-efficacy, and depression, respectively.

Demographic information was collected at the beginning of the questionnaire. Of the 146 participants, 30 were male, 116 were female, and 0.9% were non-binary. Sixty-three participants were from the UK, and 83 were international students. Fifty-eight participants lived with their parents or at home, and 88 lived away from their family/home.

Measures

Loneliness

Participants' subjective feelings of loneliness were measured by the UCLA Loneliness Scale Version 3 (Russell 1996). Loneliness was measured by statements such as 'How often do you feel that you lack companionship?' and 'How often do you feel close to people?'. This 20-item questionnaire uses a 4-point Likert scale, 1 = 'Never' and 4 = 'Often', to represent the frequency of the statements. 9 out of 20 items would be reversed to keep the score in a continuous meaning. Then, the responses were summed up to calculate and generate a total score. The total range is from 20 to 80. Higher scores indicate that participants feel lonelier.

Social Support

Social support was evaluated using the Multidimensional Scale of Perceived Social Support (MSPSS), a 12-item questionnaire developed by Canty-Mitchell and Zimet in 2000. The questionnaire comprises three subscales designed to assess support from family, friends, and significant others. Each item is rated on a 7-point Likert scale, ranging from 1 for 'Very Strongly Disagree' to 7 for 'Very Strongly Agree'. The subscale scores, ranging from 4 to 28, were calculated by summing the individual item scores, reflecting each source's support level. The total score, ranging from 12 to 84, was obtained by summing the scores of the three subscales, indicating the overall level of social support. Higher scores on the subscales and the total score indicate a higher level of perceived social support among the participants.

Self-efficacy was assessed using the New General Self-Efficacy Scale developed by Chen et al. in 2001. This 8-item questionnaire employs a 5-point Likert scale, with responses ranging from 1 for 'Strongly Disagree' to 5 for 'Strongly Agree'. The self-efficacy score, ranging from 1 to 5, was calculated by averaging the responses to the items. Higher scores on the scale indicate a higher level of self-efficacy among the participants.

Depression was measured by the Beck Depression Inventory (Beck et al. 1996). This questionnaire contains 21 items to measure depression symptoms. This questionnaire uses a 4-point Likert scale such as 0 = 'I do not feel sad' and 3 = 'I am so sad and unhappy that I cannot stand it'. The responses were summed up to form a score of a depressive state, which ranges from 0 to 63. Higher scores indicate higher levels of depression characteristics. 0–9 indicates that the participants did not have depression, 10–18 indicates they may have mild depression, 19–29 indicates that they may have moderate depression, and 30–63 indicates that they have severe depression.

Data Analysis Plan

This study used SPSS to analyse the data. The responses to the questionnaire were firstly recoded according to the instructions of each scale for any reverse score. Then, the coded responses were summed up to form the formal score for each predictor variable. Secondly, the associations between each variable were tested using a two-tailed Pearson's correlation. Linear regressions were carried out to establish the relationship between each predictor variable and the outcome variable, and multiple regression was used to indicate the interactions between predictor variables to impact the outcome variable.

Ethical Considerations

The present study received ethical approval from the university's Research Ethics Committee. All the data were kept safe and confidential. Participants were informed that their responses would be fully anonymised; they could skip any questions that they were not willing to answer, and participants could withdraw from the survey during the survey whenever they wanted. During the debriefing process, the researcher's contact information and support resources were available to participants who may have experienced negative emotions during the survey.

Results

Descriptive Data

The mean, standardised deviation, range, minimum and maximum values of loneliness, social support, self-efficacy, and depression were stated in Table 4.8. The sample mean of depression is 13.08, which is in the range of mildly depressive symptoms from 10 to 29, indicating this sample is under clinical diagnosis of depression.

The outcome variable, depression, was slightly left skewed, with the sample mean of 13.86 in the range of 0 to 63. The skewness and kurtosis index calculated by SPSS were used to indicate the normality of the data. If the skewness is between −2 and + 2, and kurtosis is between −7 and + 7, then it is acceptable to consider the data to have a normal distribution. Though self-efficacy and depression have higher skewness and kurtosis than other variables, it was still acceptable to consider the

Table 4.8 Descriptive data

Measures	Mean	SD	Range	Minimum	Maximum
Loneliness	46.83	10.10	51	26	77
Social support	61.04	14.33	72	12	84
Self-efficacy	3.64	0.72	4	1	5
Depression	13.08	10.17	50	0	50

N = 146

data to be in the acceptable range of normal distribution and meet the criteria for parametric assumptions.

Correlation

Correlations were carried out to indicate the strength of linear association between predictors, loneliness, social support, and self-efficacy and the outcome, depression. A strong positive correlation was found between loneliness and depression r (105) = 0.67, $p < 0.01$, stating that when loneliness increases, depression will also increase. A moderate negative association was found between social support and depression r (105) = −0.55, $p < 0.01$, suggesting that when social support increases, depression will decrease. A strong negative correlation was found between self-efficacy and depression r (105) = −0.62, $p < 0.01$, indicating that when self-efficacy increases, depression will decrease.

Correlations were also carried out to test association within mental status predictor variables. A strong negative correlation was found between loneliness and social support r (105) = -0.67, $p < 0.01$, suggesting that when loneliness increases, social support decreases. A moderate negative correlation was found between loneliness and self-efficacy r (105) = −0.48, $p < 0.01$, indicating that when loneliness increases, self-efficacy decreases. A moderate positive correlation was found between social support and self-efficacy r (105) = 0.59, $p < 0.01$, suggesting that when social support increases, self-efficacy also increases (Table 4.9).

All the mental status predictor variables are significantly correlated with depression, indicating that predictor variables of mental status all have significant linear associations with depression. Thus, the essential requirement of regression analysis can be satisfied.

Table 4.9 Correlations between each variable

Measures	Loneliness	Social support	Self-efficacy	Depression
Loneliness				
Social support	−0.67**			
Self-efficacy	−0.48**	0.59**		
Depression	0.67**	−0.55**	−0.62**	

** Significant at p < 0.01 level, 2-tailed, N = 146

Further correlations were carried out to test the associations between the three sources of social support and depression. The three sources of social support were others, family, and friends. A weak significant correlation was found between social support from the special one and depression, r (105) = −0.38, $p < 0.01$, indicating that when social support from the one increase, the depression will decrease. A weak but significant correlation was found between depression and social support from family, r (105) = −0.39, $p < 0.01$, and a moderately significant correlation between depression and social support from friends, r (105) = −0.60, $p < 0.01$. The result revealed that all three sources of social support have significant associations with depression.

Multiple regression

Multiple regression was used to investigate to what extent the three predictor variables, loneliness, social support, and self-efficacy can explain the level of depression and to what extent three mental factors can explain depression with the impact of each other. According to Field (2017), eight assumptions were needed to be satisfied for further regression, including (1) predictor variables and outcome variables should have linear associations; (2) independence of errors which was checked through the Durbin-Watson test; (3) homoscedasticity; (4) normally distributed errors; (5) predictors were uncorrelated with external variables; (6) variables should be in the same type, all quantitative or all categories; (7) no perfect multicollinearity; and (8) no zero variance. All eight assumptions were satisfied by analysing the sample data through SPSS. Thus, the sample was deemed appropriate to run further regression analysis.

Analysis using multiple regression indicated $R^2 = 0.57$, F (2, 103) = 67.24, $p < 0.001$. For the three predictor variables, loneliness can significantly explain the depression, unstandardised $\beta = 0.49$, $p < 0.001$, indicating that when the loneliness score increases by 1, the depression level will increase by 0.49. Self-efficacy can also significantly predict the depression, unstandardised $\beta = -5.50$, $p < 0.001$, suggesting that when self-efficacy increases by 1 unit, the depression will decrease by 5.50. The result revealed that social support cannot significantly predict depression in this model, unstandardised $\beta = -0.18$, $p = 0.063$. In this model, the result suggested that loneliness and self-efficacy are two predictor variables that can significantly predict depression after accounting for social support.

Discussion

The present investigation examined the associations among loneliness, social support, self-efficacy, and depression in university students. Additionally, the study sought to determine the extent to which these factors could influence and elucidate the depression experienced by students in the post-COVID era.

As predicted, the findings revealed a robust correlation between loneliness and depression, indicating that heightened feelings of loneliness were linked to an increased likelihood of developing depressive symptoms. This aligns with prior research that has established a strong connection between loneliness and depression, with individuals experiencing higher levels of loneliness being more susceptible to depression (Steen et al. 2022). Implementing lockdowns and social distancing measures during the pandemic resulted in heightened social isolation, particularly among young adults, leading to an increased risk of loneliness compared to pre-pandemic circumstances (Bu et al. 2020). The pandemic's adverse changes further exacerbated feelings of loneliness among young adults (Espinoza and Hernandez 2022). Consequently, young adults have had to contend with heightened feelings of loneliness during the pandemic, particularly those living alone or lacking sufficient interactions and support, which may contribute to elevated levels of depression. Further investigation is warranted to identify the risk factors associated with loneliness.

This research presents compelling evidence indicating that sleep quality substantially impacts adolescents' psychological well-being more than academic stress and attachment relationships. These findings emphasize the importance of educational institutions and caregivers prioritizing interventions to improve adolescents' sleep quality, as it may represent the most effective approach to enhancing their mental health. The results revealed that social support exhibited a moderate negative correlation with depression but did not show a significant relationship with depression in multiple regression analysis. It is suggested that students with lower levels of social support may experience higher levels of depression. Labrague et al. (2021) indicated a significant association between social support and depression.

In contrast to the pre-COVID-19 study, this research suggests that social support is not a significant predictor of depression (Dueñas et al. 2019). The study implies that social support remains a significant factor but is less influential in causing depression compared to the pre-COVID era. During the pandemic and school closures, students experienced decreased school belongingness and increased loneliness (Szelei et al. 2022). They had limited opportunities to connect with others, had to cope with life with reduced social support, and focused more on intrapersonal status rather than interpersonal relationships. They may have adapted to life with less social support and considered social support as a less critical resource in influencing their mental health.

For social support from friends, family, and significant others, it was hypothesised that all are related to depression. Friends' support was shown to be the most critical support to protect students against depression support relative to support from family and significant others. Friend's support was a buffer against depression among adolescents during the pandemic (Espinoza and Hernandez 2022). It is suggested that young people pay attention to peer connections more than family and significant others. Future research is needed to investigate the significance of friends among students.

There was also a significant inverse relationship between self-efficacy and depression. Students with higher self-efficacy were related to lower levels of depression. The result is in line with past studies such as Zeng et al. (2018), who claimed that self-efficacy is a significant factor associated with depression. Schoon and Henseke (2022) explained that lower levels of self-efficacy will increase stress levels and decrease the psychosocial resources of young adults during the pandemic, especially with the changes in life and work. Students with acute changes in life and work would have more stress and challenges. Past research revealed that students who take remote classes may have more distractions when learning (Gillis and Krull 2020), so self-efficacy, as an executing factor, can regulate daily healthy behaviours and resource management (Chong et al. 2020; Heo et al. 2022). Thus, self-efficacy could prevent related stresses and protect students against depression. The result of this study is not only consistent with past studies which revealed the relationship between self-efficacy and depression among people in the workplace and health care workers (Fida et al. 2022; Xiong et al. 2020), but also confirms that self-efficacy is also a significant predictor of depression in students.

Limitations and future directions

This research has several limitations that should be considered when interpreting the results. Firstly, the absence of baseline data to compare changes in depression and other predictor variables before and during the pandemic is a notable limitation. Additionally, the data collection for this study commenced in April, and due to time constraints, it was not feasible to collect and compare data from different periods. The study relied on online data collection using opportunistic and snowballing methods, which may have introduced bias into the sample. The gender distribution was skewed, with a ratio of 1 male to 9 females, and most participants were recruited from mental health or education-related programs, potentially leading to gender bias.

Furthermore, due to the recruitment method and time constraints, the study's sample size was limited and may not represent a normal distribution. Most participants exhibited no or mild symptoms below the clinical diagnosis of depression. At the same time, only a few had moderate or severe symptoms, indicating a need for further investigation into the population with severe depression symptoms or a diagnosed depression. The associations and impacts of loneliness, social support, and self-efficacy on depression among students with a diagnosis of depression may vary and require further exploration.

The study's voluntary and opportunistic nature may have resulted in a sample that primarily consists of students with subclinical depression. Additionally, the self-efficacy data exhibited positive and peaked kurtosis, with a mode of 4 and fewer participants scoring at 1, potentially due to the limited population accessing the study. Further research is warranted to explore populations with lower self-efficacy, and conducting qualitative interviews with students could provide a more in-depth understanding of their experiences, emotions, and support during the pandemic.

Study Three: Examination of the Emotion Regulation, Social Support, and Suicidal Ideation Among University Students

Taran Dale

Aims of this study

Although there is extensive research into ER and SI in various subgroups, there needs to be more investigation regarding university students in the UK post-COVID-19. In particular, there is a distinguished gap in research surrounding the role of social support as a moderating factor, considering that the pandemic has restructured support systems through changes in social dynamics. Therefore, this research is being carried out to investigate the relationship between ER and SI while investigating the role of social support as a moderating factor in university students in the UK. The primary hypothesis in this study anticipated that there would be a significant relationship between SI and poorer ER in students following COVID-19. The secondary hypothesis anticipated that social support would moderate the relationship between SI and ER.

Methods

Participants

Thirty-three participants were recruited through opportunity sampling. Of these, 30 provided complete data, which was analysed. Seven males and 23 females, 16 undergraduate students (53.3%) and 14 postgraduate students (46.7%), were included in this study. Participants included in this study were all aged between 18 and 50 years and fit the inclusion criteria of being university students in the UK.

Materials

The participants were required to provide demographic information (age, gender, studying status, relationship status and living situation). The participants were then shown a series of questionnaires. The first questionnaire investigated social support, the second measured ER, and finally, SI was explored.

The Multidimensional Scale of Perceived Social Support (MSPSS) was the first questionnaire used in this study (Zimet et al. 1988), which aimed to measure individuals' perceived ideas of the support they have received. This 12-item scale is separated into three subsections measuring significant others, family, and friends. The participants were required to answer the questions on a 7-point Likert scale ranging from 1 "Very Strongly Disagree" to 7 "Very Strongly Agree". The items were then added to create a score for each subscale ranging from 4 to 28. From these three subscales, the scores were added together to represent the perceived level of social support, ranging from 12 to 84. Participants who scored higher on the scale indicated receiving higher levels of social support. Cronbach's alpha was high for each subscale: significant other ($\alpha = 0.92$), family ($\alpha = 0.94$) and friends ($\alpha = 0.94$), therefore indicating high reliability.

The Emotion Regulation Questionnaire (ERQ) was utilised to assess emotion-related variables in participants (Gross and John 2003). This scale consisted of 10 items to measure ER strategies in the participants through two subscales, including suppression and reappraisal. Each statement was ranked on a Likert scale with a range of 1, "Strongly Disagree", to 7 "Strongly Agree". Higher scores on each subscale indicated higher use of that ER strategy. The Cronbach's alpha ($\alpha = 0.86$) for the reappraisal statements indicated good test–retest reliability; for the suppression items, the Cronbach's alpha for this scale indicated good reliability ($\alpha = 0.77$).

To measure suicidal thoughts in participants, Beck's Scale for Suicidal Ideation (BSSI) (Beck et al. 1988) was used. This questionnaire consisted of 19 statements in which the participants had to rate their thoughts, feelings and behaviours concerning suicidal tendencies. This scale was an adapted version of the original Scale for SI (SSI) developed by Beck and colleagues (1979), which was developed for interviews. Therefore, Beck and colleagues (1988) created a self-report version of this scale. The scoring for this measurement is 0–2, with 0 reflecting no SI and 2 suggesting more frequent levels of SI in participants. The scores were then calculated, ranging between 0 and 38. The higher the total score for the participants, the greater the chances of the participants experiencing SI. The Cronbach's alpha for this scale ($\alpha = 0.92$) indicated high levels of reliability.

Ethical Considerations

This research was ethically approved by the Institute of Education at University College London (UCL). No research was carried out before obtaining full ethical approval.

Data Analysis

The statistical software program SPSS was used to analyse data. Before data analysis, the dataset was cleaned; therefore, any missing data was excluded from the analysis. Spearman's Rho correlation was used to measure the strength of the relationship between ER and SI. A multiple regression analysis was employed to examine the role of the independent variables, ER and social support as a moderating factor, on the dependent variable, SI.

Results

Descriptives

A descriptive table was created to display the demographic information for the participants in the data analysis, including the information for each scale included in the study (please see Table 4.10).

Seven males (23.3%) and 23 females (76.7%) were included in the sample. The participants were aged 18–50 ($M = 22.63$, $SD = 2.19$).

Table 4.10 Demographic information of participants

	N	M	SD
Age	30	22.63	2.19
Gender	30	1.77	0.43
Level of study	30	1.47	0.51
MSPSS total	30	5.12	1.21
Reappraisal total	30	27.33	6.33
Suppression total	30	15.93	4.92
BSSI total	30	23.67	6.17

Note The Descriptive Table Presents the Sample Size (N), the Mean (M) and the Standard Deviation (SD)

Spearman's Rho correlations

A Spearman's Rho correlation displayed a moderately negative correlation between reappraisal items and SI. The relationship between the two variables was significant, r (28) = −0.39, p = 0.04 (Figs. 4.3 and 4.4).

Spearman's Rho correlation displayed a weak positive correlation between reappraisal items and SI. The relationship between the two variables was insignificant, r (28) = 0.16, p = 0.40.

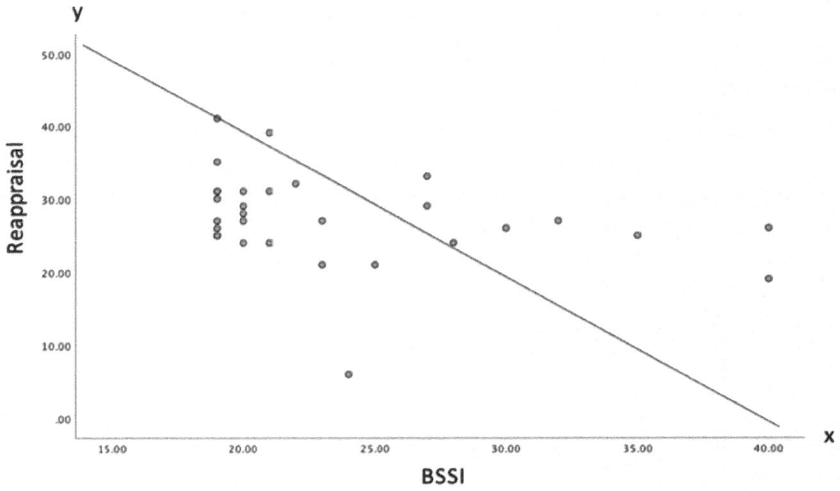

Fig. 4.3 A scatterplot demonstrating the scores discovered between reappraisal items and suicidal ideation

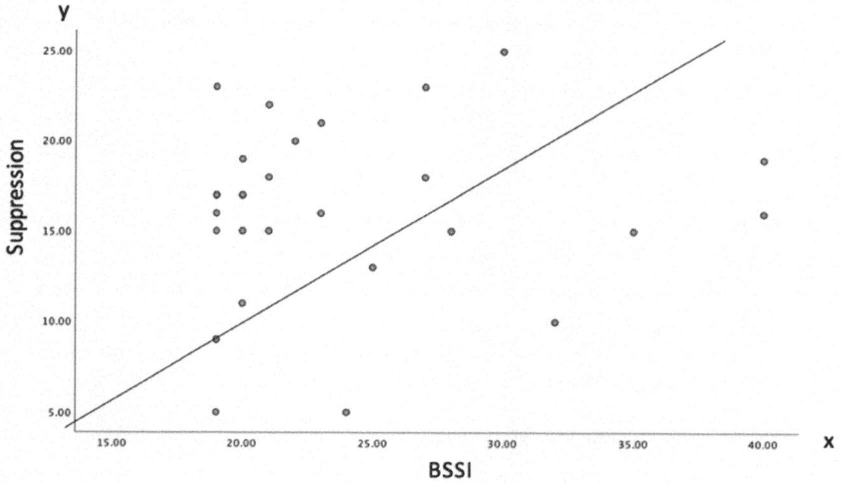

Fig. 4.4 A scatterplot showing the scores between suppression items and suicidal ideation

Multiple regression

As reappraisal was significantly correlated with SI and there was a weak correlation between suppression and SI, these variables were entered into a multiple regression, along with social support subscales (Table 4.11).

The multiple regression model shows that emotion regulation and social support account for a significant amount of variance in SI; hence, the regression model is significant. This model accounted for 90% variance ($R^2 = 0.90.$) in SI, F (11,8) = 6.28, $p = 0.007$ (Table 4.12).

This regression model highlights that suppression explains significant variance levels in SI ($p = 0.03$). The significance level for reappraisal ($p = 0.16$) indicates that reappraisal is not strongly associated with SI. This table shows that social support does not moderate the relationship between SI and ER, with a significance level of ($p = 0.47$).

Table 4.11 ANOVA table showing the significance of the multiple regression

Model	df	F	p	R square
Regression	11	6.28	0.007[b]	
Residual	8			
Total 1	19			0.896

Note Df = degrees of Freedom, F = f-test, P = p-value

Table 4.12 Multiple regression coefficient table showing suicidal ideation measured against control variables

Predictor	B	SE	B	t	P
Intercept	53.9	6.23		8.67	<0.001
Age	−0.26	0.40	−0.25	−0.66	0.53
Gender	−16.95	3.35	−0.95	−5.07	<0.001
Level of study	0.51	2.43	0.48	0.21	0.84
MSPSS total	−6.79	8.94	−1.73	0.76	0.47
MSPSS significant other subscale	1.98	3.65	0.53	0.54	0.60
MSPSS friends subscale	4.08	3.18	1.20	1.29	0.24
Reappraisal total	−0.26	0.17	−0.32	−1.53	0.16
Suppression total	0.54	0.20	0.48	2.72	0.03

Note B = Unstandardised coefficient, SE = Standard Error, β = Standardised coefficient, t = t-value and p = p value

Discussion

The principal aim of the study was to explore the relationship between ER and SI in university students in the UK while investigating social support as a moderating variable. The findings indicated a negative correlation between reappraisal and SI, therefore signifying that higher levels of reappraisal are associated with lower levels of SI, as the relationship was significant. Surprisingly, the correlation revealed no statistical significance between SI and suppression. However, there was a weak positive correlation between the two variables, thus indicating that the correlation occurred due to chance within this population. The findings from the multiple regression analysis were significant, therefore connoting that social support and ER are associated with SI. The third table from the analysis presented the significance level for variables separately, which indicated that suppression was significant; hence, the primary hypothesis was accepted.

Nevertheless, upon examination of the multiple regression analysis, it was apparent that social support was not a significant factor. Therefore, the secondary hypothesis was rejected as social support alone did not moderate the relationship between ER and SI. Considering these results, it is evident that social support combined with ER is significant. However, it is not solely associated with SI. Overall, the results indicate that reappraisal is negatively correlated with SI and that suppression plays a significant role in SI, consistent with previous research.

The present investigation established a connection between ER and SI. Although the correlation between suppression and SI was not statistically significant, utilizing of multiple regression analysis offered a more comprehensive understanding of the relationship between SI and suppression by considering additional variables and interactions. Given the significance of suppression as a variable, it is reasonable to infer that changes in suppression levels are linked to shifts in SI while considering other influencing variables. Furthermore, cognitive reappraisal was associated with lower levels of SI, consistent with prior research in this area (Laghaei et al. 2023). This study demonstrates that students exhibiting higher cognitive reappraisal levels displayed lower SI levels, emphasizing the importance of cognitive reappraisal strategies in promoting better mental health. Previous research has indicated that cognitive reappraisal can serve as a protective factor against suicidal thoughts (Duprey et al. 2021) by dismissing negative thoughts in the early stages of emotional processing. Consequently, cognitive reappraisal as an ER strategy can students' overall well-being (Kudinova et al. 2016) and is perceived as a less cognitively demanding and more effective form of ER (Ochsner et al. 2012). As the preferred ER strategy, cognitive reappraisal enables students to reframe negative thoughts and employ healthier strategies for effectively processing emotions in challenging situations.

Additionally, the multiple regression analysis indicated a heightened susceptibility to engaging in SI among individuals employing suppressive strategies, as evidenced by the significant outcomes of the model. These findings align with existing literature that underscores the adverse implications of suppression as an ER strategy, particularly concerning rumination, characterized by persistent dwelling on negative thoughts and self-blame (Luca 2019). While suppressive strategies are identified as a risk factor for SI, cognitive reappraisal is advocated by scholars in this domain. Nevertheless, suppressive strategies can be effective for individuals when confronted with overwhelming circumstances (Kaplow et al. 2014). Consequently, suppression can serve as an efficacious coping mechanism for managing emotional distress in a manner commensurate with the individual's circumstances (Parkes 1990). Employing suppressive strategies as a transient coping mechanism can afford temporary relief while contending with overwhelming emotions. Consequently, contrary to prevailing perceptions, suppression may not be inherently inadequate and can function as a beneficial provisional coping tool for individuals.

Interestingly, the results indicated a lack of significant association between suppression and SI. Despite the non-significant correlation, similar findings from previous studies have also demonstrated that heightened levels of suppression did not lead to an increase in suicidal thoughts (Franz et al. 2021). Although the multiple regression analysis revealed a significant relationship between the two variables, exploring potential explanations for the non-significant correlation between SI and suppression is crucial. Correlations, as a measure of the linear relationship between two variables (Howitt and Cramer 2008), do not account for confounding variables and their potential influence on the interplay between the measured variables (Ewert and Sibthorp 2009). This limitation needs to be revised as correlations should consider existing factors that may impact the relationship between the two variables, potentially resulting in a weak correlation. Additionally, the non-significant correlation between SI and suppression may be attributed to a small sample size. Although a weak positive relationship was observed between the two variables, the small sample size may have limited the statistical power required for the correlation to be significant (Knudson and Lindsey 2014).

Prior research has suggested that social support moderates the relationship between ER and suicidal tendencies. Demir and Sümer (2022) examined the impact of social support on suicidal tendencies and ER among university students. Their findings indicated that social support mediated the relationship between suicidal tendencies and ER, with family support being the most significant mediator. Their research underscored the importance of perceived support from friends, family, or significant others as a protective factor against suicidal behaviour, enhancing students' resilience to stressors. However, the current study's findings contradict this, as they confirm that social support did not mediate the relationship between SI and ER.

Furthermore, the results of the multiple regression analysis provided evidence that social support is associated with an increased risk of students experiencing suicidal thoughts, as the findings yielded statistical significance. Consequently, it is reasonable to infer that social support has the potential to mitigate SI, given that individuals reporting higher levels of social support also reported lower levels of SI, thereby underscoring its importance. Although social support did not act as a moderator in the relationship between ER and SI, it remains essential to acknowledge its substantial influence on the development of suicidal thoughts.

Limitations and future directions

This study utilized self-report measures to evaluate participants' thoughts and emotions using questionnaires. The use of closed questions in the questionnaires limited the participants' ability to express their subjective experiences related to ER, SI, and social support. Consequently, the researcher required a more comprehensive and detailed dataset to comprehend the underlying reasons for the participants' experiences. Alternatively, a qualitative study would have provided the opportunity to gain extensive insight and detailed descriptions of the participants' experiences and opinions. Additionally, the study's small sample size raises concerns about the generalizability of the findings, as it may only adequately represent some UK students. The limited number of participants may be attributed to the sensitive nature of the topics, which could have deterred participation. Furthermore, the inclusion of socially sensitive topics may have had adverse effects on the mental health of the students, particularly when addressing questions about SI. Research has indicated that respondents may need to be more truthful when answering sensitive questions due to fear of judgment. Therefore, including delicate topics should be approached with caution, considering the participants' vulnerability.

Future research examining the moderating role of social support on ER and SI should consider conducting a cross-cultural study to understand the differences between students from individualistic and collectivist cultures. Including students from diverse cultures would provide insights into variations in ER processes and the prevalence of SI. Investigating this link in different cultural contexts with social support as a moderating factor would be intriguing, as it would shed light on the significance of social support and its contextual differences. Studies have suggested that individuals from collectivist cultures are less likely to seek social support to avoid burdening their family and friends. In contrast, individuals from individualistic cultures rely on their social networks during challenging times. Therefore, exploring how students' perceptions of received social support vary across cultures would be valuable in enhancing researchers' understanding of the interplay between these variables and acknowledging the potential disparities in findings due to cultural differences among university students.

Furthermore, it may be beneficial to monitor the psychological well-being of participants post-study due to the sensitive nature of the research. It would be advantageous for future researchers to ensure respondents' welfare after their involvement in the study. Implementing mental health interventions for university students could be beneficial, as the study has revealed that high levels of suppression are linked to an increase in SI. Therefore, interventions that educate students on effective techniques and cognitive strategies to manage negative or intrusive thoughts are essential for improving their psychological well-being.

In conclusion, the study found that suppression was associated with increased SI, while reappraisal was linked to a lower level of SI. Future research should examine variations in students' levels of social support and how these differences impact the relationship between ER and SI in university students. This offers scholars a new perspective on the interaction between these variables in diverse contexts, thereby contributing to their knowledge base. Introducing interventions in universities would promote the adoption of effective strategies to address suppression in university students and reduce the risk of SI.

References

Ahmad N, Roslan S, Othman S, Shukor SFA, Bakar AYA (2018) The validity and reliability of psychometric profile for Depression, Anxiety and Stress Scale (DASS-21) instrument among Malaysian undergraduate students. Int J Acad Res Business Soc Sci 8(6). https://doi.org/10.6007/IJARBSS/v8-i6/4275

Aihie ON, Ohanaka BI (2019) Perceived academic stress among undergraduate students in a Nigerian university. J Educ Soc Res 9(2):56–66. https://doi.org/10.2478/jesr-2019-0013

Aldao A, Nolen-Hoeksema S, Schweizer S (2010) Emotion-regulation strategies across psychopathology: A meta-analytic review. Clin Psychol Rev 30(2):217–237

An B, Lim J (2017) Relationship among Korean university students' suicidal ideation, posttraumatic growth, self-efficacy, and cultural orientation. Int J Adv Nurs Educ Res 1(1): 83–88. https://doi.org/10.21742/ijaner.2017.2.1.15

Antúnez Z, Vinet EV (2012) Depression Anxiety Stress Scales (DASS-21): validation of the abbreviated version in Chilean university students. Terapia Psicológoca. 30:49–55

Armsden GC, Greenberg MT (1987) The inventory of parent and peer attachment: relationships to well-being in adolescence. J Youth Adolesc 16(5):427–454

Bandura A (1977) Self-efficacy: Toward a unifying theory of behavioural change. Psychol Rev 84(2):191–215

Beck AT, Kovacs M, Weissman A (1979) Assessment of suicidal intention: the Scale for Suicide Ideation. J Consult Clin Psychol 47(2):343

Beck AT, Steer RA, Brown G (1996) Beck depression inventory–II (BDI-II) [Database record]. APA PsycTests. https://doi.org/10.1037/t00742-000

Beck AT, Steer RA, Ranieri WF (1988) Scale for suicide ideation: psychometric properties of a self-report version. J Clin Psychol 44(4):499–505

Bedewy D, Gabriel A (2015) Examining perceptions of academic stress and its sources among university students: the perception of academic stress scale. Health Psychol Open 2(2):2055102915596714–2055102915596714. https://doi.org/10.1177/2055102915596714

Beiter R, Nash R, McCrady M, Rhoades D, Linscomb M, Clarahan M, Sammut S (2015) The prevalence and correlates of depression, anxiety, and stress in a sample of college students. J Affect Disord 173:90–96. https://doi.org/10.1016/j.jad.2014.10.054

British Psychological Society (2021) Code of ethics and conduct. https://doi.org/10.53841/bpsrep.2021.inf94

Brown TA, Chorpita BF, Korotitsch W, Barlow DH (1997) Psychometric properties of the Depression Anxiety Stress Scales (DASS) in clinical samples. Behav Res Ther 35:79–89

Bu F, Steptoe A, Fancourt D (2020) Who is lonely in lockdown? Cross-cohort analyses of predictors of loneliness before and during the COVID-19 pandemic. Public Health 186:31–34. https://doi.org/10.1016/j.puhe.2020.06.036

Buysse DJ, Reynolds CF, Monk TH, Berman SR, Kupfer DJ (1989) The Pittsburgh Sleep Quality Index (PSQI): a new instrument for psychiatric research and practice. Psychiatry Res 28:193–213

Camacho A, Cordero ED, Perkins T (2016) Psychometric properties of the DASS-21 among Latina/o college students by the US-Mexico border. J Immigr Minor Health 18(5):1017–1023. https://doi.org/10.1007/s10903-016-0415-1

Canty-Mitchell J, Zimet GD (2000) Psychometric properties of the multidimensional scale of perceived social support in urban adolescents. Am J Community Psychol 28(3):391–400. https://doi.org/10.1023/a:1005109522457

Cao CH, Dang CY, Zheng X, Chen WG, Chen IH, Gamble JH (2023) The psychometric properties of the DASS-21 and its association with problematic internet use among Chinese college freshmen. Healthcare (Basel) 11(5):700. https://doi.org/10.3390/healthcare11050700

Chavez-Baldini U, Wichers M, Reininghaus U, Wigman JT, Genetic risk and outcome of psychosis investigators (2020) Expressive suppression in psychosis: the association with social context. Plos one 15(3):e0230102

Chehri A, Brand S, Goldaste N, Eskandari S, Brühl A, Bahmani SD, Khazaie H (2020). Psychometric properties of the Persian Pittsburgh Sleep Quality Index for adolescents. Int J Environ Res Public Health 17(19). https://doi.org/10.3390/ijerph17197095

Chen G, Gully SM, Eden D (2001) Validation of a new general self-efficacy scale. Organ Res Methods 4(1):62–83. https://doi.org/10.1177/109442810141004

Chen W, Zhang D, Liu J, Pan Y, Sang B (2019) Parental attachment and depressive symptoms in Chinese adolescents: the mediation effect of emotion regulation. Aust J Psychol 71(3):241–248. https://doi.org/10.1111/ajpy.12239

Chen W, Zhang D, Pan Y, Cheng G, Liu G (2016) Research on parental attachment and depression of adolescents: the mediating role of psychological Suzhi. J Psychol Sci 39(6):1282–1289. https://doi.org/10.16719/j.cnki.1671-6981.20160601

Chervonsky E, Hunt C (2019) Emotion regulation, mental health, and social wellbeing in a young adolescent sample: a concurrent and longitudinal investigation. Emotion 19(2):270

Chong YY, Chien WT, Cheng HY, Chow KM, Kassianos AP, Karekla M, Gloster A (2020) The role of illness perceptions, coping, and self-efficacy on adherence to precautionary measures for COVID-19. Int J Environ Res Public Health 17(18):6540. https://doi.org/10.3390/ijerph17186540

Compas BE, Jaser SS, Bettis AH, Watson KH, Gruhn MA, Dunbar JP, ... Thigpen JC (2017) Coping, emotion regulation, and psychopathology in childhood and adolescence: A meta analysis and narrative review. Psychol Bull 143(9):939–991

Curcio G, Ferrara M, De Gennaro L (2006) Sleep loss, learning capacity and academic performance. Sleep Med Rev 10(5):323–337

De Lise F, Bacaro V, Crocetti E (2023) The social side of sleep: a systematic review of the longitudinal associations between peer relationships and sleep quality. Int J Environ Res Public Health 20(3):2017. https://doi.org/10.3390/ijerph20032017

Demir B, Sümer ZH (2022) The mediator role of perceived social support in the relationship between difficulties in emotion regulation and suicide tendency. Curr Psychol:1–10

Department of Health and Social Care (2022) England returns to Plan A as regulations on face coverings and COVID Passes change today. GOV.UK. https://www.gov.uk/government/news/odelli-returns-to-plan-a-as-regulations-on-face-coverings-and-covid-passes-change-today. Accessed 30 June 2022

Dueñas JM, Fernández M, Morales-Vives F (2019) What is the protective role of perceived social support and religiosity in suicidal ideation in young adults? J Gen Psychol 147(4):432–447. https://doi.org/10.1080/00221309.2019.1697638

Duprey EB, Handley ED, Manly JT, Cicchetti D, Toth SL (2021) Child maltreatment, recent stressful life events, and suicide ideation: A test of the stress sensitivity hypothesis. Child Abuse Negl 113:104926

Eichhorn BR (2014) Common method variance techniques. Cleveland State University, Department of Operations & Supply Chain Management, vol 1(11). SAS Institute Inc, Cleveland, OH

Espinoza G, Hernandez HL (2022) Adolescent loneliness, stress and depressive symptoms during the COVID-19 pandemic: the protective role of friends. Infant Child Develop 31(3). https://doi.org/10.1002/icd.2305

Ewert A, Sibthorp J (2009) Creating outcomes through experiential education: the challenge of confounding variables. J Exp Educ 31(3):376–389
Fallone G, Acebo C, Arnedt JT, Seifer R, Carskadon MA (2001) Effects of acute sleep restriction on behaviour, sustained attention, and response inhibition in children. Percept Mot Skills 93(1):213–229. https://doi.org/10.2466/PMS.93.5.213-229
Fida R, Paciello M, Watson D, Nayani R (2022) The protective role of work self-efficacy on wellbeing during COVID-19 pandemic: results from a longitudinal year-long study. Pers Individ Differ 197:111760. https://doi.org/10.1016/j.paid.2022.111760
Ford BQ, Troy AS (2019) Reappraisal reconsidered: A closer look at the costs of an acclaimed emotion-regulation strategy. Curr Dir Psychol Sci 28(2):195–203
França FDP, Dias TL (2021) Validity and reliability of the perceptions of academic stress scale. Psicologia: Teoria e Prática 23(1):1–21. https://doi.org/10.5935/1980-6906/ePTPPA13041
Franz PJ, Kleiman EM, Nock MK (2021) Reappraisal and suppression each moderate the association between stress and suicidal ideation: preliminary evidence from a daily diary study. Cogn Ther Res:1–8
Gillis A, Krull LM (2020) COVID-19 remote learning transition in Spring 2020: class structures, student perceptions, and inequality in college courses. Teach Sociol 48(4):283–299. https://doi.org/10.1177/0092055x20954263
Goldstein AN, Walker MP (2014) The role of sleep in emotional brain function. Annu Rev Clin Psychol 10(1):679–708. https://doi.org/10.1146/annurev-clinpsy-032813-153716
Greenberg MT (2009) Mark T. Greenberg Ph.D. Bennett Chair of Prevention Research Director, Prevention Research Center. https://emdrtherapyvolusia.com/wp-content/uploads/2016/12/Attachment_Inventory-Article.pdf
Gross JJ (1998) The emerging field of emotion regulation: An integrative review. Rev Gen Psychol 2(3):271–299
Gross JJ, John OP (2003) Individual differences in two emotion regulation processes: implications for affect, relationships, and well-being. J Pers Soc Psychol 85(2):348
Guo Ch (2022) Assessing the Chinese version of Pittsburgh Sleep Quality Index in non-clinical adolescents. Curr Psychol (New Brunswick, N.J.). https://doi.org/10.1007/s12144-022-03581-2
Heo H, Bonk CJ, Doo MY (2022) Influences of depression, self-efficacy, and resource management on learning engagement in blended learning during COVID-19. Internet High Educ 54:100856. https://doi.org/10.1016/j.iheduc.2022.100856
Hirshkowitz M, Whiton K, Albert SM, Alessi C, Bruni O, DonCarlos L, Hazen N, Herman J, Adams Hillard PJ, Katz ES, Kheirandish-Gozal L, Neubauer DN, O'Donnell AE, Ohayon M, Peever J, Rawding R, Sachdeva RC, Setters B, Vitiello MV, Ware JC (2015) National sleep foundation's updated sleep duration recommendations: final report. Sleep Health 1(4):233–243. https://doi.org/10.1016/j.sleh.2015.10.004
Ho KY, Lam KKW, Xia W, Chung JOK, Cheung AT, Ho LLK, Chiu SY, Chan GCF, Li WHC (2021) Psychometric properties of the Chinese version of the Pittsburgh Sleep Quality Index (PSQI) among Hong Kong Chinese childhood cancer survivors. Health Qual Life Outcomes 19(1):1–176. https://doi.org/10.1186/s12955-021-01803-y
Howitt D, Cramer D (2008). Introduction to SPSS in psychology: for version 16 and earlier. Pearson Education
Jiang S, Ren Q, Jiang C, Wang L (2021) Academic stress and depression of Chinese adolescents in junior high schools: moderated mediation model of school burnout and self-esteem. J Affect Disord 295:384–389. https://doi.org/10.1016/j.jad.2021.08.085
Jiang XS, Wang Y, Singer JA (2023) Self-defining memories and past academic stress in Chinese and American college students: a replication and extension of Wang and Singer (2021). Memory (hove) 31(3):346–356. https://doi.org/10.1080/09658211.2022.2154941
John OP, Gross JJ (2004) Healthy and unhealthy emotion regulation: personality processes, individual differences, and life span development. J Pers 72(6):1301–1334

Johnson H (2021) Examining the differences in perceived stress, academic success, and potential protective factors between first-generation college students and continuing-generation college students. Middle Tennessee State University ProQuest Dissertations Publishing, 28415919p

Ju M, Tao Y, Lu Y, Ding L, Weng X, Wang S, Fu Q, Li X (2019) Evaluation of sleep quality in adolescent patients with osteosarcoma using Pittsburgh Sleep Quality Index. Eur J Cancer Care 28(4):e13065. https://doi.org/10.1111/ecc.13065

Kaplow JB, Gipson PY, Horwitz AG, Burch BN, King CA (2014) Emotional suppression mediates the relation between adverse life events and adolescent suicide: Implications for prevention. Prev Sci 15:177–185

Kelley NJ, Glazer JE, Pornpattananangkul N, Nusslock R (2019) Reappraisal and suppression emotion-regulation tendencies differentially predict reward-responsivity and psychological well-being. Biol Psychol 140:35–47

Klonsky ED, Dixon-Luinenburg T, May AM (2021) The critical distinction between suicidal ideation and suicide attempts. World Psychiatry 20(3):439

Knudson DV, Lindsey C (2014) Type I and type II errors in correlations of various sample sizes. Compr Psychol 3:03-CP

Kudinova AY, Owens M, Burkhouse KL, Barretto KM, Bonanno GA, Gibb BE (2016) Differences in emotion modulation using cognitive reappraisal in individuals with and without suicidal ideation: an ERP study. Cogn Emot 30(5):999–1007

Labrague LJ, de Los Santos JAA, Falguera CC (2021) Social and emotional loneliness among college students during the COVID-19 pandemic: the predictive role of coping behaviours, social support, and personal resilience. Perspect Psychiatr Care 57(4):1578–1584. https://doi.org/10.1111/ppc.12721

Laghaei M, Mehrabizadeh Honarmand M, Jobson L, Abdollahpour Ranjbar H, Habibi Asgarabad M (2023) Pathways from childhood trauma to suicidal ideation: mediating through difficulties in emotion regulation and depressive symptoms. BMC Psychiatry 23(1):1–13

Larche CL, Plante I, Roy M, Ingelmo PM, Ferland CE (2021) The Pittsburgh Sleep Quality Index: reliability, factor structure, and related clinical factors among children, adolescents, and young adults with chronic pain. Sleep Disord:5546484. https://doi.org/10.1155/2021/5546484

Lee B, Kim YE (2022) Validity of the depression, anxiety, and stress scale (DASS-21) in a sample of Korean university students. Curr Psychol (New Brunswick, N.J.) 41(6):3937–3946. https://doi.org/10.1007/s12144-020-00914-x

Li JY, Li J, Liang JH, Qian S, Jia RX, Wang YQ, Xu Y (2019) Depressive symptoms among children and adolescents in china: a systematic review and meta-analysis. Med Sci Monitor 25:7459–7470. https://doi.org/10.12659/MSM.916774

Liu X, Tang M, Hu L, Wang A, Wu H, Zhao G, Gao C, Li W (1996) The reliability and validity of the Pittsburgh Sleep Quality Index. Chin J Psychiatry 29(2):103–107 [In Chinese]

Lovibond PF (1998) Long-term stability of depression, anxiety, and stress syndromes. J Abnorm Psychol 107:520–526. https://doi.org/10.1037/0021-843X.107.3.520

Lovibond PF, Lovibond SH (1995a) The structure of negative emotional states: comparison of the Depression Anxiety Stress Scales (DASS) with the beck depression and anxiety inventories. Behav Res Ther 33(3):335–343. https://doi.org/10.1016/0005-7967(94)00075-U

Lovibond SH, Lovibond PF (1995a) Manual for the depression anxiety & stress scales, 2nd edn. Psychology Foundation, Sydney

Luca M (2019) Maladaptive rumination as a transdiagnostic mediator of vulnerability and outcome in psychopathology. J Clin Med 8(3):314

Luszczynska A, Gutierrez-Dona B, Schwarzer R (2005) General self-efficacy in various domains of human functioning: Evidence from five countries. Int J Psychol 40(2):80–89

Ma A, Yang Y, Guo S, Li X, Zhang S, Chang H (2022) Adolescent resilience and mobile phone addiction in Henan Province of China: Impacts of chain mediating, coping style. PLoS ONE 17(12):e0278182. https://doi.org/10.1371/journal.pone.0278182

Miller AE, Racine SE (2022) Emotion regulation difficulties as common and unique predictors of impulsive behaviours in university students. J Am Coll Health 70(5):1387–1395

Misra M, Joshi H, Sarwal R, Rao KD (2022) Exit strategies from lockdowns due to COVID-19: a scoping review. BMC Public Health 22(1):488. https://doi.org/10.1186/s12889-022-12845-2

Muris P (2002) Relationships between self-efficacy and symptoms of anxiety disorders and depression in a normal adolescent sample. Pers Individ Differ 32(2):337–348

Neacsiu AD, Fang CM, Rodriguez M, Rosenthal MZ (2018) Suicidal behaviour and problems with emotion regulation. Suicide Life Threat Behav 48(1):52–74

Ochsner KN, Silvers JA, Buhle JT (2012) Functional imaging studies of emotion regulation: a synthetic review and evolving model of the cognitive control of emotion. Ann N Y Acad Sci 1251(1):E1–E24

Page AC, Hooke GR, Morrison DL (2007) Psychometric properties of the Depression Anxiety Stress Scales (DASS) in depressed clinical samples. Br J Clin Psychol 46(Pt. 3):283–297. https://doi.org/10.1348/014466506X158996

Parkes KR (1990) Coping, negative affectivity, and the work environment: additive and interactive predictors of mental health. J Appl Psychol 75(4):399

Passos MH, Silva HA, Pitangui AC, Oliveira VM, Lima AS, Araújo RC (2017) Reliability and validity of the Brazilian version of the Pittsburgh Sleep Quality Index in adolescents. Jornal de Pediatria 93(2):200–206. https://doi.org/10.1016/j.jped.2016.06.006

Peltz JS, Rogge RD, Connolly H, O'Connor TG (2017) A process-oriented model linking adolescents' sleep hygiene and psychological functioning: the moderating role of school start times. Sleep Health 3:465–471. https://doi.org/10.1016/j.sleh.2017.08.003

Qidwai W, Ishaque S, Shah S, Rahim M (2010) Adolescent lifestyle and behaviour: a survey from a developing country. PLoS ONE 5(9):e12914. https://doi.org/10.1371/journal.pone.0012914

Russell DW (1996) UCLA loneliness scale (version 3): reliability, validity, and factor structure. J Pers Assess 66(1):20–40. https://doi.org/10.1207/s15327752jpa6601_2

Schoon I, Henseke G (2022) Social Inequalities in young people's mental distress during the COVID-19 pandemic: do psychosocial resource factors matter? Front Public Health 10. https://doi.org/10.3389/fpubh.2022.820270

Setia MS (2016) Methodology series module 3: CROSS-sectional studies. Indian J Dermatol 61(3):261

Setyowati A, Chung MH (2021) Validity and reliability of the Indonesian version of the Pittsburgh Sleep Quality Index in adolescents. Int J Nurs Pract 27(5):e12856–n/a. https://doi.org/10.1111/ijn.12856

Sharma S (2018) Perceived academic stress among students. Res Rev Int J Multidiscip 3(8):421–425. https://doi.org/10.5281/zenodo.1401248

Steen OD, Ori APS, Wardenaar KJ, van Loo HM (2022) Loneliness associates strongly with anxiety and depression during the COVID pandemic, especially in men and younger adults. Sci Rep 12(1). https://doi.org/10.1038/s41598-022-13049-9

Szabo M (2010) The short version of the Depression Anxiety Stress Scales (DASS-21): factor structure in a young adolescent sample. J Adolesc (London, England.) 33(1):1–8. https://doi.org/10.1016/j.adolescence.2009.05.014

Szelei N, Devlieger I, Verelst A, Spaas C, Jervelund SS, Primdahl NL, Skovdal M, Opaas M, Durbeej N, Osman F, Soye E, Colpin H, de Haene L, Aalto S, Kankaanpää R, Peltonen K, Andersen AJ, Hilden PK, Watters C, Derluyn I (2022) Migrant students sense of belonging and the covid-19 pandemic: implications for educational inclusion. Soc Incl 10(2). https://doi.org/10.17645/si.v10i2.5106

Tang X, Tang S, Ren Z, Wong DFK (2019) Prevalence of depressive symptoms among adolescents in secondary school in mainland China: a systematic review and meta-analysis. J Affect Disord 245:498–507. https://doi.org/10.1016/j.jad.2018.11.043

Teismann T, Forkmann T, Brailovskaia J, Siegmann P, Glaesmer H, Margraf J (2018) Positive mental health moderates the association between depression and suicide ideation: a longitudinal study. Int J Clin Health Psychol 18(1):1–7

Tonsing KN (2014) Psychometric properties and validation of Nepali version of the Depression Anxiety Stress Scales (DASS-21). Asian J Psychiatr 8(1):63–66. https://doi.org/10.1016/j.ajp.2013.11.001
Trompetter HR, De Kleine E, Bohlmeijer ET (2017) Why does positive mental health buffer against psychopathology? An exploratory study on self-compassion as a resilience mechanism and adaptive emotion regulation strategy. Cogn Ther Res 41:459–468
Voderholzer U, Piosczyk H, Holz J, Landmann N, Feige B, Loessl B, Kopasz M, Doerr JP, Riemann D, Nissen C (2011) Sleep restriction over several days does not affect long-term recall of declarative and procedural memories in adolescents. Sleep Med 12:170–178. https://doi.org/10.1016/j.sleep.2010.07.017
Wang K, Shi H, Geng F, Zou L, Tan S, Wang Y, Neumann DL, Shum DK, Chan RK (2016) Cross-cultural validation of the depression anxiety stress scale–21 in China. Psychol Assess 28(5):e88–e100. https://doi.org/10.1037/pas0000207
Watermeyer R, Crick T, Knight C, Goodall J (2021) COVID-19 and digital disruption in UK universities: afflictions and affordances of emergency online migration. High Educ 81(3):623–641. https://doi.org/10.1007/s10734-020-00561-y
Werner-Seidler A, Perry Y, Calear AL, Newby JM, Christensen H (2017) School-based depression and anxiety prevention programs for young people: A systematic review and meta analysis. Clin Psychol Rev 51:30–47
Winsler A, Deutsch A, Vorona RD, Payne PA, Szklo-Coxe M (2015) Sleepless in fairfax: the difference one more hour of sleep can make for teen hopelessness, suicidal ideation, and substance use. J Youth Adolesc 44:362–378. https://doi.org/10.1007/s10964-014-0170-3
World Health Organization (2021) Mental health of adolescents. https://www.who.int/news-room/fact-sheets/detail/adolescent-mental-health
Xiong H, Yi S, Lin Y (2020) The psychological status and self-efficacy of nurses during COVID-19 outbreak: a cross-sectional survey. Inquiry J Health Care Organ Provision Financ 57:004695802095711. https://doi.org/10.1177/0046958020957114
Yu H-Q, Zhou Z-K (2002) 4–6th graders' attachment to parents and its associations with peers relations. Psychol Dev Educ 18(4):36–40
Zarotti N, Povah C, Simpson J (2020) Mindfulness mediates the relationship between cognitive reappraisal and resilience in higher education students. Pers Individ Differ 156:109795
Zeek ML, Savoie MJ, Song M, Kennemur LM, Qian J, Jungnickel PW, Westrick SC (2015) Sleep duration and academic performance among student pharmacists. Am J Pharm Educ 79(5):63–63. https://doi.org/10.5688/ajpe79563
Zeifman RJ, Antony MM, Kuo JR (2020) When being imperfect just won't do: exploring the relationship between perfectionism, emotion dysregulation, and suicidal ideation. Pers Individ Differ 152:109612
Zeng B, Zhao J, Zou L, Yang X, Zhang X, Wang W, Zhao J, Chen J (2018) Depressive symptoms, post-traumatic stress symptoms and suicide risk among graduate students: the mediating influence of emotional regulatory self-efficacy. Psychiatry Res 264:224–230. https://doi.org/10.1016/j.psychres.2018.03.022
Zhang J, Paksarian D, Lamers F, Hickie IB, He J, Merikangas KR (2017) Sleep patterns and mental health correlates in US adolescents. J Pediatr 182:137–143. https://doi.org/10.1016/j.jpeds.2016.11.007
Zhang X, Xu H, Gu J, Lau JTF, Hao C, Zhao Y, Davis A, Hao Y (2016) Depression, suicidal ideation, and related factors of methadone maintenance treatment users in Guangzhou, China. AIDS Care 28(7):851–856. https://doi.org/10.1080/09540121.2015.1124981
Zhang Y-L, Zhang Y-L, Zhang Y-X, Wang J-L, Hung C-Y (2011) Reliability and validity of Chinese version of revised inventory of parent and peer attachment in junior students. Chin Ment Health J 25(1):66–70
Zhu X, Haegele JA, Liu H, Yu F (2021) Academic stress, physical activity, sleep, and mental health among Chinese adolescents. Int J Environ Res Public Health 18(14):7257

Zimet GD, Dahlem NW, Zimet SG, Farley GK (1988) The multidimensional scale of perceived social support. J Pers Assess 52(1):30–41

Mrs. Yuefei Jiang has a Master of Science in the Psychology of Education from University College London, UK, and a Master of Arts in Linguistics and Applied Linguistics from Fudan University, China. She was a senior journalist and received the China Journalism Award, the most authoritative journalism award in the country. As a mother, Yuefei has been exposed to numerous instances of children struggling with psychological issues. Specifically, several cases of suicides among Chinese teenagers—a serious and concerning issue in China—sparked her profound concern for adolescent mental health. This motivated her to pursue a conversion psychology programme. Drawn to Dr. Elsie Ong because of a shared concern over adolescent suicide, Yuefei chose her as a supervisor. Under Elsie's mentorship, Yuefei initiated a study examining the interplay between mental health, sleep quality, academic stress, and attachment relationships in Chinese high school students. it represents her initial foray into this critical area and marks her first step in the field of psychology.

Miss. Taran Dale completed her Master's degree in Educational Psychology at University College London. She has a specific interest in mental health, which led her to explore suicidal ideation and emotion regulation, specifically in university students within her degree. Her passion for understanding the complex dynamics between learning and mental health has shaped her academic journey. Taran's invaluable experiences working alongside educational psychologists have provided her with a deep understanding of the challenges individuals face by striving to navigate the complex terrain of mental wellbeing within the educational context. Her academic pursuits have consistently reflected an insatiable curiosity, coupled with an earnest desire to venture into the uncharted territories of the human mind.

Dr. Elsie Ong is a Lecturer and a Dissertation Supervisor in UCL. She has worked in many universities in Asia and the UK for over ten years. Elsie is active in leading research that focuses on the mental health of young adults; especially those going through university transitions. Her expertise in cognitive neuroscience and psychology has also initiated further exploration on the underlying causes of mental health problems and later sparkles potentials for suicide preventions and interventions. Elsie is devoted to the study of psychological wellbeing in young adults and has published her research through internationally renowned conferences and reputed journals such as Frontiers in psychiatry. These experiences have helped to keep her most up to date on the latest development in preventions and interventions in mental health.

Chapter 5
The Importance of Digital Technology

Elsie Ong and Molly Bass

Overview

Recent advancements in digital technologies have the potential to significantly transform the landscape of clinical research and treatment, particularly in the context of mental health issues experienced by young individuals. Additionally, the impact of social media on mental health has been extensively studied, with findings often indicating its negative influence on individuals' psychological well-being and various aspects of their lives. Research focusing on university students has highlighted their heightened susceptibility to mental health issues and their reliance on social media platforms (Power 2005).

This chapter explores the implications of digital developments, including the excessive using the internet as an information source and its role in facilitating help-seeking behaviours among young people. **Study One** will delve into using mobile phone and digital technologies by young people in this post-pandemic era for mental health and defining their self-identities. While optimism surrounds the potential of these tools to address challenges related to the availability, accessibility, and costs of existing mental health services, there is a need for further exploration and optimization before their integration into routine clinical care. The second study (**Study Two**) aims to investigate the influence of social media on the eating behaviours of university students, specifically about the mental health challenges stemming from extensive social media use.

E. Ong (✉)
Department of Psychology and Human Development, IOE—UCL's Faculty of Education and Society, University College London, London, WC 1E 6BT, UK
e-mail: Elsie.ong@ucl.ac.uk

M. Bass
Faculty of Health, Education and Society, University of Northampton, Northampton, UK
e-mail: molly.bass@northampton.ac.uk

E. Ong (ed.), *The Emergence of the Digital World*,
https://doi.org/10.1007/978-981-97-3098-8_5

The study employed three quantitative scale answer questionnaires on the independent variable of social media and the dependent variables of mental health and eating habits, along with a qualitative open-ended question distributed to university students. The findings revealed both positive and negative impacts of social media on the participants' daily lives, indicating a moderately strong relationship between social media use and the variables under consideration. However, it is important to acknowledge the presence of other variables that may influence eating habits, and the study encountered limitations related to response rates and participant reluctance to provide certain information, which may have affected the reliability of the overall findings.

We will finish by highlighting some important factors in the design, use, and evaluation of these digital resources.

How Important is Digital Technology to Young People?

Information and communication technologies have significantly changed among young people in recent decades. Traditional television viewing has decreased among this demographic, with current broadcasting statistics confirming a decline in scheduled television consumption compared to other age groups (British Audience Research Board 2018). Instead, young people are increasingly turning to streaming and downloading platforms such as YouTube and Netflix for their viewing habits. Accurate data on these behaviours is challenging, but a 2023 survey of parents and children in the UK revealed that 98% of yadditive explanouth aged 16–24 own a mobile phone (Ofcom 2023). New technologies present challenges and opportunities, with a growing recognition that new media and communication devices can serve as platforms for health interventions tailored to young people (Saadeh et al. 2021).

During the COVID lockdown, many individuals relied heavily on the internet and smart devices, such as tablets, laptops, and mobile phones, due to social and spatial distancing measures. This increased reliance on smart devices has been observed to lead to a form of addiction, characterized by a compulsive physiological need for and use of habit-forming substances (Saadeh et al. 2021). Much screen time for young people is now occupied accessing the internet. The Office for National Statistics 2018 internet access survey shows the most common internet activities for 16–24 year olds compared with those aged 25–34 (Chart 4.19). Younger people are more likely to be engaged in social networking and finding information (Ofcom 2023). The most common reasons for using the internet in the 16–24 age group were for emailing, social networking, watching videos, and listening to music (Fig. 5.1).

Fig. 5.1 98% of 16–24 year olds in the UK own a smartphone <*Source* Office for National Statistics (2023) Internet Access. Households and Individuals>

The Power of Social Media

The internet profoundly impacted societal development since its inception in the late 1960s (Beranek 2007). Initially designed for file sharing, it quickly evolved into a widely utilized communication platform, contributing to the prevalent use of social media in contemporary society (Naughton 2016). Furthermore, the modern internet has facilitated accessibility in various domains such as online shopping, banking, and professional activities (Hoffman et al. 2004). Consequently, the multifaceted utility of the internet has led to heightened dependence (Al-Rafee and Rouibah 2010), potentially resulting in excessive internet usage. Therefore, a study is needed to investigate the extent of this excessive usage and dependence and its implications for individuals' psychological well-being, specifically in terms of anxiety, depression, and stress (Figs. 5.2 and 5.3).

Some argue that the proliferation of social media platforms and the ability to observe others may have more adverse than beneficial effects on individuals (Kamal et al. 2015). University students have reported comparing their lifestyles and appearances with public figures they aspire to emulate and peers of the same age, leading to negative feelings about their image (Nicholls and Miller 1984). This increased opportunity for comparison can result in negative outcomes such as depression, anxiety, low self-esteem, and disordered eating (Jed 2023). Suzanne Higgs' article "Social Norms and Their Influence on Eating Behaviours" highlights the significant impact of social norms on food choices and consumption, emphasizing their influence on behaviour through associations with social judgment and self-perception (Higgs 2015). Consequently, numerous studies have explored the various factors influencing eating behaviours, each reflecting the influence of social media in distinct ways. However, it is essential to understand the relationship between social media and its influence on eating habits and behaviours, particularly among university students who are the most frequent social media users. It is reasoned that social media will affect students' eating habits and mental health.

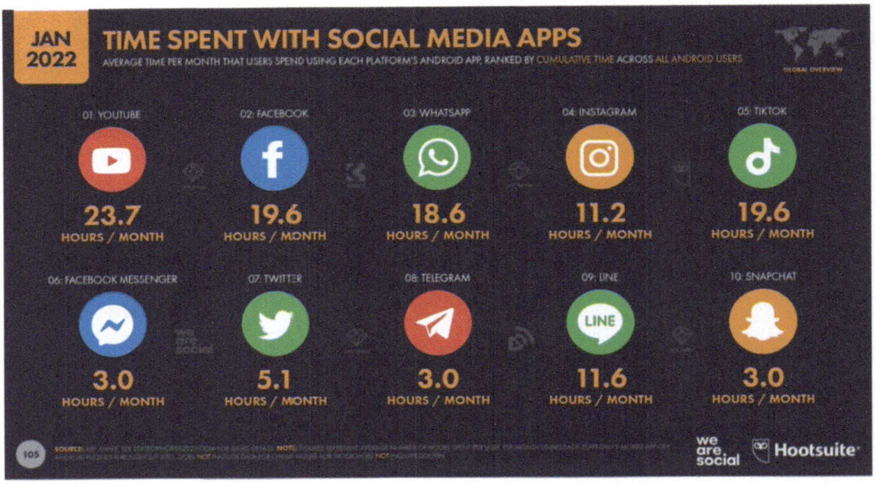

Fig. 5.2 Obtained from https://wearesocial.com/au/blog/2022/01/digital-2022-another-year-of-bumper-growth/

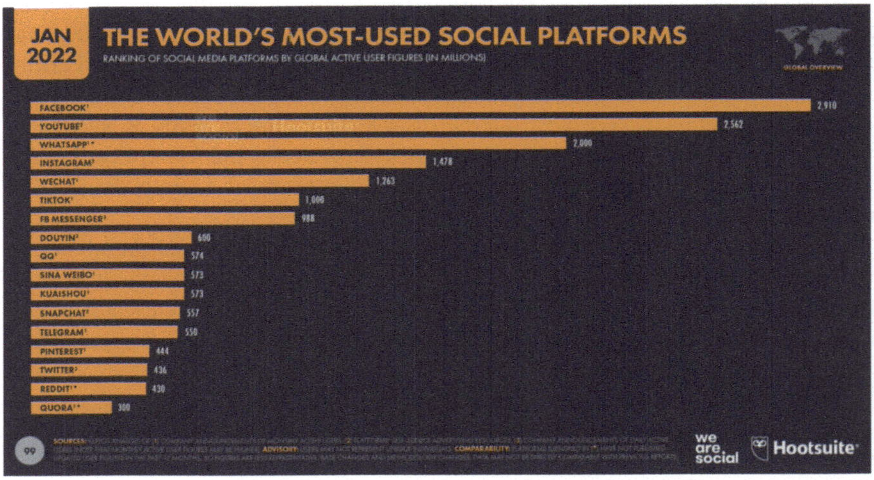

Fig. 5.3 Obtained from https://wearesocial.com/au/blog/2022/01/digital-2022-another-year-of-bumper-growth/

Eating Behaviours

"Eating behaviours" is a broad term that includes various factors such as food choices, feeding practices, dieting, and issues like obesity, eating disorders, and feeding disorders (LaCaille 2013). Eating habits are unique to each individual and can vary based on their specific circumstances (McCarthy et al. 2017). Prior research has shown that eating habits continually evolve, deviating from past norms. Modern lifestyles, characterized by decreased physical activity and time constraints due to work and family responsibilities, often lead individuals to skip meals or choose quick, convenient food options (Daryaee 2012). This significant shift in dietary patterns from previous generations calls for contemporary research that considers relevant societal factors and potential influences on these habits (Petty 2017). As a result, individuals' eating habits are constantly changing, adapting in response to their environment and associated influences.

Parental influence plays a key role in developing eating habits, as parents often make food choices for the family and serve as role models for dietary preferences and behaviours. They use feeding practices to reinforce the establishment of eating patterns and behaviours they consider appropriate (Evers 1997). These eating habits, established during childhood, are likely to continue into early adulthood. Numerous studies have investigated the development of eating habits and the influences that shape them as individuals transition into adulthood, including the impact of their environment and the eating patterns of others to accommodate their lifestyle. The most significant influence on eating habits and behaviours often comes from observing others (Birch et al. 2007).

The COVID-19 pandemic led to changes in many habits of young people due to disruptions in daily life, such as remote work and learning, and changes in diet. Some individuals experienced irregular mealtimes, increased snacking, or skipped meals. Many resorted to emotional eating as a coping mechanism for stress and anxiety. However, some young people used the pandemic to develop cooking skills and experiment with healthier recipes. The closure of restaurants and limited dining options led to a greater reliance on food delivery and takeout services, impacting dietary choices and financial expenditures. The pandemic also prompted a heightened focus on nutrition and dietary supplements. Unfortunately, the stress and changes in eating habits contributed to body image concerns and, in some cases, the development or worsening of eating disorders among young people. As we move forward from the pandemic, it is crucial to comprehensively address these changes, considering both physical and psychological well-being, and to provide support and resources to help young people establish healthy sleep and eating habits.

Digital Technology and Mental Health

Internet addiction is characterized by strong urges to use the internet and distress when these urges are not fulfilled (Shaw and Black 2008). It is estimated that approximately 14% of internet users exhibit signs of addiction, with the issue first gaining attention in 1995 (Tao et al. 2010). Despite this, internet addiction has not been officially recognized as a disorder and is not included in any editions of the DSM (Tateno et al. 2019). Nevertheless, various theories have been proposed to explain the reasons behind individuals developing internet addiction.

Skinner's (1963) theory of positive reinforcement posits that behaviour will persist if it leads to positive outcomes, such as feelings of pleasure. Longstreet et al. (2019) suggest that the positive reinforcement experienced by individuals when using the internet can lead to excessive use and subsequent addiction. This reinforcement is often derived from social media platforms, which allow individuals to communicate and socialize, seek social support, and form emotional connections without physical interaction (Demircioğlu and Köse 2018). Additionally, receiving likes and comments on social media posts has been shown to elicit positive emotions, further incentivizing individuals to use these platforms. This suggests that the internet's facilitation of convenient socialization may lead to reliance and subsequent addiction, in line with Skinner's theory of positive reinforcement (Skinner 1963).

In addition to positive reinforcement, it has been suggested that individuals who have experienced bullying may turn to the internet as an escape from reality, potentially leading to reliance and addiction (Jia et al. 2018). Furthermore, internet gaming addiction has been identified as both a type and a cause of internet addiction. Users of online gaming platforms have been found to experience negative effects when unable to access these games, including sleep disturbances and mood swings (Jiang 2014). Moreover, individuals who engage in online gaming are more likely to develop internet addiction and experience associated negative consequences (Baturay and Toker 2019; Jiang 2014).

There are many factors associated with internet addiction such as poor relationships, or an escape from reality and responsibility (Baturay and Toker 2019). Individuals with internet addiction are also linked to disturbed sleeping pattern, with 68.7% of those in a UK study claiming to suffer from poor quality of sleep due to their excessive internet use (Sohn et al. 2021). This negative effect on sleep has been replicated in alternative studies such as Gupta et al (2020), suggesting that there is a relationship between poor sleep and internet addiction.

There are a variety of concerns that have been said to be associated with internet addiction. It has been shown that internet addiction can lead to poor relationships, as well as people neglecting their responsibilities to use the internet (Baturay and Toker 2019). In addition to this, it has been demonstrated that those with an internet addiction are likely to experience a disturbed sleeping pattern, with 68.7% of those in a UK studying claiming to suffer from poor quality of sleep due to their excessive internet use (Sohn et al. 2021). This negative effect on sleep has been replicated in further studies such as Gupta et al (2020), suggesting that there is a relationship between poor sleep and Internet addiction.

Internet Addiction and Psychological Well-Being

Excessive use of the internet can have detrimental effects on an individual's mental health, leading to symptoms of anxiety, depression, and stress. Research conducted on a sample of 300 students in Turkey demonstrated a correlation between internet addiction and increased levels of depression, anxiety, and stress (Akin and Iskender

2011). While anxiety and depression are prevalent in both genders, females tend to exhibit these symptoms more frequently (Droogenbroeck et al. 2018). This gender difference is particularly pronounced in depression, with females being more susceptible to it than males (Gaus et al. 2015). However, conflicting studies suggest that this gender disparity diminishes with age, as individuals over the age of 80, regardless of gender, are equally likely to experience anxiety and depression (Pachana et al. 2011). Furthermore, some research suggests that gender differences in psychological well-being are insignificant, indicating that males and females are equally affected (Emslie et al. 2002).

Recent studies, such as that conducted by Younes et al. (2016), have replicated the association between internet addiction and poor psychological well-being. However, it is important to note that this study focused solely on medical students, with a majority of female participants, limiting the generalizability of the findings. Conversely, alternative research on 200 college students has suggested that feelings of depression can lead to excessive internet use, creating a cycle of depression perpetuated by internet usage (Kumar and Mondal 2018) (Fig. 5.4).

There is contradictory evidence regarding the impact of internet use on psychological well-being. Some studies suggest increased internet use is associated with improved psychological well-being, particularly in older adults. For example, a study of 5,203 adults over 65 found that frequent internet use was linked to stronger social support, reduced feelings of loneliness, and overall better psychological well-being (Heo et al. 2015). Similarly, other research has shown a negative correlation between internet use and depression (Lifshitz et al. 2018), contradicting previous findings. This is because greater internet use in this digital world has been found to help young people maintain relationships and reduce social anxiety. However, it has also

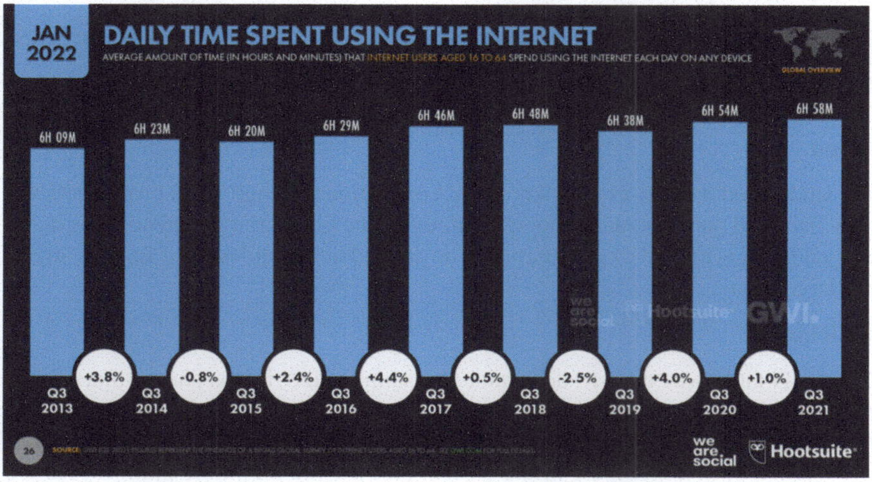

Fig. 5.4 Obtained from https://wearesocial.com/au/blog/2022/01/digital-2022-another-year-of-bumper-growth/

been linked to increased bullying (Subrahmanyam and Greenfield 2008; González-Cabrera et al. 2018). However, there is limited research on the impact of internet use on psychological well-being among UK students especially in a university setting. One study of 179 university students in the UK found no significant correlation between excessive internet use and psychological well-being, contradicting findings from other countries (Alheneidi and Smith 2020). Notably, this study composed of female first-year university students aged 18–21, which may limit its generalizability. Therefore, more research on whether internet use has positive or negative implications for the psychological well-being of young people would be needed.

Study One: The Impact of Excessive Internet Use on Psychological Well-Being of Young Adults

Elsie Ong

Aims and objectives of the current study

The issue of Internet addiction has been discussed since 1955, and its effects on psychological well-being have been debated ever since (Tao et al. 2010). This study examines the relationship between Internet addiction, depression, anxiety, and stress among 80 university students recruited through a random sample. The main hypothesis is that Internet addiction would be negatively correlated with overall psychological well-being (in self-reported measures of depression, anxiety, and stress). A second hypothesis is that there would be a gender and age difference in self-perceived levels of anxiety, depression, and stress.

Keywords Internet addiction, Psychological well-being, Depression, Anxiety, Stress

Method

Design

This study used a quasi-experimental and correlational design. This cross-sectional study involved participants giving quantitative data, where the independent variable was gender, age, and internet addiction. The dependent variables were anxiety, stress, and depression.

Participants

Cohen's D table was used to determine the sample size, it was shown that having an effect size of 0.5, a power ratio of 0.8, and a probability of 0.05, 102 participants would be ideal for the research to hold statistical significance. Participants voluntarily signed up to participate in the current study using an online platform named SONA. There was no payment, but participants were rewarded one degree-related credit for their participation. Participants were excluded from the study if they stated they were suffering from extreme mental distress at the time of the research. 112 participants were initially recruited. However, 32 of these participants were excluded due to having stated that they were suffering from mental distress before completing the study. The final sample consisted of 80 participants, of which 15 were males and 65 were females. The mean age for male participants was 24 ($SD = 9$), with a mean age of 29 for females ($SD = 11$). Participant's ages ranged from 18 to 55 years old ($M = 27.86$, $SD = 10.81$).

Materials

Participants completed a demographic questionnaire followed by two questionnaires that assessed internet addiction and psychological well-being.

The study utilized **Young's 20-item Internet Addiction Test (IAT)** to evaluate internet addiction. Each item on the IAT is scored on a scale from 1 to 5, with a composite score ranging from 20 to 100, where a higher score indicates a greater level of internet addiction. A score equal to or greater than 40 was used to identify individuals meeting the criteria for internet addiction. In the mediation model, a continuous scale of IAT scores was employed. The internal consistency of the IAT within the study population was found to be excellent (Cronbach's $\alpha = 0.834$).

Depressive symptoms were assessed using The Depression, Anxiety and Stress Scale (**DASS-21**), a self-report questionnaire consisting of 21 items, with 7 items per subscale for depression, anxiety, and stress. Participants rated each item on a scale from 0 to 3, and sum scores were calculated by adding and multiplying the scores by a factor of 2. The total DASS score ranges from 0 to 120, and the subscale scores range from 0 to 42. Cut-off scores of 60 for the total DASS score and 21 for the depression subscale were used to indicate high or severe symptoms based on the severity ratings proposed by Lovibond and Lovibond (1995). The reliability of the DASS-21 within the study population was found to be high (αdass_T1 = 0.95 for total DASS, αdass_T1 = 0.91 for depression subscale, αdass_T2 = 0.92 for total DASS, αdass_T2 = 0.86 for depression subscale).

Scores for the **Internet Addiction Test (IAT)** were calculated using the overall score from the questionnaire. However, the DASS-21 scale used slightly different scoring techniques determine the result for each subcategory. The first subcategory of anxiety was calculated by adding the sum of questions 2, 4, 7, 9, 15, 19, and 20. For depression, the sum of questions 3, 5, 10, 13, 16, 16, and 21 were used. The total stress score was calculated using questions 1, 6, 8, 11, 12, 14, and 18. Finally, to calculate an overall psychological well-being score, a total of the answers to all the questions from question 1 to question 21 was used.

Procedure

Participants completed the study online via JISC online surveys or the SONA systems. First, participants were directed to a participant information sheet and a consent form. On the demographic page, they were asked their age and gender identity and asked questions on whether they were experiencing any extreme mental distress recently. Then, participants completed the Internet Addiction Test and the DASS-21 scale. After completing both surveys, participants were taken to the debrief sheet with a full explanation of the study, and mental health hotlines if needed. Participants were also thanked for their participation. The completion time for participants was around 20 min.

Analysis

Statistical Package for Social Sciences (SPSS) v28 (IBM) was used as the analysis software to investigate if each hypothesis had a significant relationship. Before performing statistical analyses, some tests were conducted to check for parametric assumptions. These include using histograms and box plots to determine if the data were normal, and checks for outliers. As the assumption of normality was not met and the data was ordinal, the non-parametric alternatives were used in this study for statistical analysis. Thus, for the first four hypotheses, a Spearman's Rho correlational analysis was carried out, with a Mann–Whitney test being run for the final hypotheses.

Ethical Considerations

The current investigation was conducted by the ethical guidelines outlined by the British Psychological Society (2021). Before participating in the study, individuals were provided with comprehensive information regarding the study's objectives and the utilization of their data in compliance with the Data Protection Act (2018). This ensured that participants could provide informed consent before commencing the study. Given that participants were informed in advance about the potential discussion of sensitive topics such as anxiety and depression, measures were taken to minimize the risk of psychological harm by allowing them to withdraw before addressing these topics. Furthermore, participants were required to confirm their age of 18 or older, ensuring their consent was fully informed. They were also informed that they could withdraw from the study at any point before submitting their responses and that their data would be kept anonymous. Following the study, participants were provided with a debriefing form to reiterate the study's objectives and to offer guidance to mental health support resources if necessary. Ethical approval for the study was obtained from the Psychology Ethics Committee at the University.

Results

Internet Addiction and Overall Psychological well-being

The total score of the DASS-21 was used to calculate an overall psychological well-being score. Overall, the IAT scores for all participants had a mean of 30.80 ($SD =$ 12.96), and the DASS-21 scores overall had a mean of 30.78 ($SD = 23.69$). Table 1 shows males had a higher score overall on the DASS-21 ($M = 37.73$, $SD = 29.12$), reflecting lower psychological well-being than female participants ($M = 29.17$, SD $= 22.21$). Males also scored higher on the IAT ($M = 33.60$, $SD = 12.84$), which indicates more internet addiction than females ($M = 30.15$, $SD = 13$) (Table 5.1).

A correlational analysis was conducted using Spearman's rho, a non-parametric test, to examine the current hypothesis, due to the data not meeting the assumptions

Table 5.1 Descriptive statistics of DASS-21 scores compared to IAT scores by gender

	Male				Female			
	Mean	Standard deviation	95% lower CI	95% upper CI	Mean	Standard deviation	95% lower CI	95% upper CI
DASS	37.73	29.12	21.61	53.86	29.17	22.21	23.67	34.67
IAT	33.60	12.84	26.49	40.71	30.15	13.00	26.93	33.37

required for Pearson's r. The data does not adhere to the assumptions necessary for a parametric test, as it is not normally distributed.

To further investigate the hypothesis and determine the significance of any results, a Mann–Whitney test was employed as the data did not satisfy the assumptions for a t-test. The data utilized for this statistical analysis includes nominal (gender) and ordinal (DASS-21 scores) variables. Additionally, the DASS-21 scores are not normally distributed, although no outliers are present, as previously discussed in the hypotheses (Table 5.2).

Total DASS-21 scores of males ($Mdn = 34.00$) were higher than that of females ($Mdn = 26.00$). The Mann–Whitney test indicated that these results were not statistically significant at a p value of 0.05 ($U = 413$, $z = -0.919$ $p = 0.358$), with a small effect size $r = 0.11$. Therefore, the null hypothesis was accepted, as there was no significant difference in DASS-21 scores between males and females.

Age, Internet Addiction, and Overall Psychological well-being

Table 5.3 presents the descriptive statistics for age groups with IAT scores and total DASS-21 scores. The figures indicate that participants aged 30 and below exhibited higher scores on the DASS-21 scale (M = 36.11, SD = 24.89) compared to those over the age of 30 (M = 20.30, SD = 17.13). Furthermore, participants aged 30 and below also demonstrated higher scores on the IAT scale (M = 34.68, SD = 11.45) compared to participants aged over 30 (M = 23.19, SD = 12.54). These results suggest that younger participants are more inclined to engage in excessive internet use and have lower overall psychological well-being. Conversely, it has been suggested that the opposite is true for older participants (Table 5.4).

A significant and moderate positive correlation was found between the total DASS-21 score and the overall IAT score ($r_s(78) = 0.527$, $p < 0.001$.) suggesting a relationship between higher internet addiction and lower psychological well-being. It is shown that males scored higher on the depression elements of the DASS-21 test

Table 5.2 Mann–Whitney test statistics to compare gender with overall mental-well-being

	DASS total
Mann–Whitney U	413.000
Wilcoxon W	2558.000
Z	−0.919
Asymp. Sig. (2-tailed)	0.358

Table 5.3 Descriptive statistics for age groups compared to Internet Addiction (IAT) and overall psychological well-being (DASS-21 total)

	Age							
	30 and under				Over 30			
	Mean	Standard deviation	95% lower CI	95% upper CI	Mean	Standard deviation	95% lower CI	95% upper CI
DASS total	36.11	24.89	29.25	42.98	20.30	17.13	13.52	27.07
IAT total	34.68	11.45	31.52	37.83	23.19	12.54	18.22	28.15

Table 5.4 Spearman's Rho correlation between Internet Addiction (IAT) and overall psychological well-being (DASS-21)

			IAT total	DASS total
Spearman's rho	IAT total	Correlation coefficient	1.000	0.527**
		Sig. (2-tailed)		<0.001
		N	80	80
	DASS total	Correlation coefficient	0.527**	1.000
		Sig. (2-tailed)	<0.001	
		N	80	80

**Correlation is significant at the 0.01 level (2-tailed)

($M = 13.9$, $SD = 12.00$) than females ($M = 8.98$, $SD = 8.20$). This shows that males have shown higher rates of depression than females in this study. The standard deviation for both males and females for the depression score is moderate, suggesting the data is relatively spread from the mean for both males and females (Table 5.5).

A correlational analysis was employed to examine the hypothesis, and a scatterplot is presented in the appendices. Spearman's Rho was utilized due to the absence of outliers for either variable. Consequently, the non-parametric Spearman's Rho was employed because neither variable satisfied the assumptions for a parametric test. The analysis revealed a moderately positive and statistically significant correlation

Table 5.5 Descriptive statistics of IAT scores compared to depression scores by gender

	Male				Female			
	Mean	Standard deviation	95% lower CI	95% upper CI	Mean	Standard deviation	95% lower CI	95% upper CI
Depression total	13.9	12.00	7.00	20.00	8.98	8.20	6.95	11.02
IAT total	33.60	12.84	26.49	40.71	30.15	13.00	26.93	33.37

between total IAT scores and total depression scores (rs(78) = 0.583, $p < 0.001$) (Table 5.6).

Internet Addiction and Anxiety

Table 5.7 shows the descriptive statistics for this hypothesis and the descriptive statistics for anxiety results have shown that males show higher rates of anxiety ($M = 9.20$, $SD = 9.91$) than females ($M = 7.91$, $SD = 7.92$) according to the DASS-21 test. However, the means for both genders are not vastly different, suggesting that anxiety scores may not differ largely between genders (Table 5.8).

Table 5.6 Spearman's Rho correlation between internet addiction (IAT total) and depression (depression total)

			IAT total	Depression total
Spearman's rho	IAT total	Correlation coefficient	1.000	0.583**
		Sig. (2-tailed)		<0.001
		N	80	80
	Depression total	Correlation coefficient	0.583**	1.000
		Sig. (2-tailed)	<0.001	
		N	80	80

** Correlation is significant at the 0.01 level (2-tailed)

Table 5.7 Descriptive statistics of IAT scores compared to anxiety scores by gender

	Male				Female			
	Mean	Standard deviation	95% lower CI	95% upper CI	Mean	Standard deviation	95% lower CI	95% upper CI
Anxiety total	9.20	9.91	3.71	14.69	7.91	7.92	5.94	9.87
IAT total	33.60	12.84	26.49	40.71	30.15	13.00	26.93	33.37

Table 5.8 Spearman's Rho output for correlation between internet addiction (IAT) and anxiety (anxiety total)

			IAT total	Anxiety total
Spearman's rho	IAT total	Correlation coefficient	1.000	0.401**
		Sig. (2-tailed)		<0.001
		N	80	80
	Anxiety total	Correlation Coefficient	0.401**	1.000
		Sig. (2-tailed)	<0.001	
		N	80	80

** Correlation is significant at the 0.01 level (2-tailed)

The Spearman's Rho analysis revealed a moderate, significant, positive correlation between The total IAT scores and total anxiety scores reveals a relationship between excessive internet use and higher rates of anxiety ($r_s(78) = 0.401, p < 0.001$.)

Internet Addiction and Stress

Based on the mean of Internet Addiction and Stress: males ($M = 14.67, SD = 11.00$) and for females ($M = 12.28$, $SD = 7.99$), it was revealed males scored higher on the DASS-21 for overall stress. Therefore, as males also have shown higher scores on the IAT test, stress increases as internet addiction does, suggesting a correlation between these two variables (Table 5.9).

The analysis has shown that there is a significant positive correlation between total IAT scores and total stress scores ($r_s(78) = 0.512, p > 0.001$) (Table 5.10).

Discussion

Internet Addiction and Overall Psychological well-being

Numerous previous studies have provided evidence for a positive association between internet addiction and adverse overall psychological well-being. For example, Akin and Iskender (2011) found that students in Turkey exhibited higher levels of negative psychological well-being when they displayed signs of internet addiction. The current study, conducted in the UK, has replicated these findings, suggesting they may be applicable across different cultures. The results of this study align with

Table 5.9 Descriptive statistics for IAT total scores compared to stress scores by gender

	Male				Female			
	Mean	Standard deviation	95% lower CI	95% upper CI	Mean	Standard deviation	95% lower CI	95% upper CI
Stress total	14.67	11.00	8.58	20.76	12.28	7.99	10.30	14.26
IAT total	33.60	12.84	26.49	40.71	30.15	13.00	26.93	33.37

Table 5.10 Spearman's Rho output for correlation between internet addiction (IAT) and stress (stress total)

			IAT total	Stress total
Spearman's rho	IAT total	Correlation coefficient	1.000	0.512**
		Sig. (2-tailed)		<0.001
		N	80	80
	Stress total	Correlation coefficient	0.512**	1.000
		Sig. (2-tailed)	<0.001	
		N	80	80

** Correlation is significant at the 0.01 level (2-tailed)

those of Younes et al. (2016), who observed a strong positive correlation between negative psychological well-being and internet addiction in a sample of 600 participants. Although the present study's statistical analysis revealed a moderate positive correlation, this discrepancy may be attributed to the smaller sample size utilized.

Additionally, other research has indicated a link between internet usage and psychological well-being. For instance, recent studies have reported disrupted sleep patterns due to excessive internet use, likely harming an individual's psychological well-being. Consequently, it can be inferred that while internet addiction may not directly cause negative psychological well-being, it may contribute to factors that do so. However, some previous research has yielded conflicting results compared to the present study. One study of university students found no significant correlation between excessive internet use and negative psychological well-being, contradicting the significant result found in the present study. Furthermore, internet use may improve psychological well-being by providing social connections through social networking sites.

Internet Addiction and Depression

The findings indicate a substantial moderate association between internet addiction and symptoms of depression. The correlation coefficient between depression and internet addiction was found to be higher than that of other correlation analyses, suggesting that internet addiction has a more pronounced impact on depressive symptoms than on anxiety, stress, and overall psychological well-being. While this study suggests a significant impact of internet addiction on depressive symptoms, previous research has yielded conflicting results. For instance, Lifshitz et al. (2018) reported a negative correlation between internet use and depression, indicating a positive impact of internet use on depressive symptoms. However, it is important to note that Lifshitz et al. (2018) focused on participants over 50 years old, making comparisons with the present study's younger participants challenging. Similarly, Bashir and Bhat (2017) found that internet use, particularly through social media, increased in positive emotions, which contrasts with the current research findings. However, the lack of distinction between internet addiction and excessive internet use in previous studies may contribute to inconsistent results.

In contrast, a study of 200 college students by Kumar and Mondal (2018) supported the current study's findings by demonstrating that excessive internet use was associated with feelings of depression. Both studies share similar participant demographics, which may explain the convergence of results. However, it is important to note that both studies are correlational, and as such, it is difficult to determine the direction of the relationship between internet addiction and depression.

Internet Addiction and Anxiety

There was a moderate positive association between internet addiction and anxiety. Limited research has been conducted on the potential correlation between anxiety and internet addiction, with much of the existing literature focusing on overall psychological well-being and depression. However, it has been suggested that internet use may alleviate feelings of social anxiety in adolescents (Subrahmanyam and Greenfield 2008; Yang et al. 2021), which contradicts the findings of this study. Conversely, it has also been proposed that internet use could contribute to heightened levels of social anxiety as a result of cyberbullying (González-Cabrera et al. 2018). These conflicting results were observed in an adolescent population, indicating a substantial amount of contradictory evidence regarding the relationship between anxiety and internet addiction.

Internet Addiction and Stress

The study revealed a significant moderate positive correlation between internet addiction and stress, indicating a connection between the two variables. These findings are consistent with previous research, as scholars have reported similar results. For example, previous studies have indicated that individuals experience heightened stress levels when they cannot fulfil their internet usage urges (Shaw and Black 2008). This aligns with the current study's findings, suggesting that stress may arise when individuals addicted to the internet are unable to access online resources. Moreover, research has shown that feelings of stress can lead to an increased likelihood of internet addiction, as individuals may perceive the internet as an escape from everyday stressors, thereby intensifying their usage (Jia et al. 2018). While these findings align with the current study's results, the direction of causality between stress and internet addiction still needs to be more conclusive, as the study utilized correlational analysis, precluding the determination of causation. Additionally, prior research has suggested that excessive internet use may lead to neglect of daily responsibilities, subsequently contributing to feelings of stress (Baturay and Toker 2019). Therefore, while internet addiction may not directly cause stress, it may lead to factors that contribute to stress, thus explaining the observed relationship between the two variables.

Gender and Overall Psychological well-being

Despite a slight variance in the means, the study found no statistically significant difference in the DASS-21 scores between males and females. The small effect size further indicates that there is likely no association between gender and overall psychological well-being. While some previous research contradicts these findings, suggesting that women are more prone to anxiety and depression than men (Droogenbroeck et al. 2018), it is important to note that the sample used in Droogenbroeck's research was not very representative, consisting only of males and females aged 15 to 25, which is not comparable to the broader age range in the present study. Additionally, other previous research aligns with the current study's findings, indicating that although there may appear to be gender differences in anxiety and depression, these differences are not significant (Emslie et al. 2002). This suggests that gender may not have influenced the DASS-21 scores in the present study. Instead, it is possible that internet addiction had an impact on psychological well-being, anxiety, stress, and depression scores, as it showed a significant relationship with these variables, unlike gender. However, further previous research has indicated that females are more likely to experience depression than males (Gaus et al. 2015). Still, this tendency is suggested to diminish with age, indicating that as individuals grow older, symptoms of anxiety and depression become similar between genders (Pachana et al. 2011). Given the conflicting nature of previous research and its inconsistency with the present study's findings, it is recommended that gender differences in psychological well-being be further investigated.

Age, Internet Addiction, and Overall Psychological well-being

The findings of this study suggest that older individuals tend to exhibit better overall psychological well-being and are less likely to be addicted to the internet. In comparison, younger individuals are more likely to have poorer psychological well-being and show signs of internet addiction. Previous research has also indicated a potential correlation between age, internet addiction, and psychological well-being. For example, a study of individuals over the age of 65 demonstrated positive psychological well-being and a lack of internet addiction, while younger college-aged individuals were more likely to experience negative psychological well-being and signs of internet addiction. However, it is important to note that this study did not employ statistical analysis to determine the significance of the differences in means. While previous research has suggested the significance of these results, further investigation is warranted to confirm their significance.

Several limitations should be acknowledged in this study. Firstly, self-reporting may introduce potential biases due to participants' honesty and interpretation of the Likert scale. Additionally, the relatively small and predominantly female sample, and the use of volunteer sampling may limit the generalizability of the findings. Furthermore, the study did not account for extraneous variables, making it difficult to establish causality. Lastly, the study's recruitment primarily from one university in England may further limit the generalizability of the results to the broader population.

Study Two: Exploring the Influence That Social Media Has on Eating Behaviours in University Students

Molly Bass and Elsie Ong

Aims and objectives of the current study

Numerous factors shape individuals' eating behaviours, including social and cultural influences, mood, and hunger levels. Income level is also a significant determinant of eating habits, as individuals with higher incomes may have access to kitchen technology that facilitates cooking substantial meals. In comparison, those with lower incomes may encounter challenges in accessing such resources. Additionally, the ease of obtaining essential food for a healthy diet can be influenced by transportation to shops, with car or bike owners having an advantage over those reliant on public transportation or walking.

The objectives of this research encompass understanding the correlation between social media usage and its impact on the eating habits of university students. The study will explore the connection between the rise of social media and its adverse effects on individuals' psychological well-being. We will specifically focus on eating habits, examining body image and the potential impact of social media content on individuals' self-perception and dietary choices.

While there is a substantial body of research on individuals' eating habits and the influence of social media, there needs to be more information or research specifically focusing on young adults who are most affected. By filling these gaps, new insights can be generated to facilitate better support for those impacted. Social media is increasingly shaping individuals' communication and personality development (Moreno and Whitehill 2014), affecting adolescents and those in their social circles. Understanding these experiences can aid in improving overall well-being. Therefore, the findings of this research will contribute to bridging existing gaps in knowledge and promoting interventions and solutions to address common challenges individuals faced.

Method

Design

This research utilized a mixed methods approach involving the administration of three distinct multiple-choice quantitative questionnaires about eating habits, mental health, and social media. A qualitative research question was included after the questionnaires to gather more specific insights into individuals' perceptions of how social media impacts their mental health and eating habits. Adopting a mixed methods approach was crucial in comprehending the diverse experiences of the participants rather than simply classifying them as university students. This approach facilitated a deeper understanding of the specific factors influencing university students. It yielded valuable insights for future investigations on the impact of social media usage on their eating habits.

The chosen investigative approach is survey research, which entailed the self-administration of questionnaires to university students, encompassing items aligned with the research objectives. The three questionnaires aimed to gather data on participants' mental health, eating behaviours, frequency of social media usage, and its effects on them. With a total of 57 participants, this sample size enabled comparisons regarding the influence of social media on their eating habits, as well as variations in participants' opinions and behaviours. This approach addressed the research question concerning social media's influence on university students' eating behaviours. In this study, the independent variable was social media, as it was compared to the dependent variable of eating behaviour and mental health, as well as participants' current feelings due to their social media usage.

Participants

Participants were recruited via a university research participation platform, SONA, where some module credits can be obtained via active participation in research within the Faculty. Using a sample size calculator, 30 participants (rounded down from 34) were needed to ensure the detection of a significant effect (where effect size = 0.5, sig level = 0.05, and power = 0.8). However, 57 participants were obtained via convenience sampling. The inclusion criteria specified that participants must be university students aged 18–25.

Materials

Mental health

Participants' mental health was assessed using the **Patient Health Questionnaire (PHQ-9)**, a 9-item instrument was developed by Spitzer et al. (1990). This questionnaire delves into the participants' emotional state, including their mood, sleep patterns, self-perception, and behaviour. Responses were measured on a 4-point Likert scale, with 1 indicating "nearly every day" and 4 indicating "Not at all." The total score was calculated by summing the responses, with lower scores indicating greater impact on mental health and higher scores suggesting less current struggle with mental health.

The PHQ-9 comprises 9 questions, each with 4 response options. All questions were negatively framed, with "Not at all" yielding 4 points, "several days" yielding 3 points, "more than half the days" yielding 2 points, and "nearly every day" yielding 1 point. Consequently, higher scores indicate a more positive outlook, while lower scores indicate a more negative outlook. A high score on the social media scale and low scores on the Adult Eating behaviours Questionnaire and the PHQ-9 would indicate a relationship between these variables. Additionally, examining participants' supporting statements regarding the impact of social media on their health or eating habits can provide further evidence of the correlation between these variables.

Eating habits

The eating habits were assessed using the **'adult eating behaviour questionnaire'**, a 20-item instrument developed by Hunot et al. (2016) to gauge individuals' attitudes towards their dietary intake. The questionnaire employs a 5-point Likert scale to measure responses to both positive and negative statements. Positive statements (items 1, 2, 3, 10, 13, 15, and 20) were rated on a scale of 1 to 5, with 1 indicating strong disagreement and 5 indicating strong agreement. Examples of positive statements include "I love food," "I enjoy eating," and "eating food makes me happy." Conversely, negative statements (items 4, 5, 6, 7, 8, 9, 11, 12, 14, 16, 17, 18, and 19) were rated in reverse, with 1 representing strong agreement and 5 representing strong disagreement. Examples of negative statements include "I eat more when I am annoyed," "I eat more when I am upset," and "I eat less when I am anxious." The total scores from the questionnaire indicate individuals' overall positive or negative relationship with food and their eating habits.

Social media

The "**Social Media Scale**" questionnaire comprises 27 items divided into 9 sections: tolerance, withdrawal, persistence, escape, problems, deception, displacement, and conflict (Regina et al. 2016). Each section contains three statements, and participants must select the statement that best aligns with their experiences. The statements were designed to gauge the impact of social media on individuals' daily lives, with the first statement indicating a predominantly negative effect (scoring 1), the second indicating a moderate effect (scoring 2), and the third suggesting some impact without significant disruption to daily life (scoring 3). A lower score on the questionnaire indicates a more negative relationship with social media use. The questionnaire is complementary to other measures in understanding participants' relationship with social media and its relevance to the research question. Additionally, the questionnaire was adapted from its original reference to "school" to "university" for this study.

Open-Ended question

There was an added open-ended question ''Has social media affected your mental health or eating habits in any way? Please elaborate." This gathered more information to back up the scores from the quantitative multiple-choice questions, allowing them to elaborate on their thoughts and feelings giving more information on how they feel their mental health and eating habits have been affected by social media.

Procedure

Informed consent was obtained through the consent form, which was attached to the questionnaire. This ensured that the individuals have read and understood what they were going to be doing, and what will happen with the data they provide. The participants were debriefed through the participant information sheet and the debrief form. The information sheet stated the purposes of the study, what they will be doing, and what will happen to their data once the study is completed, informing them of what is about to come when participating in the study. The debrief form offered support information to the participants, providing links to multiple mental health support. The data were collected via a university research participation platform called SONA. This link was shared in group chats, and on the universities Facebook groups and asked to share to friends who attend the university, creating a snowball affect.

Ethics

The BPS code of ethics and conduct emphasizes four primary ethical principles, which this study adheres to. Respect for participants is demonstrated by maintaining their anonymity, providing comprehensive information about the study before they participate, offering support through links to relevant services for sensitive topics, and allowing them to withdraw their participation up to three weeks after completing the study if they feel uncomfortable. The study also upholds a responsibility to the participants by obtaining informed consent, ensuring their anonymity and confidentiality, and respecting their privacy during the questionnaire process. Integrity is maintained through honesty in proposing the research question, conducting the research, and reporting the data provided by the participants. The study also addresses ethics by informing participants about the risks and benefits of participation, providing access to support resources if they struggle with sensitive topics, and assuring them of the strict confidentiality and secure storage of their personal data by the General Data protection Regulations (2018) and the UK Data Protection Act (2018).

Analytical plan

All quantitative analysis was conducted using the SPSS v27. The different parametric assumptions have been met in this study, the data has a normal distribution, the data from the group of university students has the same variance, the data has a linear relationship, and the data is overall independent. This exploratory analysis was used to identify potential relationships between the dependant variable eating behaviour/mental health and the independent variable social media. Multiple regression analysis was used to determine the relationship between the independent variable (social media) and the two dependent variables (mental health and eating habits) while controlling for other variables' effect.

Results

The results of a multiple linear regression test show a significant effect of social media on eating habits. The test shows a P-value of 0.001 which means that the null hypothesis can be rejected at the 0.05 significance level, suggesting that the data is not normally distributed. All participants were full time undergraduate students over the age of 18, they accessed the questionnaire through SONA a platform which the University shares. Overall, 57 participants completed three questionnaires about social media use, mental health, and their relationship with food regarding their eating habits (Table 5.11).

The different measures of variability show a moderate to high variance within the responses to each questionnaire. This was expected as the study attempts to understand the use of social media with individuals' eating habits; being unaware of how much they use social media alters the understanding of whether it impacts their day-to-day lives.

The confidence interval for the adult eating behaviour questionnaire shows a 95% chance that the population parameter falls between 59.68 and 65.37. The confidence interval for the patient health questionnaire shows that there is a 95% chance that the population parameter falls between 21.22 and 24.57, and finally the confidence interval for the social media scale shows that there is a 95% chance that the population parameter falls between 13.61 and 16.67 (Table 5.12).

This Pearsons r correlation test shows that the p-value is 0.494 which leads to the assumption that it is statistically significant, which means that the correlation coefficient is unlikely to have occurred by chance. There is a correlation coefficient of 0.092, 063 and 0.252 which indicates a low to moderate positive relationship between the two variables. This means that as one of the variables increase so do the others. However, the relationship suggests that the two variables are almost significantly related.

Table 5.11 Descriptives

			Statistic	Std. error
Adult_eating_behaviour_questionnaire	Mean		62.5263	1.41910
	95% confidence interval for mean	Lower bound	59.6835	
		Upper bound	65.3691	
	5% trimmed mean		63.2671	
	Median		63.0000	
	Variance		114.789	
	Std. deviation		10.71398	
	Minimum		1.00	
	Maximum		90.00	
	Range		89.00	
	Interquartile range		9.00	
	Skewness		−3.197	0.316
	Kurtosis		19.537	0.623
Patient_health_questionnaire	Mean		22.8947	0.83572
	95% confidence interval for mean	Lower bound	21.2206	
		Upper bound	24.5689	
	5% trimmed mean		22.8860	
	Median		23.0000	
	Variance		39.810	
	Std. deviation		6.30953	
	Minimum		9.00	
	Maximum		36.00	
	Range		27.00	
	Interquartile range		9.00	
	Skewness		0.072	0.316
	Kurtosis		−0.381	0.623
Social_media_scale	Mean		15.1404	0.76435
	95% confidence interval for mean	Lower bound	13.6092	
		Upper bound	16.6715	
	5% trimmed mean		15.4561	
	Median		16.0000	
	Variance		33.301	
	Std. deviation		5.77073	
	Minimum		0.00	
	Maximum		24.00	
	Range		24.00	
	Interquartile range		6.00	

(continued)

Table 5.11 (continued)

		Statistic	Std. error
	Skewness	−0.925	0.316
	Kurtosis	0.458	0.623

Table 5.12 Correlations

		Patient_health_ questionnaire	Adult_eating_ behaviour_ questionnaire	Social_media_ scale
Patient_health_ questionnaire	Pearson correlation	1	0.092	0.063
	Sig. (2-tailed)		0.494	0.641
	N	57	57	57
Adult_eating_ behaviour_ questionnaire	Pearson correlation	0.092	1	−0.252
	Sig. (2-tailed)	0.494		0.058
	N	57	57	57
Social_media_ scale	Pearson correlation	0.063	−0.252	1
	Sig. (2-tailed)	0.641	0.058	
	N	57	57	57

Data from open-ended questions

At the end of the three questionnaires, I included one qualitative open-ended question ''Has social media affected your mental health or eating habits in any way? Please elaborate''. However, 10 participants responded 'no' without elaboration, and 4 participants expanded and discussed that they feel that if social media has affected them in anyway it is positively, being easy to access things and making it easier to communicate with their friends believing their relationship with social media is a healthy one that does not impact their everyday life.

Whereas most individuals who participated in my study elaborated on how social media has affected their mental health and eating habits. Some individuals believed it only affected their eating habits, others believed it only affected their mental health, and others stated it has affected both as any problem has risen with one it has also risen with the other. Many responses explain how social media is prominent in their everyday lives and how it distracts them from things they should be focusing on. The responses discuss the unrealistic ideologies which are presented to them often on an everyday basis, this affecting the way they view their success and the stage they are at within their life, as well as others comparing themselves to others wanting to make changes to their image and hoping to look the way that they see others online.

Although most of these responses relay a negative relationship between social media and eating habits, few shared that social media has affected them positively, widening their knowledge of food and exercise in a good way, helping them make the changes they have already wanted to make.

Discussion

The results of this study suggest a moderate association between the influence of social media on eating behaviours among college students. It is implied that while the connection is not particularly strong, there is a noticeable link between the variables. Other contributing factors may also play a role in the varied eating patterns reported by the participants in this investigation. The study's reliability supports the comprehension of the relationship between eating behaviours and social media, as rejecting the null hypothesis indicates a somewhat significant but not overwhelmingly strong connection between the two.

Attitudes were marginally, though not significantly, more negative towards eating behaviours and mental health when individuals extensively use social media. This suggests that social media affects individuals' eating habits and may lead to struggles with their mental health. This has potential implications for individuals who frequently use social media, as they may not be aware of the correlation between its use and negative attitudes towards food and mental health issues, potentially leading to future repercussions. Prior research has indicated that college students are more likely to experience mental health challenges due to their extensive use of social media. Studies have also elucidated that social media usage can adversely affect individuals' eating habits. Therefore, the correlation between the responses to these questionnaires aligns with previous research.

Analyzing the individual responses from each questionnaire provides insight into the diverse characteristics and experiences of the participants with social media, as well as potential struggles with mental health and eating habits. For instance, some participants scored low, indicating an unhealthy relationship with food and mental health, and also exhibited low scores on the social media scale, suggesting an excessive and unhealthy reliance on social media. Conversely, those who scored high on all questionnaires displayed a positive relationship with food, mental health, and healthy use of social media. Additionally, individuals who scored low on eating habits and mental health questionnaires but high on the social media scale indicated that their struggles were not directly linked to social media, and vice versa. However, the predominant responses indicate a correlation between individuals' social media usage and their mental health in relation to eating habits.

The variability in responses was anticipated due to the lack of information regarding the frequency of social media usage by each participant, despite reporting its effects on their daily lives. As a researcher, I can make inferences about the frequency of social media usage based on their responses. However, the lack of reported usage contributed to the expected diversity and disparity in individual responses. The respondents who provided detailed responses described their experiences with social media, its impact on them, and how it affected their mental health and eating habits. A minority of respondents indicated that social media did not influence their mental health or eating habits. Some participants expressed a positive view of social media, stating that it was their primary means of connecting with friends and that they would feel isolated without it. While acknowledging high screen time, they believed their social media use was healthy and did not significantly affect their daily lives.

Social media has affected the mental health and eating habits of certain individuals. Those who reported negative impacts on their mental health described an unhealthy relationship with social media, leading to adverse effects. Several respondents used the term "toxic" to describe their addiction to specific apps, which hindered their ability to complete tasks and affected their motivation. They also mentioned feeling upset and having negative thoughts about themselves and their progress, attributing these feelings to unrealistic ideals and comparisons with others online. The pandemic was also cited as contributing to negative self-perception, as social media became a primary source of entertainment and interaction during lockdown, leading to increased usage and exposure to potentially harmful content.

Many respondents discussed how social media affected their eating habits, with some using it as a distraction from eating or experiencing binge eating due to excessive usage. Others mentioned being influenced by online content to try new foods, adopt gym routines, and make positive lifestyle changes. However, some individuals felt insecure and pressured to change their diet or appearance to conform to online norms, leading to negative impacts on their mental health and eating habits. Several participants highlighted the negative effects of social media on their mental health and eating habits, including negative self-image, self-esteem issues, anxiety, and disordered eating behaviours. These findings underscore the significant impact of social media on individuals' well-being and emphasize the need for further exploration and understanding of these effects.

The responses indicate that social media has significantly affected the participants' relationship with their mental health and overall well-being. Access to various platforms has led individuals to compare their lives with others, causing them to question their circumstances. Some respondents expressed a desire to make changes and are actively seeking ways to improve their mental health and eating habits, such as by reducing their social media usage and unfollowing accounts that trigger negative comparisons. While each response varied, it is evident that social media substantially impacts university students and their eating habits.

The findings of this study align closely with previous research, such as the study "Using Social Media to Change Eating Habits Without Conscious Effort" (Higgs (2015), which highlighted similar issues among participants. However, this study contributes by exploring the experiences of individuals before the influence of enforced behaviours, shedding light on the impact of social media use on the mental health and eating habits of young adults.

The results of this study align with those of another research in the same field. For instance, Higgs (2015) in the article "Social Norms and Their Influence on Eating behaviours" found that social media significantly impacts individuals, particularly young ones, influencing their behaviour even when not directly engaged with social media. This study's social media scale questionnaire also supports this influence, indicating that university students frequently use social media, with some individuals more affected than others. The study further reveals that social media affects their focus, interests, and personal relationships, corroborating previous research and providing additional evidence of its influence.

This study's primary focus was investigating social media's impact on eating behaviours. It concluded that exposure to others' eating habits online, often showcasing only the positive aspects of their lives, bodies, and diets, tends to have a negative impact. However, it also noted the potential for positive influence, as individuals may use this exposure to make healthy changes. The study found that frequent social media use was associated with participants' negative eating habits and self-perception.

The study included 57 participants, a sufficient sample size to ensure statistical power and representativeness. While the participants' age and gender were not specified, they were all university students. The data collection methods were reliable and valid, minimizing errors and biases. The use of three questionnaires related to the independent variable (social media scale) and two dependent variables (Patient Health Questionnaire and Adult Eating behaviours Questionnaire) allowed for examining their relationships. The Pearson's r correlation and multiple linear regression analysis conducted in the study demonstrated a significant relationship between social media use and its influence on participants' mental health and eating habits.

In my research, several considerations must be made when interpreting the results as strong and statistically significant. A few participants exhibited consistent response patterns, such as three individuals providing the same answer for every question. This raises concerns about the reliability of their responses compared to those who offered varied responses. Additionally, the frequency of social media usage among these individuals is not known, making it difficult to conclude the impact of social media on their lives. In the third questionnaire, a significant number of participants declined to answer questions related to deception and conflict, with over 50% opting out. This raises doubts about the accuracy of the scores, as those who did not respond may have lower scores due to their non-participation. It is important to note that the participants were exclusively from the University of Northampton, all within a similar age group known for frequent social media use. This limits the generalizability of the findings to other demographics and life stages.

Limitation and future directions

The qualitative data collected in my research yielded limited implications. Employing mixed methods was beneficial in comprehending the effects of social media on eating behaviours among university students. About this inquiry, 14 participants chose not to respond, suggesting potential discomfort with the sensitive nature of the question. Additionally, 10 participants answered 'no,' impacting the comparison of their responses to the scale questions, as it hindered the ability to correlate their scores with their rationale for perceiving no impact. Consequently, in future studies, more open-ended questions are recommended as this single question could significantly influence the study's findings, leading to the rejection of the null hypothesis due to the strong relationship between the variables. However, rephrasing the question to encourage participants who responded negatively to elaborate on their reasons, thereby gaining deeper insights into their experiences and encouraging greater participation. Furthermore, imposing a minimum word requirement for responses to gain a comprehensive understanding of each participant's experience.

For future studies, exploring individuals of similar age groups who do not attend university may be better, as their responses may differ, providing insights into their distinct relationship with social media. Additionally, studying older generations would offer valuable insights into their life experiences and potentially different social media relationships, thereby enhancing understanding of its influence on mental health and eating habits. In subsequent research, investigating older adult is recommended as their use of social media platforms is minimal. Exploring any mental health issues or negative eating patterns and linking these to their social media use could provide valuable insights into the influence of social media. Erica Chen's article, "Online Social Media and Mental Health Among Older Adults," examines the mental health of individuals about their social media use before and after the Covid-19 outbreak. It highlights that the individuals she studied had a minimal relationship with social media before the pandemic. Still, during the lockdown, their reliance on social media increased significantly, becoming a habit that persisted even years after the pandemic.

Chen's study also explores the psychological well-being of individuals about their condition before the increase in social media usage. She argues that there is a growing prevalence of feelings of loneliness, social disconnection, and depression among older adults (Chen et al. 2022), indicating the influence of social media on their mental health. This comparison highlights the changing effects of social media on the psychological well-being of older adults. Consequently, further investigation into this subject, encompassing younger adults, will yield a more comprehensive understanding of the correlation between social media and mental health and its association with eating behaviours.

Conclusion

The primary objective of the study one was to investigate the potential association between overall psychological well-being and internet addiction. The study revealed a statistically significant correlation between negative psychological well-being and internet addiction, indicating a reciprocal influence as hypothesized. Additionally, the research demonstrated that higher levels of internet addiction were significantly linked to increased levels of depression, anxiety, and stress as distinct variables, consistent with prior research. Moreover, the study concluded that gender does not seem to have a substantial impact on overall psychological well-being. However, this finding may be influenced by the limited representation of males in the study and necessitates further examination with a more extensive male sample. In summary, the study's findings supported most of the hypotheses, including the primary hypothesis. While the hypothesis regarding the impact of gender on overall psychological well-being was not upheld, this outcome may be attributed to a sampling error and requires further investigation. The study provided evidence confirming the correlation between internet addiction and overall psychological well-being, highlighting the potential adverse effects of excessive internet use on psychological well-being.

After the investigation on internet addiction and psychological well-being, the second study aimed to explore the impact of social media on eating behaviours in university students using a mixed methods research approach. The findings indicated a moderately strong correlation between these variables, suggesting that social media positively correlates with eating habits and can negatively impact frequent users. The study confirmed the hypothesis that social media significantly affects eating behaviours. For future research, it is recommended to investigate the influence of social media on individuals of different genders and age groups, as well as those at various life stages. Additionally, future studies should establish a cause-and-effect relationship between the variables, gather more comprehensive participant demographics, and increase the sample size to provide a more representative sample from the general population. Furthermore, future research should explore the impact of age and gender on psychological well-being and internet addiction, as conflicting results have been found in previous studies. It is also suggested to include participants who do not strictly identify as male or female in future studies to gain a more comprehensive understanding of the impact of gender on psychological well-being.

References

Akin A, Iskender M (2011) Internet addiction and depression, anxiety and stress. Int Online J Educ Sci 3(1):138–148. https://doi.org/10.12691/ajphr-3-5-3

Al-Rafee S, Rouibah K (2010) The fight against digital piracy: an experiment. Telematics Inform 27(3):283–292. https://doi.org/10.1016/j.tele.2009.12.002

Alheneidi H, Smith AP (2020) Effects of the internet use on wellbeing and academic attainment of students starting university. Int J Humanit Soc Sci Educ 7(5):20–34. https://doi.org/10.20431/2349-0381.0705003

Bashir H, Bhat SA (2017) Effects of social media on mental health: a review. Int J Indian Psychol 4(3):125–131. https://doi.org/10.25215/0403.134

Baturay MH, Toker S (2019) Internet addiction among college students: some causes and effects. Educ Inf Technol 24(5):2863–2885. https://doi.org/10.1007/s10639-019-09894-3

Beranek LL (2007) Who really invented the internet? Sound Vibr 41(1):6–15

Birch L, Savage JS, Ventura A (2007) Influences on the development of children's eating behaviours: from infancy to adolescence. Can J Dietetic Pract Res Publ Dietitians of Canada = Revue Canadienne de La Pratique et de La Recherche En Dietetique : Une Publication Des Dietetistes Du Canada 68(1):s1–s56. https://www.ncbi.nlm.nih.gov/pmc/articles/PMC2678872/

British Psychological Society (2021) BPS code of human and research ethics. https://www.bps.org.uk/sites/www.bps.org.uk/files/Policy/Policy%20-%20Files/BPS%20Code%20of%20Human%20Research%20Ethics.pdf

Chen E, Wood D, Ysseldyk R (2022) Online social networking and mental health among older adults: a scoping review. Can J Aging/La Revue Canadienne Du Vieillissement:1–14. https://doi.org/10.1017/s0714980821000040

Daryaee T (2012) Food, purity and pollution: Zoroastrian views on the eating habits of others. Iran Stud 45(2):229–242. https://doi.org/10.1080/00210862.2011.617157

Data Protection Act (2018) Data Protection Act 2018. GOV.UK. https://www.legislation.gov.uk/ukpga/2018/12/contents/enacted Accessed 20 Mar 2022

Demircioğlu ZI, Köse AG (2018) Effects of attachment styles, dark triad, rejection sensitivity, and relationship satisfaction on social media addiction: a mediated model. Curr Psychol 40(1):414–428. https://doi.org/10.1007/s12144-018-9956-x

Droogenbroeck FV, Spruyt B, Keppens G (2018) Gender differences in mental health problems among adolescents and the role of social support: results from the Belgian health interview surveys 2008 and 2013. BMC Psychiatry 18(6):1–9. https://doi.org/10.1186/s12888-018-1591-4

Emslie C, Fuhrer R, Hunt K, Macintyre S, Shipley M, Stansfeld S (2002) Gender differences in mental health: evidence from three organisations. Soc Sci Med 54(4):621–624. https://doi.org/10.1016/S0277-9536(01)00056-9

Evers C (1997) Empower children to develop healthful eating habits. J Am Diet Assoc 97(10):S116. https://doi.org/10.1016/s0002-8223(97)00742-6

Gaus V, Kiep H, Holtkamp M, Burkert S, Kendel F (2015) Gender differences in depression, but not in people with epilepsy. Seizure 32:37–42. https://doi.org/10.1016/j.seizure.2015.07.012

González-Cabrera J, León-Mejía A, Beranuy M, Gutiérrez-Ortega M, Álvarez-Bardón A, Machimbarrena JM (2018) Relationship between cyberbullying and health-related quality of life in a sample of children and adolescents. Qual Life Res 27(10):2609–2618. https://doi.org/10.1007/s11136-018-1901-9

Gupta R, Taneja N, Anand T, Gupta A, Gupta R, Jha D, Singh S (2020) Internet addiction, sleep quality and depressive symptoms amongst medical students in Delhi, India. Community Mental Health J 57(4):771–776. https://doi.org/10.1007/s10597-020-00697-2

Heo J, Chun S, Lee S, Lee KH, Kim J (2015) Internet use and well-being in older adults. Cyberpsychol Behav Soc Netw 18(5):268–272

Higgs S (2015) Social norms and their influence on eating behaviours. Appetite 86:38–44. https://doi.org/10.1016/j.appet.2014.10.021

Hoffman DL, Novak TP, Venkatesh A (2004) Has the internet become indispensable? Commun ACM 47(7):37–42. https://doi.org/10.1145/1005817.1005818; https://doi.org/10.1089/cyber.2014.0549

Jia J, Li D, Li X, Zhou Y, Wang Y, Sun W, Zhao L (2018) Peer victimization and adolescent internet addiction: the mediating role of psychological security and the moderating role of teacher-student relationships. Comput Hum Behav 85:116–124. https://doi.org/10.1016/j.chb.2018.03.042

Jiang Q (2014) Internet addiction among young people in china: internet connectedness, online gaming, and academic performance decrement. Internet Res 24(1):2–20. https://doi.org/10.1108/IntR-01-2013-0004

Kamal T, Tariq M, Ishtiaq M, Nawab K, Idrees M (2015) An investigation into the negative impacts of social media on academic performance of youth, 34p. https://core.ac.uk/download/pdf/234652672.pdf

Kumar M, Mondal A (2018) A study on internet addiction and its relation to psychopathology and self-esteem among college students. Ind Psychiatry J 27(1):61–66. https://doi.org/10.4103/ipj.ipj_61_17

LaCaille L (2013) Eating behaviour. In: Gellman MD, Turner JR (eds) Encyclopedia of behavioural medicine. Springer, New York, NY. https://doi.org/10.1007/978-1-4419-1005-9_1613

Lifshitz R, Nimrod G, Bachner YG (2018) Internet use and well-being in later life: a functional approach. Aging Ment Health 22(1):85–91. https://doi.org/10.1080/13607863.2016.1232370

Longstreet P, Brooks S, Gonzalez ES (2019) Internet addiction: when the positive emotions are not so positive. Technol Soc 57:76–85. https://doi.org/10.1016/j.techsoc.2018.12.004

Lovibond SH, Lovibond PF (1995) Manual for the depression anxiety & stress scales, 2nd edn. Psychology Foundation

McCarthy MB, Collins AM, Flaherty SJ, McCarthy SN (2017) Healthy eating habit: a role for goals, identity, and self-control? Psychol Mark 34(8):772–785. https://doi.org/10.1002/mar.21021

Moreno MA, Whitehill JM (2014) Influence of social media on alcohol use in adolescents and young adults. Alcohol Res Curr Rev 36(1):91–100. https://www.ncbi.nlm.nih.gov/pmc/articles/PMC4432862/

Naughton J (2016) The evolution of the internet: from military experiment to general purpose technology. J Cyber Policy 1(1):5–28. https://doi.org/10.1080/23738871.2016.1157619

Nicholls JG, Miller AT (1984) Reasoning about the ability of self and others: a developmental study. Child Dev 55(6):1990. https://doi.org/10.2307/1129774

Ofcom (2023) Share of children owning mobile phones in the United Kingdom (UK) in 2023, by age group [Graph]. In Statista. https://www.statista.com/statistics/1326211/children-owning-mobile-phone-by-age-uk/. Accessed 11 Jan 2024

Pachana NA, McLaughlin D, Leung J, Byrne G, Dobson A (2011) Anxiety and depression in adults in their eighties: do gender differences remain? Int Psychoger 24(1):145–150. https://doi.org/10.1017/S1041610211001372

Petty L (2017) Comparing diets with your grandparents'. the hub|high speed training. https://www.highspeedtraining.co.uk/hub/changes-in-eating-habits/#:~:text=Over%20the%20last%20century%2C%20our

Power EM (2005) Les odellingts de la saine alimentation chez les Canadiens à faible odelli. Can J Public Health 96(S3):S42–S43. https://doi.org/10.1007/bf03405200

Saadeh H, Al Fayez RQ, Al Refaei A, Shewaikani N, Khawaldah H, Abu-Shanab S, Al-Hussaini M (2021) Smartphone use among university students during COVID-19 quarantine: an ethical trigger. Front Public Health 9. https://doi.org/10.3389/fpubh.2021.600134

Shaw M, Black DW (2008) Internet addiction. CNS Drugs 22(5):353–365. https://doi.org/10.2165/00023210-200822050-00001

Skinner BF (1963) Operant behaviour. Am Psychol 18(8):503–515. https://doi.org/10.1037/h0045185

Sohn SY, Krasnoff L, Rees P, Kalk NJ, Carter B (2021) The association between smartphone addiction and sleep: a UK cross-sectional study of young adults. Front Psychiatry 12:629407. https://doi.org/10.3389/fpsyt.2021.629407

Subrahmanyam K, Greenfield P (2008) Online communication and adolescent relationships. Future Child 18(1):119–146

Tao R, Huang X, Wang J, Zhang H, Zhang Y, Mengchen L (2010) Proposed diagnostic criteria for internet addiction. Addiction 105(2):556–564. https://doi.org/10.1111/j.1360-0443.2009.02828.x

Tateno M, Teo AR, Ukai W, Kanazawa J, Katsuki R, Kubo H, Kato TA (2019) Internet addiction, smartphone addiction, and hikikomori trait in Japanese young adult: social isolation and social network. Front Psych 10:1–11. https://doi.org/10.3389/fpsyt.2019.00455

Understanding social comparison on social media|JED (2023) The Jed Foundation. https://jedfoundation.org/resource/understanding-social-comparison-on-social-media/#:~:text=As%20social%20media%20sites%20update. Europepmc.org. https://europepmc.org/books/n/nap9566/ddd0000009/?extid=25077212&src=med&fid=ddd0000011

Yang X, Hu H, Zhao C, Xu H, Tu X, Zhang G (2021) A longitudinal study of changes in smart phone addiction and depressive symptoms and potential risk factors among Chinese college students. BMC Psychiatry 21(1). https://doi.org/10.1186/s12888-021-03265-4

Younes F, Halawi G, Jabbour H, El Osta N, Karam L, Hajj A, Rabbaa Khabbaz L (2016) Internet addiction and relationships with insomnia, anxiety, depression, stress and self-esteem in university students: a cross-sectional designed study. PLoS 11(9):1–13. https://doi.org/10.1371/journal.pone.0161126

Dr. Elsie Ong is a Lecturer and a Dissertation Supervisor in UCL. She has worked in many universities in Asia and the UK for over ten years. Elsie is active in leading research that focuses on the mental health of young adults; especially those going through university transitions. Her expertise in cognitive neuroscience and psychology has also initiated further exploration on the underlying causes of mental health problems and later sparkles potentials for suicide preventions and interventions. Elsie is devoted to the study of psychological wellbeing in young adults and has published her research through internationally renowned conferences and reputed journals such as Frontiers in psychiatry. These experiences have helped to keep her most up to date on the latest development in preventions and interventions in mental health.

Chapter 6
Mental Health Service and Intervention

Elsie Ong and Wan San Wendy Wang

Overview

The issue of mental healthis a significant concern that impacts individuals globally, with young adults being particularly susceptible. In England, the government has recognized the importance of addressing mental health issues among young adults and has taken steps to enhance mental health services. This chapter will examine the prevalent mental health services offered to young adults in England, emphasizing their key components, challenges, and potential areas for improvement.

Recent advancements in digital technologies can potentially transform clinical research and treatment. This chapter will explore these developments and their relevance to young individuals facing mental health challenges. This includes considering the internet as an information source and its potential to facilitate help-seeking among young people. Furthermore, the chapter will discuss the progress in utilizing smartphone and wearable technologies to monitor symptoms, detect early signs of relapse, and even provide clinical intervention. While there is optimism that these tools will address issues related to the availability, accessibility, and increasing costs of existing mental health services, there is still much to be learned to optimize these approaches before they are integrated into routine clinical care. Additionally, this section will highlight important considerations in designing, utilizing, and evaluating these digital resources.

The COVID-19 pandemic has negatively impacted the mental health of university students by exacerbating the severity of mental health conditions such as anxiety and depression. Still, rates of diagnosis and treatment remain low. It is reasoned

E. Ong (✉) · W. S. W. Wang
Department of Psychology and Human Development, IOE—UCL's Faculty of Education and Society, University College London, London, WC 1E 6BT, UK
e-mail: Elsie.ong@ucl.ac.uk

W. S. W. Wang
e-mail: wan.wang.21@alumni.ucl.ac.uk

E. Ong (ed.), *The Emergence of the Digital World*,
https://doi.org/10.1007/978-981-97-3098-8_6

that digital intervention strategies may potentially address difficulties students have encountered in seeking and obtaining treatment for their mental health. In this chapter, **Study One** was conducted on 73 participants to complete an online quantitative questionnaire. Self-report measures of socioeconomic status, perceived stress levels, and attitudes towards seeking psychological professional help were collected and analyzed using multiple regression. **Study Two** was conducted to investigate students' post-pandemic mental health, and obstacles that prevent students from seeking support, and to expand on the current understanding of digital interventions by investigating student experiences with them. Mixed methods research was conducted on 100 university students, using the Zung Self-Rated Depression and Anxiety Scales and open-ended questions on student experiences with digital interventions. Results indicate that although digital interventions have been helpful towards students' self-management of their mental health, rates of depression and anxiety within student populations remain high. Further research may investigate how digital interventions can be made more approachable and accessible to students to encourage as a preventative strategy and a more urgent form of intervention.

Keywords University students, Mental health, Intervention, International students

Young Adults' Perceptions on Mental Health Services

The mental health of university students has deteriorated during the COVID-19 pandemic, yet many students have not received the necessary treatment or diagnosis for their mental health issues (Ebert et al. 2018). Accessing mental health services provided by universities in the United States has been challenging for some students, with issues such as a shortage of available treatment services, limited resources, and a lack of immediate support from university therapists (Levin et al. 2022). Despite the increased demand for mental health support, the provision of face-to-face support from university therapists has not kept pace, resulting in long waiting lists for Counselling and therapy treatments (Levin et al. 2017). This delay in treatment is particularly concerning for students in urgent need of support (Levin et al. 2022). Some studies suggest that the lack of treatment for mental health conditions may be due to students' attitudes rather than structural barriers, such as transportation difficulties (Loya et al. 2010). Research has shown that a significant percentage of students are reluctant to seek external intervention for their mental health issues, preferring to handle their problems on their own, even when treatment is readily available (Ebert et al. 2019). Students also report feeling stigmatized and embarrassed about seeking mental health treatment, which has hindered their help-seeking behaviour (Yeung et al. 2021). Additionally, international students may face challenges in accessing mental health resources due to a lack of awareness of available support at their institutions (Loya et al. 2010).

Factors Affecting Help-Seeking in Mental Health Services

Social Economical Status

The global impact of the coronavirus pandemic was profound, leading to the UK government's unprecedented decision to impose a national lockdown in March 2020, a measure not seen since World War II. It took two years for the restrictions to be fully lifted (Brown and Kirk-Wade 2021; Jones 2021; Office for National Statistics 2022). Historical evidence from World War II suggests that prolonged lockdowns can have enduring effects on the population. Psychological interventions and strategies, such as mindfulness training, meditation, and various therapeutic approaches, can play a crucial role in mitigating and addressing emotional distress. However, certain individuals may exhibit resistance to seeking psychological assistance from professionals. Research indicates that individuals with low socioeconomic status (SES) are less inclined to seek psychological support for various reasons, a topic that warrants further exploration. Consequently, individuals from such backgrounds who experience moderate to severe stress during challenging times and are resistant to seeking help from mental health professionals may face detrimental effects on their mental well-being.

Perceived Stress and Socioeconomic Status

The definition of socioeconomic status (SES) needs to be more consistent, making it easier to conceptualize. The American Psychological Association (APA) suggests measuring SES through education level, household composition, income, and occupation to assess poverty and life outcomes. While earlier research focused on structural determinants, SES now encompasses lifestyle factors, social psychology, and other variables. SES influences health through the social gradient, financial status, psychological well-being, social exclusion, and other factors. It is based on an individual's ability to access goods, services, and social resources, closely linked to ideologies, life experiences, and achievements, shaping attitudes (Zhang et al. 2022). Education level as an SES indicator is easier to measure in self-report questionnaires and applicable to anyone, regardless of employment or household situations. However, it does not reflect the quality of education and may vary across generations and countries, requiring consideration of birth cohort effects (Galobardes 2006). Research shows a strong link between higher education and better mental health in adulthood, as higher education leads to greater earnings and access to resources, enabling healthier lifestyles with fewer chronic stressors (Mirowsky and Ross 2012; Selvitopu and Kaya 2021). High SES individuals have an improved quality of life and mental well-being, while those with low SES have limited access to resources to cope with chronic stressors (Halpern-Manners et al. 2016; Niemeyer et al. 2019).

Income is also a determinant of SES, with lower income associated with exposure to challenging environments, negative emotions, and severe stress (Dunkel

Schetter et al. 2013). Financial worries are significantly linked to psychological stress, particularly for those who are financially vulnerable (Ryu and Fan 2022). Low SES is associated with higher cortisol and adrenaline levels, as indicated by research focusing on income and education components of SES (Cohen et al. 2006). The pandemic's collateral effects have resulted in a cost-of-living crisis, exacerbated by unprecedented international conflicts. This crisis decreased 'real' disposable incomes, causing heightened stress among the public. Research indicates that a significant portion of adults have reported symptoms of depression and difficulties in meeting financial obligations, particularly mortgage and energy bills. This situation raises concerns about the mental well-being of individuals with low socioeconomic status (SES) during these consecutive crises. While individuals with high SES may not have experienced similar financial instability, they are believed to be better equipped to manage stressful situations. However, studies have shown that higher SES workers report increased stress levels while working compared to lower SES individuals. Work-related stress is the most prevalent type of stress reported in the UK, followed by financial stress. The severity of stress may vary, but all SES groups experience demanding life circumstances, highlighting research gaps. Income instability has been found to have a significant impact on mental health disorders such as anxiety, depression, and stress. Lifestyle factors, including unhealthy practices, are also considered determinants of SES, contributing to mental health inequalities among those with low SES. Despite its significance, socioeconomic status is not commonly included in psychological research due to challenges in defining and operationalizing it. Collecting subjective and objective socioeconomic status from participants is recommended to address this, as both are significantly correlated. Additionally, many studies on the effects of socioeconomic status on mental health are cross-sectional, and longitudinal studies often focus on physical health-related variables rather than psychological effects. When socioeconomic status is studied, it is typically hypothesized that it either causes health issues, health outcomes are the reasons behind SES, or both SES and health issues result from another variable.

Stress and Help-Seeking Attitudes

In recent years, there has been an increased emphasis on the importance of mental health services and the promotion of mental wellbeing. However, despite these efforts, there continues to be a stigma surrounding therapy and psychological practices within society (Department of Health and Social Care 2021). This stigma is often rooted in negative stereotypes about individuals with mental health issues, which can deter those in need from seeking help and contribute to their stress. The process of seeking mental health support involves identifying an issue, seeking help, and taking steps to access psychological assistance (Koydemir-Özden 2010). The underutilization of mental health services has been linked to mental health stigma, behavioural obstacles, and poor mental health literacy (Chatmon 2020; Clement et al. 2015). Jorm (2000) introduced the concept of mental health literacy, defining it as possessing knowledge and understanding of mental disorders to aid in their detection, treatment, and prevention. However, a study by Tambling et al. (2021) suggests that individuals with mental health literacy may be more likely to internalize stigma, leading to delays in seeking timely care for mental health issues. Interestingly, there were no significant differences in mental health literacy based on income or education level, indicating that mental health literacy is not the sole factor influencing poor help-seeking attitudes among individuals with lower socioeconomic status.

Mental health stigma plays a significant role in deterring individuals from seeking professional help for stressors, serving as a prominent barrier. However, a systematic review by Clement et al. (2015) aimed to understand the impact of mental health stigmas on help-seeking behaviours related to mental health issues and stress. The review, which included 144 studies, concluded that stigma had a small to moderately sized negative effect on help-seeking, with certain groups such as youth, ethnic minorities, health professionals, men, and military personnel being disproportionately affected by stigmas.

Socioeconomic status also influences help-seeking attitudes. Picco et al. (2016) found that opinions about seeking help are often shaped by various attitudinal and sociodemographic variables, leading to treatment gaps, delays, and unmet needs. Their study evaluated the Attitude towards Seeking Professional Psychological Help scale and identified several subgroups significantly related to the scale, including income and education, both of which are indicators of socioeconomic status. Lower-income and lower-education individuals were found to have higher scores in preferring to cope alone and lower scores in the value of seeking professional help, which may be attributed to poor mental health literacy. Numerous studies consistently indicate the significance of socioeconomic status (SES) in shaping individuals' beliefs and willingness to seek help. Wardle and Steptoe (2003) found that individuals with high SES tend to hold more positive beliefs about help-seeking and are more open to receiving assistance. Kahneman (2011) also noted that higher SES individuals are less likely to report feeling stressed and more willing to seek psychological help, although this does not necessarily translate to improved psychological well-being, suggesting that high SES individuals may have difficulty enjoying their resources.

Contrary to this perspective, some argue that individuals, regardless of SES, may be willing to seek help when experiencing moderate to severe levels of stress. Cramer (1999) proposed a help-seeking behaviour model, indicating that individuals are increasingly likely to seek Counselling when experiencing distress. However, Wilson (2010) found that young people are more likely to avoid seeking help when experiencing psychological distress symptoms, highlighting a negative relationship between perceived stress and attitudes towards help-seeking. However, Orji and Abikoye (2019) found that perceived stress is not predictive of attitudes towards professional psychological help, as there was no significant relationship between the two variables. They suggested that participants may resist seeking help due to social and availability issues. Koydemir-Özden (2010) also found no association between attitudes and psychological well-being, cautioning against the risk of social desirability bias in responses.

It is important to note that much of the research discussed has yet to be conducted in the UK, and there may be cultural differences in results. Additionally, research often focuses on the elderly or young, neglecting the broader population. There are significant gaps in research, as studies rarely focus solely on perceived stress and attitudes towards seeking help as primary variables. Furthermore, when investigated, attitudes toward seeking help are often included in cross-sectional studies, making it difficult to establish causality. Given the conflicting results from previous studies, these findings underscore the complexity of the relationship between perceived stress and attitudes toward psychological help-seeking. This highlights the importance of further research in this area.

Study One: The Relationship Between Perceived Stress, Socioeconomic Status and Attitudes Towards Seeking Psychological Professional Help

Elsie Ong and Wan San Wendy Wang

Aims and objectives of the current study

Attitudes are influenced by past learning, experiences, and surroundings, and these attitudes directly impact our behaviours. Previous studies have suggested a complex connection between perceived stress and attitudes toward mental health. Negative attitudes toward mental health are often rooted in stigmas, whether they are self-stigmatization or public stigma, which arise from discriminatory or unfavourable perceptions of individuals with mental health issues. Research has demonstrated that stigmas and negative attitudes can worsen perceptions of stress among individuals. The aftermath of the COVID-19 pandemic and recent economic challenges are frequently discussed as having had an impact on mental health in the United Kingdom.

This study aimed to examine the link between perceptions of stress and socioeconomic status, and attitudes toward seeking professional help for mental health issues. The primary objective of this research is to investigate the relationship between stress and socioeconomic status, as well as attitudes toward psychological help. There is substantial evidence to support the idea that individuals with low socioeconomic status may be less inclined to seek professional psychological help due to issues related to accessibility or stigma. Previous research has also explored how each aspect of socioeconomic status is negatively associated with stress. Furthermore, findings support the notion that attitudes in general, including attitudes toward seeking mental health-related help, are influenced by socioeconomic status. However, much of the data on the relationship between stress and attitudes toward seeking help is either limited or inconsistent and does not account for socioeconomic status. Therefore, this study aims to investigate whether such a relationship exists. The study will measure perceived stress and then analyze the relationship between the two independent variables, socioeconomic status, and attitudes.

Hypotheses:

H[1] predicts that it is more than likely that there will be a relationship between perceived stress and attitudes towards seeking psychological professional help.
H[2] predicts that it is a likely that there will be a relationship between perceived stress and socioeconomic status.
H[3] predicts that it is more than likely that there will be a relationship between socioeconomic status and attitudes towards seeking psychological professional help.

Method

The research employed a cross-sectional correlational design on the participants. The primary aim was to explore the influence of socioeconomic status on mental health help-seeking behaviours and perceived stress. In this context, perceived stress is the dependent variable, while socioeconomic status and mental health help-seeking behaviours are the independent variables.

Participants

Participants were enlisted through volunteer and opportunity sampling methods, utilizing social media and the university research participation platform, SONA. This approach allows university students to engage in research and receive academic credit. The sample size was determined based on Power analysis calculation and Tabachnick and Fidell (2019), suggesting a target number of 75 participants. All participants completed the questionnaire except two whom exhibited acquiescence bias and substantial missing data in the perceived stress measure, leading to their exclusion from the study. Of the remaining 73 participants, 58 were female (79.5%) and 15 were male (20.5%). Additionally, 34 participants were university students. The distribution of socioeconomic status within the sample was as follows: 23 individuals (31.5%) with low socioeconomic status, 45 (61.6%) with middle socioeconomic status, and 5 (6.8%) with high socioeconomic status. The ethnic background of the participants included 14 Asian/Asian British individuals (19.2%), 24 Black/Black British Caribbean/African individuals (32.9%), 1 Hispanic/Latino individual (1.4%), 1 mixed/multiple ethnic group individual (1.4%), and 33 White individuals (45.2%). The study excluded individuals under the age of 18.

Materials

The study utilized the JISC online survey platform to administer a questionnaire. The initial section of the questionnaire included demographic inquiries related to gender, ethnicity, and socioeconomic status. Participants were then asked to respond to questions regarding their perceived stress levels and mental health help-seeking behaviours using two self-report questionnaires. Socioeconomic status was determined by factors such as income, occupation, wealth, and education. For participants unsure of their socioeconomic status, a classification calculator developed by the Office for National Statistics (2022b) was provided.

The Perceived Stress Scale (PSS) was used to evaluate participants' stress levels, assessing the frequency of stress and perceived stressful situations over the previous month (Cohen et al. 1983; Cohen and Williamson 1998). The ten-item questionnaire utilized a 5-point Likert scale, with scores ranging from 0 (never) to 4 (very often). One example of an item from the PSS is 'In the last month, how often have you felt difficulties were piling up so high that you could not overcome them?'. First the positive questions are reverse scored and there are four in total (questions: 4, 5,7 and 8). PSS scores are then obtained by adding all the responses, generating a figure between 0 and 40 with higher scores reflecting more severe levels of stress. The PSS scores were calculated by summing the responses, resulting in a score between 0 and 40, with higher scores indicating more severe stress levels. The PSS was chosen for its ability to measure general stress rather than specific life events, aligning with the study's objectives. Additionally, it has been widely used in clinical practice and empirical research across various populations (Baik et al. 2019).

The Attitudes Towards Seeking Professional Psychological Help Scale in Short Form (ATSPPH-SF) was adapted from the original 29-item scale by Fischer and Farina in 1995. The shortened version consists of 10 items rated on a 4-point Likert scale which ranges from 3-Strongly Agree to 0 for Strongly Disagree. There are both positively and negatively phrased items, therefore items 2, 4, 8, 9 and 10 are reversed scored. An example of an item: 'There is something admirable in the attitude of a person who is willing to cope with his or her conflicts and fears without resorting to professional help'. The scale assesses individuals' attitudes towards seeking professional psychological help, with higher scores indicating more favourable views of receiving help.

The ATSPPH-SF has been widely used and has demonstrated sound psychometric properties, making it applicable in both Eastern and Western societies. It has been utilized to assess patients' attitudes towards mental health treatment and intentions of seeking psychological help in the future, demonstrating its effectiveness in clinical practice and academic research (Elhai et al. 2008). The psychometric properties of the ATSPPH-SF have been examined, with studies reporting satisfactory internal consistency reliability and validity (Torres et al. 2021; Rayan et al. 2020). Additionally, investigations into the factor structure of the ATSPPH-SF have revealed multidimensionality, with varying components related to coping, the value of seeking professional help, and openness to seeking psychological professional help (Picco et al. 2016; Elhai et al. 2008).

Data Collection

The study was uploaded to the university's research participation platform, and the study advertisement and link were shared on various social media platforms. Participants were given an information sheet and asked to complete an online consent form. They then created a unique participation ID by combining the first two letters of their first name and surname with two random numbers. This ID code was used for any communication with the researcher. Participants were then asked to provide demographic information, including socioeconomic status, gender, and ethnic background. They completed the PSS-10 and ATSPPH-SF-10 questionnaires, totalling 23 questions. Upon completion of the study, participants were provided with a debrief form.

Ethics

The research adhered to the ethical guidelines the American Psychological Association (APA) and the British Psychological Society (BPS) outlined. The core ethical principles of respect, integrity, competence, and responsibility, as defined by the BPS, were upheld throughout the study. The study received ethical approval from the Psychology Research Ethics Committee at the University, and all participants were over 18. Participants were fully informed about the nature and aims of the study, their right to withdraw at any time, and how their data would be handled. No deception was used in the study.

Confidentiality

To maintain confidentiality, participants generated their own unique identification code, and their personal information was not revealed. The study operated in accordance with the General Data Protection regulations, and participants were informed about the management of their data. After data collection and analysis, the unique participation codes were removed, and all personal information was destroyed.

Analytical Plan

The data was analyzed using the SPSS software. Two participants exhibited acquiescence bias in their responses, and their data was removed from the analysis. Descriptive statistics were used to calculate means and standard deviations, and demographic data was analyzed and presented in tables. Multiple linear regression and ANOVA were conducted to assess the relationship between attitudes towards psychological professionals and socioeconomic status with perceived stress levels.

Results

First, the data was tested to find if the parametric assumptions of multiple linear regression were met. This enables the relationship between the variables to be explored, as perceived stress scores could be used to predict SES and attitudes. The descriptive statistics are provided in Table 6.1, The mean scores for attitudes towards professional psychological help ($M = 18.86$, $SD = 5.13$) and perceived stress scores ($M = 20.41$, $SD = 7.16$) categorised means by low, middle, high SES.

A two-tailed Spearman's rho correlation test found relationship between attitudes seeking help and socioeconomic status, ($Rs = 0.068$, $p = 0.57$) for perceived stress and attitudes towards help seeking ($n = 73$, $Rs = -0.14$, $p = 0.25$). For perceived stress and socioeconomic status ($Rs = -0.297$, $p = 0.01$), and these were the only two variables that were significantly correlated, even though the strength of the

Table 6.1 Descriptive statistics of perceived stress and attitudes towards psychological professionals in relation to socioeconomic status—means, standard deviations and skewness (n = 73)

95% confidence interval					
Measure	Mean	Standard deviation	Lower bound	Upper bound	Skewness
PSS	20.41	7.16	2	29	−0.41
ATSPPH	18.86	5.13	4	34	−0.26
Low SES					
PSS	23.39	5.89	20.84	25.94	−0.20
ATSPPH	17.91	5.98	15.33	20.50	−0.71
Middle SES					
PSS	19.33	7.35	17.12	21.54	−0.22
ATSPPH	18.82	5.51	17.17	20.47	−0.11
High SES					
PSS	16.4	7.26	7.37	25.42	1.04
ATSPPH	20.40	2.19	17.68	23.12	−0.85

relationship is small. R^2 would mean that 8% of perceived stress is accountable for by socioeconomic status. However, this also means that hypothesis two would be rejected as though there is a negative relationship between perceived stress and attitudes, the effect is too small to be significant. There is a 95% confidence that F (3,70) = 3.95, p. = 024, $R^2 = 0.101$, which would mean SES and ATSPPH justifies 10% of perceived stress, but this is of statistical significance. Which implies that this model is not a suitable fit as there is no significant link between the three variables, thus the null hypothesis should be accepted.

Discussion

The primary hypothesis of this study posits a connection between perceived stress levels and socioeconomic status, while the secondary hypothesis suggests a relationship between perceived stress levels and attitudes towards seeking professional psychological help. The third hypothesis proposes a significant relationship between socioeconomic status and attitudes toward seeking professional help. Additionally, the research aims to investigate whether stress can serve as a predictor for both independent variables.

The findings reveal a modest yet significant negative association between perceived stress and socioeconomic status, consistent with prior scholarly investigations. Hypothesis 1 was confirmed, as the research identified a correlation between perceived stress and socioeconomic status, albeit with a weak relationship. These results contribute to the existing body of research on the impact of socioeconomic status, which has been extensively explored in previous studies (Steele et al. 2007). This enhanced understanding of socioeconomic status enables conclusions to be drawn regarding those most susceptible to aid in improving their psychological wellbeing and functioning. It also facilitates the refinement of psychological interventions to better cater to the needs of individuals with low and high socioeconomic status. However, Hypothesis 2 was refuted, as the detected correlation was more likely due to chance, although it was negative as anticipated in the literature review. Similarly, Hypothesis 3 was also rejected, as the weak yet positive correlation observed was not likely to be of significance, contradicting previous research on socioeconomic status and attitudes towards psychological help.

The study identified a pattern within the means of socioeconomic status, with individuals of low socioeconomic status exhibiting lower mean scores on attitudes towards seeking professional psychological help compared to those of middle and high socioeconomic status, aligning with most research on these variables. The unequal distribution of participants across socioeconomic subgroups, with low socioeconomic status comprising 31.7% and high socioeconomic status only 6.8% of the sample, may have influenced the study's findings. The subgroup size differences may have impacted the high standard deviations for perceived stress within each subgroup and the overlapping confidence intervals. Therefore, an increased sample size could have mitigated these issues and allowed for a better explanation of the relationships between the variables. Despite plausible research supporting the relationship between the variables, the findings did not align with the researcher's expectations. Research by Businelle et al. (2013) suggests that reducing exposure to stressors and/or improving coping with life stresses can enhance mental health and reduce health disparities.

The current research has a significant limitation in that not all participants may have utilized the calculator provided in the questionnaire. It is suggested that the questionnaire should have gathered participant income, education level, household occupants, and calculated the socioeconomic status (SES) instead. Galobardes (2006) proposed that participants are more willing to participate in a study that does not directly request their income or education levels, which is why the SES calculator was external. Participants are not obligated to answer all questions and have the right to skip items if they wish, so the questionnaire should not be modified to encourage participants to respond; instead, missing data should be removed (Décieux et al. 2015). It is recommended for future studies to measure both subjective and objective SES, as it has been previously established that they are directly related (Navarro-Carrillo et al. 2020; American Psychological Association 2015). Additionally, differences in perceptions of their reality and accurate SES could be observed to determine if individuals with varying subjective and objective SES differ in perceived stress levels compared to those whose objective and subjective SES are the same. Destin et al. (2017) utilized multiple findings from different fields of identity research to recognize how individuals interpret their own SES identity, suggesting that uncertainty about one's SES is correlated with lower mental wellbeing. This finding is similar to Zang and Bardo's (2018) study, which found that SES is not linked to health, but subjective social status is. This approach could also enhance the quality of the responses. However, the reliability and accuracy of the study has been significantly impacted by the lack of consistency in the measurement of socioeconomic status (Huang et al. 2017).

Previous research has concluded that socioeconomic status is difficult to conceptualize, and it was advised that the current research should have chosen one component of SES rather than investigating socioeconomic status as a variable. Focusing the study on one component of SES, such as level of education or income, would have made the variable easier to quantify and more suitable for statistical testing. There is sufficient research to demonstrate that each component is directly associated with perceived stress levels and attitudes towards seeking help. As SES is not dichotomous (ranked low, middle, and high), it was unsuitable for most statistical tests, including multiple linear regression. To ensure its suitability, middle and high SES had to be combined via dummy coding. The current research suggests that in the future, SES can still be effectively used through this method, and is supported by Alkharusi (2012) or through multiple logistics regression. Although SES is considered a qualitative variable, it can still be used within quantitative research. Despite the difficulties, SES is a determinant that is becoming increasingly relevant, as useful findings can be implemented in real life through policy-making and systematic changes to help reduce the impact of socioeconomic disparities across the UK.

Another limitation of this study is that 34 out of the 73 participants were recruited from a university where the majority of students were aged 18 to 25. To ensure the generalizability of the findings to the broader population, the study should have aimed for a more balanced representation of participants across different age groups. The questionnaire used in the study did not include age as a demographic variable, which may have influenced the results. For instance, Chen et al. (2017) found that older individuals were less likely to use problem-focused coping strategies and exhibited lower levels of positive affect. Additionally, only 20.5% of the sample identified as male, which does not accurately represent the general population. This is significant because stress affects genders differently, with women being more susceptible to emotional exhaustion and reporting higher levels of stress. Furthermore, certain communities and individuals may face barriers to seeking psychological help, and gender differences in help-seeking behaviours have been well-documented. Given the existing concentration of research in this area, it may be more beneficial for academics to focus on intersectionality aspects, as research consistently shows that ethnic minorities, sexual minorities, and individuals living in deprived neighbourhoods report higher levels of stress. Additionally, gender may also play a role in attitudes towards seeking psychological help, as the relationship is multifaceted and cannot be explained by a single factor. Furthermore, the correlational design of the current research limits the ability to establish causality, despite identifying significant relationships within the data. This is a significant drawback of correlational research.

Conclusion

In conclusion, this study aimed to investigate the impact of perceived stress on attitudes towards seeking professional psychological assistance and socioeconomic status, and to discern the interrelationships among these variables. The findings revealed a weak positive correlation between perceived stress and socioeconomic status, consistent with existing research. However, no other significant associations were observed, leading to the rejection of two hypotheses. Previous studies have also failed to establish a link between perceived stress and attitudes towards seeking professional psychological help. While this outcome is not uncommon, qualitative, or longitudinal investigations may offer insights into the stress-attitude relationship. These comprehensive research approaches may uncover common themes relevant to the stress-attitude connection. It has been suggested that stress could be better elucidated through related concepts such as social support, coping strategies, and mental health literacy. Methodological limitations, including unreliable measurement of socioeconomic status among participants, constrained the study's findings. There needs to be a standardized operational definition of socioeconomic status in this area. Most studies on these three variables employ similar quantitative, cross-correlational methodologies, which can inform future research. Although this study did not identify moderately significant relationships, recommendations were made for future research, including the reliable measurement of socioeconomic status and the inclusion of subjective social status.

Study Two: Students' Preference on Digital Intervention for Mental Health

Wan San Wendy Wang and Elsie Ong

Aims and objectives

Existing literature predominantly highlights the state of students' mental health amid COVID-19—there is a research gap regarding students' mental health as they return and readjust to a post-pandemic life. The first aim of this investigation is to examine the mental health and well-being of university students in the later stages of the COVID-19 pandemic. To eliminate barriers to receiving mental health support, there must be a more nuanced understanding of the reasons preventing students from seeking and receiving help and how these can be overcome. Therefore, the second aim is to examine university students' experiences with digital mental health interventions throughout the pandemic—such as their rates and consistency of usage, satisfaction with its effect on mental health, the experienced obstacles to help-seeking, or obstacles encountered with using interventions. Current literature focuses more on the effectiveness of digital intervention strategies, with lesser understanding on students' perspectives of seeking in-person treatment or digital interventions. Even though digital interventions have been demonstrated to overcome some reasons students are hesitant to seek in-person treatment, a large proportion of students are not familiar with digital interventions.

The third aim of this investigation is to compare the experiences of international and local students, with regard to their mental health and personal experiences with digital interventions. Existing literature regarding digital interventions has predominantly focused on student populations, with few studies comparing the experiences of international versus non-international student groups. As international students may struggle with different circumstances, this information is important for institutions who wish to address all student barriers to receiving treatment—international students possibly have different experiences with their mental health and face different barriers to receiving or seeking treatment.

Methods

Design

The current research utilized a mixed methods approach, with participants completing an online questionnaire on the QUALTRICS platform. The questionnaire included both quantitative and qualitative components, with the qualitative section comprising open-ended questions to capture participants' experiences with digital interventions in their own words, providing a deeper understanding of their perspectives.

Measures

The study assessed students' mental health and well-being using three measures: symptoms of anxiety, symptoms of depression, and stress. Depression and anxiety were evaluated using the **Zung Self-Rating Depression Scales and Zung Self-Rating Anxiety rating scales** (Zung 1971), which utilize diagnostic criteria to assess various manifestations of these conditions. Each scale consisted of 20 items, for each of which participants were asked to indicate from a 4-point scale how often they felt a certain way within the last few days. 1 indicated "None, or a little of the time" and 4 indicated "most of the time, or never". For example, an item in the SAS screening for cognitive symptoms is "I feel afraid for no reason" (Zung 1965). Previous research has demonstrated the sensitivity and validity of the Zung Self-Rated Depression scales in identifying the clinical severity of depression, with the SDS showing a strong correlation with the widely used Hamilton Rating Scale for depression (Biggs et al. 1978). The SAS has been found to possess internal consistency, convergent validity, and concurrent validity, and is effective in detecting symptoms of clinical anxiety (Dunstan et al. 2017), demonstrating higher sensitivity compared to other anxiety rating scales such as the DASS (Dunstan et al. 2017).

Lastly, stress levels were measured using the Perceived Stress Scale (Cohen et al. 1983). This instrument is designed for self-evaluation of an individual's personal stress levels and comprises 10 questions that ask about the individual's feelings and thoughts over the preceding month. Responses are self-rated on a scale of 0 to 4, with 0 representing "Never" and 4 representing "Always". An example item is "How often have you felt that you could not control the important things in your life?". The Perceived Stress Scale was selected to gauge the degree to which university students perceive their life circumstances as unpredictable and uncontrollable, and consequently stressful. The 10-item Perceived Stress Scale was chosen over the 14-item Perceived Stress Scale due to its superior psychometric properties, internal consistency, reliability, and validity (Lee 2012).

Procedure

Participants were asked about their motivations for initiating digital interventions, their reasons for not utilizing them, and their preferences for in-person versus online interventions. The survey also prompted participants to identify and specify the types of digital interventions with which they have had experience. A list of examples was provided for participants to select from, along with an additional textbox for inputting other interventions. Examples included computerized cognitive behavioural therapy, gamified interventions, and mindfulness apps designed for mobile phones.

Ethics consideration

In this study, participants must provide full informed consent before completing an online QUALTRICS survey. They were informed about the potential for discomfort due to sensitive items in the Zung Depression Self-Rating scale and were given the option to withdraw from the study at any time.

Results

The investigation focused on the mental health of university students in the post-pandemic period. Raw scores from the SDS, SAS, and PSS were converted into index scores using Zung's scoring system and compared against a conversion chart. Higher scores indicated greater severity of anxiety and depression (Dunstan and Scott 2019). The results revealed that 77% of students scored above the normal range of 40 points on the Zung Self-Rating depression scale, indicating a spectrum of depressive disorder. Most students fell within the range of mild to moderate depression. Additionally, 57% of students scored above the normal range of 45 points on the Zung Self-Rating anxiety scale, indicating mild to moderate anxiety disorder levels. On the perceived stress scale, most students obtained scores within the range for experiencing a moderate to high level of perceived stress (Tables 6.2 and 6.3).

Examining university students' experiences with digital mental health interventions throughout the pandemic

26% of students ($n = 100$) did not have experience with digital interventions at all. 72% of international students ($n = 36$) and 76% of local students ($n = 64$) have had experience using some form of digital interventions within the last year to improve/treat their mental health. The most used form of digital intervention was found to be mobile applications, including the use of meditation, relaxation, or mental health coaching apps. Just over 25% of participants used mobile apps on their own, or in addition to other forms of digital interventions. Specifically, the most used app among students was Headspace, a meditation app intended for relaxation and relief of stress. Following this, online therapy and online counselling were the next most used digital interventions among students, with 17% and 16% of participants indicating their use of these, respectively. 86% of students using digital interventions were using them

Table 6.2 Students' self–rated symptoms of anxiety, depression, and perceived stress

	International student (%)	Local student (%)	All students (%)
Depressive disorder			
Normal	27	21	21
Mild	39	39	39
Moderate	18	28	25
Severe	16	12	13
Anxiety disorder			
Normal	52	38	43
Mild to moderate	24	43	36
Moderate to severe	18	16	17
Extreme	6	3	4
Perceived stress			
Low	24	8	14
Moderate	48	74	65
Severe	28	18	21

Table 6.3 Student demographics

Variable	Frequency	Percentage (%)
International student	36	36
Local student	64	64
Experience with digital interventions	74	74
No experience	26	26
International students, experience	26	72
International students, no experience	10	28
Local students, experience	49	76
Local students, no experience	15	24

on their own, while 14% were receiving support from digital interventions and face-to-face intervention. It was the most common for students to engage with digital interventions once a week for between 1 and 20 min. The second most frequent engagement with interventions was once a month (Table 6.4).

Participants were asked to rate on a scale of 1–10 their experienced effect that digital interventions had on their mood right after use, 1 being not at all and 10 being a great improvement. Most individuals felt the beneficial effects of the interventions on their mood directly after use. 93% of participants felt some improvement in their stress levels right after use. 87% of individuals felt that they were at least somewhat satisfied with their experiences (Table 6.5).

Both international and local student groups generally show a preference for in-person interventions over digital interventions. Some participants expressed no

Table 6.4 Students ratings of their satisfaction, and effectiveness of digital interventions

	International students	Local students	Overall rating	% satisfied/ improvement
Satisfaction with digital interventions (rated from 1–10)	6.85	6.15	6.4	87
Improvement on mood (rated from 1 to 10)	5.71	6.04	5.8	94
Improvement on stress (rated from 1 to 10)	6.15	5.70	5.9	93

Table 6.5 Student preferences on mode of intervention

	International student (%)	Local student (%)	Overall (%)
Preference for face to face	51	65	60
Preference for digital	35	21	26
No preference	14	14	14

specific preference for either digital or in-person interventions. International students exhibited a slightly stronger preference for digital interventions compared to local students, while local students showed a stronger preference for face-to-face interventions. For various reasons, nearly one-third of students favored digital therapy and intervention over in-person therapy. Attitudinal barriers were identified as a factor preventing some students, particularly international students, from seeking in-person support (Loya et al. 2010). This was especially observed in participants who were international students. For instance, one student stated they "sometimes feel way too anxious for the idea of face-to-face interventions". Other students find it difficult to talk about their mental health issues in face-to-face settings—one student mentioned they "find that it's really awkward [for me] to bring up mental health in real life". Another student mentioned they just feel "much more comfortable to do it online, I wouldn't want to go in person, I just feel like there's more privacy that way. Another recurring theme was the accessibility of digital interventions instead of in-person treatment—regarding affordability and ease of physical access. Students felt that "it's free and more affordable on the internet", "digital interventions have helped me a lot when I needed it and couldn't access f2f", "real life interventions involve considerable travel", "convenience, especially on a busy schedule".

Few individuals were using online therapy alongside traditional face to face therapy, suggesting individuals usually select one or the other. With regards to the reasons students chose in person interventions or digital interventions, it was revealed that the severity of their anxiety and depression strongly influenced the decision and preference they have towards in person interventions or digital interventions. This varies from individual to individual. For some students, digital interventions are a way for them to obtain the support they need when it is too mentally or physically taxing for them to seek out face to face help. One student stated that *"On days where I am at my lowest and simply cannot leave the house"* they would turn to using digital interventions. Or when *"Sometimes I feel too anxious for the idea of face-to-face interventions so I think I would prefer digital"*.

As for the most common reasons why students did not use digital interventions, international students reported a lack of knowledge on where to access resources. They "did not know about these forms of interventions", and they "don't know where to find the right resources". Meanwhile, local students predominantly said they "did not feel a need to use them".

A comparison of international and local student populations

A Two-Way Analysis of Variance (ANOVA) was performed to evaluate the presence of a statistically significant difference in means of student's symptoms of anxiety and depression, based on whether students were international, and the use of digital interventions. Before conducting the two-way ANOVA, parametric assumptions were tested. The Shapiro–Wilk test of normality was non-significant for all 3 dependent variables, with $p > 0.05$ so the assumption for the normal distribution of variables was met. Levene's test for equality and variance showed that the data met assumptions for homogeneity of variance, so equal variance could be assumed for the dependent variables of anxiety, depression, and stress.

The Two Way ANOVA revealed that there was no main effect of using digital interventions on students' symptoms of depression and anxiety. There was also no statistically significant interaction between the effects of being an international student and using digital interventions, $F(1, 90) = 0.037$, $p > 0.05$. An analysis of simple main effects showed that there was no main effect of being an international or local student on symptoms of depression and anxiety.

Discussion

The findings of the study revealed that the prevalence of depression and anxiety among students remains notably high, consistent with previous research conducted during the COVID-19 pandemic (Radwan et al. 2021). Approximately 38% of surveyed students exhibited moderate to severe levels of depression, while 21% reported similar levels of anxiety. These results are in line with studies indicating that over 70% of students experienced heightened anxiety symptoms during the pandemic (Son et al. 2020), underscoring the imperative for universities to continue enhancing their mental health resources for students.

The study did not indicate a significant impact of utilizing digital interventions in the past year on students' reported symptoms of depression and anxiety. Nevertheless, the findings reported that most students (87%) who had utilized digital interventions expressed satisfaction with their experience and reported improvements in their stress levels and mood immediately following usage, irrespective of their status as international or local students. It is plausible that the observed improvements in stress and mood among these students may have coincided with concurrent amelioration of their symptoms of depression and anxiety through the use of digital interventions, potentially resulting in reduced severity of these symptoms. This proposition finds support in a meta-analysis encompassing 24 studies involving 1431 students from diverse academic disciplines, which concluded that digital interventions were effective in alleviating anxiety symptoms and reducing levels of depression and cortisol in university students (Regehr et al. 2013). These interventions' positive effects were consistent across variations in specific intervention components and student characteristics.

Contrary to the low rates of digital intervention utilization reported by Levin et al. (2017), this study found a much higher prevalence of digital intervention usage among participants, with 74% of students utilizing digital interventions within the past year. This shift in behaviour may be attributed to an increased receptiveness among students toward digital interventions and a greater willingness to seek support, particularly during the pandemic when in-person services are limited. This suggests that a larger proportion of individuals turned to digital interventions as a viable support option during the COVID-19 pandemic, making it an increasingly common and accessible form of support for students. This presents a valuable opportunity for universities and institutions to reach a broader audience of potential students willing to utilize digital interventions, given its adaptable self-managed format and ease of dissemination to a wide audience.

According to Loya et al. (2010), this study identified the primary reasons cited by students for not utilizing digital interventions, which included a lack of knowledge about where to access mental health resources and the types of resources available to them. This contrasts with the findings of Levin et al. (2017), who reported that students had concerns about the effectiveness of apps, a lack of interest in using apps as an intervention, and apprehensions about the privacy protection of their data. The results suggest that universities may need to exert more effort in promoting digital therapeutic intervention platforms to assist students in accessing technology-based support. However, some students preferred to address their issues independently, even if treatment was readily available, similar to the findings of Ebert et al. (2019). Universities should be prepared for the possibility that some students will choose to manage their problems independently, regardless of the available interventions. In such cases, universities should consider the type of support they wish to provide to these students.

The findings of this study indicate that students favored combining digital interventions with face-to-face interventions, which aligns with the results of a more recent study by Levin et al. (2022), where both students and therapists preferred using mobile apps alongside traditional in-person interventions. Levin et al. (2022) also noted that while students found mobile apps helpful while awaiting therapy, they did not view it as a replacement for traditional therapy or Counselling. Similarly, the results of this study indicated that 60% of students preferred in-person support and intervention, while only 26% preferred online support. Both international and local students expressed this preference. In contrast to the findings of Ebert et al. (2019), where students expressed feeling embarrassed to seek mental health support, the most common reason students preferred digital interventions over face-to-face interventions was attributed to feelings of anxiety and nervousness about in-person intervention. This is consistent with the findings of Loya et al. (2010), which emphasized that attitudinal barriers to treatment should not be overlooked as contributors to untreated mental health conditions, in addition to structural barriers.

A notable trend is the tendency of students to seek interventions when they are already approaching burnout, struggling significantly with their mental health symptoms, and in urgent need of help. This contrasts with studies that have found students were less likely to seek help as levels of psychological distress increased. Conversely, the intention to use an online intervention increased at higher levels of distress (Ryan et al. 2015). Therefore, it may be worthwhile to further explore the potential of promoting digital interventions to students as a preventive strategy rather than solely as an intervention for those who are already reaching a breaking point in their mental health struggles. Given the waiting times and barriers students face to receive in-person treatment, there is a clear need to explore alternative options that are more accessible and approachable for students.

The third objective of the research was to specifically investigate whether there was any association between being an international or local student and their mental health and engagement with digital interventions. The study found no significant impact of being an international or local student on the experienced symptoms of depression and anxiety. Moreover, there were no statistically significant differences between international and local students in terms of the severity of their self-reported anxiety, depression, and perceived stress. This indicates positive outcomes regarding diversity, equity, and inclusion initiatives within universities and higher education, aligning with the findings of Kivelä et al. (2022), who observed that international students were not disproportionately affected by the COVID-19 pandemic compared to other students. This finding contrasts with previous studies (Kivelä et al. 2022; Yeung et al. 2021) that suggested international students experience higher levels of anxiety and depression. Those studies indicated that international students were more likely to experience overwhelming depression compared to their peers. It is plausible that in this investigation, individuals struggling with their mental health received adequate support to alleviate their symptoms.

Limitations

The findings of this study are subject to certain methodological limitations that should be considered when interpreting the results. Firstly, there was an overrepresentation of females, particularly in Western countries, similar to a previous study. Additionally, the study focused on international student populations, predominantly of East Asian backgrounds. Still, the data collected indicated an equal distribution between students of East Asian and Caucasian backgrounds, which may impact the results due to cultural differences in attitudes towards mental health. The study relied on self-assessed rating scales rather than clinical interviews, which may lead to a greater dependence on participants' self-reported satisfaction with digital interventions and potential response bias. Furthermore, the study was not longitudinal, making it challenging to assess participants' improvements or changes in symptoms and establish causal relationships.

The mental health services available to young adults have improved in recent years, reflecting a growing recognition of the importance of young people's mental well-being. The purpose of the two studies was to examine the relationship between students' self-reported level of Perceived Stress and their attitudes towards Seeking Professional Help, as well as to explore students' preference for digital intervention for mental health and investigate the post-pandemic mental health status of university students. The findings indicated no significant relationship between students' use of digital interventions and their level of anxiety and depression. However, students reported an improvement in their stress levels and mood directly after using digital interventions, regardless of their international or local student status. The findings also indicated a high usage rate of digital interventions among students, demonstrating their increasing relevance as a more common and accessible form of support, especially in the form of mobile apps. Students were not using digital interventions due to a lack of knowledge regarding the kinds of digital interventions available to them and where to access these mental health resources, but they are open to using them. Addressing challenges such as limited resources, lengthy waiting times, and regional disparities, and further developing preventative measures, specialized care, and digital support platforms will contribute to a more comprehensive and effective mental health service provision for young adults.

Conclusion

The mental health services available to young adults have improved in recent years, reflecting a growing recognition of the importance of young people's mental well-being. However, it is unclear how young people see the provision of mental health services. Therefore, the purpose of conducting the two studies was to examine the relationship between students' self-reported Perceived Stress and their attitudes toward Seeking Professional Help. With the growing trend of digitalization in everyday lives, this chapter also explored students' preference for digital intervention for mental health, thus investigating the post-pandemic mental health status of the universities and comparing international and local student populations. Overall. We have found no significant relationship between students' use of digital interventions and students' levels of anxiety and depression. However, students rated an improvement in their stress levels and mood directly after using digital interventions, regardless of whether they were international or local students. Compared to existing studies, the current findings indicated a high usage rate of digital interventions among students, demonstrating their increasing relevance as a more common and accessible form of support for students, especially in mobile apps and online help. Moreover, our findings indicated that the predominant reason students were not using digital interventions was due to a lack of knowledge regarding the kinds of digital interventions available to students and a lack of understanding of where to access these mental health resources, though they were open to using them. This is important in seeking to eliminate barriers to treatment for students to allow digital interventions to reach their full potential. In the future, universities can work to promote these more widely among student populations and to increase accessibility for digital interventions. Future studies could investigate the possibility of conducting longitudinal studies to try and establish a relationship between the symptoms of depression and anxiety in students and their use of digital interventions.

Despite progress, challenges such as limited resources, lengthy waiting times, and regional disparities continue to affect the quality and accessibility of face-to-face services. Addressing these challenges and developing preventative measures, specialized care, and digital support platforms will contribute to a more comprehensive and effective mental health service provision for young adults.

References

Alkharusi H (2012) Categorical variables in regression analysis: a comparison of dummy and effect coding. Int J Educ 4(2):202. https://doi.org/10.5296/ije.v4i2.1962

American Psychological Association (2015) Measuring socioeconomic status and subjective social status. https://www.apa.org/pi/ses/resources/class/measuring-status

Biggs JT, Wylie LT, Ziegler VE (1978) Validity of the zung self-rating depression scale. Br J Psychiatry 132(4):381–385. https://doi.org/10.1192/bjp.132.4.381

Brown J, Kirk-Wade E (2021) Coronavirus: a history of English lockdown laws. https://researchbriefings.files.parliament.uk/documents/CBP-9068/CBP-9068.pdf

Businelle MS, Mills BA, Chartier KG, Kendzor DE, Reingle JM, Shuval K (2013) Do stressful events account for the link between socioeconomic status and mental health? J Public Health 36(2):205–212. https://doi.org/10.1093/pubmed/fdt060

Chatmon BN (2020) Males and mental health stigma. Am J Men's Health 14(4). https://doi.org/10.1177/1557988320949322

Chen Y, Peng Y, Xu H, O'Brien WH (2017) Age differences in stress and coping: problem-focused strategies mediate the relationship between age and positive affect. Int J Aging Human Dev 86(4):347–363. https://doi.org/10.1177/0091415017720890

Clement S, Schauman O, Graham T, Maggioni F, Evans-Lacko S, Bezborodovs N, Morgan C, Rüsch N, Brown JSL, Thornicroft G (2015) What Is the impact of mental health-related stigma on help-seeking? A systematic review of quantitative and qualitative studies. Psychol Med 45(01):11–27. https://doi.org/10.1017/s0033291714000129

Cohen S, Williamson G (1998) Perceived stress in a probability sample of the United States. In: Spacapan S, Oskamp S (eds) The social psychology of health. Sage, pp 31–67

Cohen S, Doyle WJ, Baum A (2006) Socioeconomic status is associated with stress hormones. Psychosom Med 68(3):414–420. https://doi.org/10.1097/01.psy.0000221236.37158.b9

Cohen S, Kamarck T, Mermelstein R (1983) A global measure of perceived stress. J Health Soc Behav 24(4):385–396. https://doi.org/10.2307/2136404

Cramer KM (1999) Psychological antecedents to help-seeking behaviour: a reanalysis using path modelling structures. J Counsel Psychol 46(3):381–387. https://doi.org/10.1037/0022-0167.46.3.381

Décieux J, Mergener A, Neufang K, Sischka P (2015) Implementation of the forced answering option within online surveys: Do higher item response rates come at the expense of participation and answer quality? Psihologija 48(4):311–326. https://doi.org/10.2298/psi1504311d

Department of Health and Social Care. (2021) Mental health recovery plan backed by £500 million. Gov.uk. https://www.gov.uk/government/news/mental-health-recovery-plan-backed-by-500-million#:~:text=Under%20the%20plan%20NHS%20talking

Destin M, Rheinschmidt-Same M, Richeson JA (2017) Status-based identity. Perspect Psychol Sci 12(2):270–289. https://doi.org/10.1177/1745691616664424

Dunkel Schetter C, Schafer P, Lanzi RG, Clark-Kauffman E, Raju TNK, Hillemeier MM (2013) Shedding light on the mechanisms underlying health disparities through community participatory methods. Perspect Psychol Sci 8(6):613–633. https://doi.org/10.1177/1745691613506016

Dunstan DA, Scott N (2019) Clarification of the cut-off score for Zung's self-rating depression scale. BMC Psychiatry 19(1). https://doi.org/10.1186/s12888-019-2161-0

Dunstan DA, Scott N, Todd AK (2017) Screening for anxiety and depression: reassessing the utility of the Zung Scales. BMC Psychiatry 17(1). https://doi.org/10.1186/s12888-017-1489-6

Ebert DD, Franke M, Kählke F, Küchler AM, Bruffaerts R, Mortier P, Karyotaki E, Alonso J, Cuijpers P, Berking M, Auerbach RP, Kessler RC, Baumeister H (2018) Increasing intentions to use mental health services among university students: results of a pilot randomised controlled trial within the world health organisation's world mental health international college student initiative. Int J Methods Psychiatric Res 28(2). https://doi.org/10.1002/mpr.1754

Ebert DD, Mortier P, Kaehlke F, Bruffaerts R, Baumeister H, Auerbach RP, Alonso J, Vilagut G, Martínez KU, Lochner C, Cuijpers P, Kuechler AM, Green J, Hasking P, Lapsley C, Sampson NA, Kessler RC (2019) Barriers of mental health treatment utilisation among first-year college students: first cross-national results from the who world mental health international college student initiative. Int J Methods Psychiatric Res 28(2). https://doi.org/10.1002/mpr.1782

Elhai JD, Schweinle W, Anderson SM (2008) Reliability and validity of the attitudes toward seeking professional psychological help scale-short form. Psychiatry Res 159(3):320–329. https://doi.org/10.1016/j.psychres.2007.04.020

Galobardes B (2006) Indicators of socioeconomic position (chapter 1). J Epidemiol Commun Health 60(1):7–12. https://doi.org/10.1136/jech.2004.023531

Halpern-Manners A, Schnabel L, Hernandez EM, Silberg JL, Eaves LJ (2016) The relationship between education and mental health: new evidence from a discordant twin study. Soc Forces 95(1):107–131. https://doi.org/10.1093/sf/sow035

Huang S, Hou J, Sun L, Dou D, Liu X, Zhang H (2017) The effects of objective and subjective socioeconomic status on subjective well-being among rural-to-urban migrants in China: The moderating role of subjective social mobility. Front Psychol 8(819). https://doi.org/10.3389/fpsyg.2017.00819

Jones E (2021) COVID-19 and the Blitz compared: mental health outcomes in the UK. The Lancet Psychiatry 8. https://doi.org/10.1016/s2215-0366(21)00118-8

Jorm AF (2000) Mental health literacy: public knowledge and beliefs about mental disorders. Br J Psychiatry 177(05):396–401. https://doi.org/10.1192/bjp.177.5.396

Kahneman D (2011) Thinking, fast and slow. Farrar, Straus and Giroux.

Kivelä L, Mouthaan J, van der Does W, Antypa N (2022) Student Mental Health during the COVID-19 pandemic: Are international students more affected? J Am Coll Health 1–9. https://doi.org/10.1080/07448481.2022.2037616

Koydemir-Özden S (2010) Self-aspects, perceived social support, gender, and willingness to seek psychological help. Int J Ment Health 39(3):44–60. https://doi.org/10.2753/imh0020-7411390303

Lee E-H (2012) Review of the psychometric evidence of the perceived stress scale. Asian Nurs Res 6(4):121–127. https://doi.org/10.1016/j.anr.2012.08.004

Levin ME, Hicks ET, Krafft J (2022) Pilot evaluation of the stop, breathe & think mindfulness app for student clients on a college counselling centre waitlist. J Am Coll Health 70(1):165–173. https://doi.org/10.1080/07448481.2020.1728281

Levin ME, Stocke K, Pierce B, Levin C (2017) Do college students use online self-help? A survey of intentions and use of mental health resources. J Coll Stud Psychother 32(3):181–198. https://doi.org/10.1080/87568225.2017.1366283

Loya F, Reddy R, Hinshaw SP (2010) Mental illness stigma as a mediator of differences in Caucasian and South Asian college students' attitudes toward psychological counselling. J Couns Psychol 57(4):484–490. https://doi.org/10.1037/a0021113

Mirowsky J, Ross CE (2012) Education, social status, and health. Aldinetransaction

Navarro-Carrillo G, Alonso-Ferres M, Moya M, Valor-Segura I (2020) Socioeconomic status and psychological well-being: revisiting the role of subjective socioeconomic status. Front Psychol 11. https://doi.org/10.3389/fpsyg.2020.01303

Niemeyer H, Bieda A, Michalak J, Schneider S, Margraf J (2019) Education and mental health: Do psychosocial resources matter? SSM Popul Health 7:100392. https://doi.org/10.1016/j.ssmph.2019.100392

Office for National Statistics (2022b). Income, spending and wealth: How do you compare? Office for National Statistics. https://www.ons.gov.uk/peoplepopulationandcommunity/personalandhouseholdfinances/incomeandwealth/articles/incomespendingandwealthhowdoyoucompare/2022-03-09

ONS (2022) Cost of living and depression in adults, Great Britain. Office for National Statistics. https://www.ons.gov.uk/peoplepopulationandcommunity/healthandsocialcare/mentalhealth/articles/costoflivinganddepressioninadultsgreatbritain/29septemberto23october2022

Orji L, Abikoye G (2019) Perceived social support and stress as predictors of help-seeking attitude for mental health among young adults. Covenant Int J Psychol 4(1):1–15. https://doi.org/10.20370/tgcz-ch15

Picco L, Abdin E, Chong SA, Pang S, Shafie S, Chua BY, Vaingankar JA, Ong LP, Tay J, Subramaniam M (2016) Attitudes toward seeking professional psychological help: factor structure and socio-demographic predictors. Front Psychol 7(547). https://doi.org/10.3389/fpsyg.2016.00547

Radwan E, Radwan A, Radwan W, Pandey D (2021) Prevalence of depression, anxiety and stress during the COVID-19 pandemic: a cross-sectional study among Palestinian students (10–18 years). BMC Psychol 9(1). https://doi.org/10.1186/s40359-021-00688-2

Rayan A, Baker O, Fawaz M (2020) The psychometric properties of attitudes toward seeking professional psychological help scale-short form in Jordanian university students. J Muslim Mental Health 14(1). https://doi.org/10.3998/jmmh.10381607.0014.102

Regehr C, Glancy D, Pitts A (2013) Interventions to reduce stress in university students: a review and meta-analysis. J Affect Disord 148(1):1–11. https://doi.org/10.1016/j.jad.2012.11.026

Ryan G, De Silva M, Terver JS, Ochi OP, Eaton J (2015) Information systems for global mental health. Lancet Psychiat 2(5):372–373

Ryu S, Fan L (2022) The relationship between financial worries and psychological distress among U.S. adults. J Family Econ Issues 44(1). https://doi.org/10.1007/s10834-022-09820-9

Selvitopu A, Kaya M (2021) A meta-analytic review of the effect of socioeconomic status on academic performance. J Educ:1–13. https://doi.org/10.1177/00220574211031978

Son C, Hegde S, Smith A, Wang X, Sasangohar F (2020) Effects of COVID-19 on college students' mental health in the United States: interview survey study. J Med Internet Res 22(9). https://doi.org/10.2196/21279

Steele L, Dewa C, Lin E, Lee K (2007) Education level, income level and mental health services use in Canada: associations and policy implications. Healthc Policy|Politiques de Santé 3(1):96–106. https://doi.org/10.12927/hcpol.2007.19177

Tambling RR, D'Aniello C, Russell BS (2021) Mental health literacy: a critical target for narrowing racial disparities in behavioural health. Int J Ment Heal Addict. https://doi.org/10.1007/s11469-021-00694-w

Torres L, Magnus B, Najar N (2021) Assessing the psychometric proprieties of the attitudes toward seeking professional psychological help scale–short form (ATSPPH-SF) among latino adults. Assessment 28(1), 211–224. Sage J. https://doi.org/10.1177/1073191119899470

Wardle J, Steptoe A (2003) Socioeconomic differences in attitudes and beliefs about healthy lifestyles. J Epidemiol Community Health 57(6):440–443. https://doi.org/10.1136/jech.57.6.440

Wilson CJ (2010) General psychological distress symptoms and help-avoidance in young Australians. Adv Ment Health 9(1):63–72. https://doi.org/10.5172/jamh.9.1.63

Yeung TS, Hyun S, Zhang E, Wong F, Stevens C, Liu CH, Chen JA (2021) Prevalence and correlates of mental health symptoms and disorders among US International College Students. J Am Coll Health:1–7. https://doi.org/10.1080/07448481.2020.1865980

Zang E, Bardo AR (2018) Objective and subjective socioeconomic status, their discrepancy, and health: evidence from East Asia. Soc Indic Res 143(2):765–794. https://doi.org/10.1007/s11205-018-1991-3

Zhang Y, Su D, Chen Y, Tan M, Chen X (2022) Effect of socioeconomic status on the physical and mental health of the elderly: the mediating effect of social participation. BMC Public Health 22(1). https://doi.org/10.1186/s12889-022-13062-7

Zung WW (1965) A self-rating depression scale. Arch Gen Psychiatry 12(1):63. https://doi.org/10.1001/archpsyc.1965.01720310065008

Zung WWK (1971) A rating instrument for anxiety disorders. Psychosomatics 12(6):371–379. https://doi.org/10.1016/s0033-3182(71)71479-0

Dr. Elsie Ong is a Lecturer and a Dissertation Supervisor in UCL. She has worked in many universities in Asia and the UK for over ten years. Elsie is active in leading research that focuses on the mental health of young adults; especially those going through university transitions. Her expertise in cognitive neuroscience and psychology has also initiated further exploration on the underlying causes of mental health problems and later sparkles potentials for suicide preventions and interventions. Elsie is devoted to the study of psychological wellbeing in young adults and has published her research through internationally renowned conferences and reputed journals such as Frontiers in psychiatry. These experiences have helped to keep her most up to date on the latest development in preventions and interventions in mental health.

Wan San Wendy Wang has a Bachelor of Science in Psychology from McGill University and a Master of Science in Child Development from the Institute of Education University College London. She is currently working as an Assistant Psychologist at Westminster Talking Therapies, part of the Central and North West NHS Trust. She has previously been a Research Assistant at the Translational Research in Affect and Cognition Laboratory in Montreal, Canada, where her interest began in mental disorders in the context of students and young adults of various backgrounds.

Chapter 7
Future Directions and Conclusions

Elsie Ong and Kevin Conn

Summary of Chapters 1–6

In this book, Scholars and researchers have gathered data from various sources, including secondary schools and universities in different regions, such as Asia and the United Kingdom, to examine the impact of the pandemic on students. Common behavioural patterns have been identified, categorizing the impact into two main groups: academic and mental health. The effects of pandemic-related transitions on university students' mental health and well-being in residential halls have been highlighted in the early chapters. These students have experienced isolation from their social connections and family, significantly impacting their emotions, relationships, and coping strategies. As a result, they have become particularly vulnerable to mental health concerns, with increased stress and anxiety due to the COVID-19 pandemic. The findings emphasize the urgent need for interventions and preventive strategies to address the mental health of college students. Chapter 4 of the study establishes a relationship between loneliness, social support, self-efficacy, and depression among students, indicating the importance of intrapersonal and interpersonal perspectives in higher education. Students with higher loneliness, lower self-efficacy, and less social support are at a higher risk of developing mental health conditions, highlighting the need for universities to provide additional support to these students. The study also reveals that students' levels of depression were relatively high and negatively correlated with their coping resiliency, emphasizing the need for improvement

E. Ong (✉)
Department of Psychology and Human Development, IOE—UCL's Faculty of Education and Society, University College London, London, WC 1E 6BT, UK
e-mail: Elsie.ong@ucl.ac.uk

K. Conn
Executive Director Student Housing and Residential Life California State University Northridge, Northridge, CA 91330, United States
e-mail: kevin.conn@nyu.edu

E. Ong (ed.), *The Emergence of the Digital World*,
https://doi.org/10.1007/978-981-97-3098-8_7

in students' university transition experiences to facilitate their psychological well-being and coping strategies. The study also emphasizes the role of social support, coping, and resilience in helping students overcome the mental health challenges brought by the pandemic. Positive coping and higher social support among students have been shown to prevent mental health problems. The findings suggest that universities should institutionalize support mechanisms and facilitate tutors in providing emotional support alongside their academic duties. Additionally, the study highlights the need for further research and attention to cases of maladaptive coping strategies adopted by students, such as internet addiction, to deal with pandemic-related stressors.

It is clear that some students have experienced emotional distress during the pandemic but have not utilized the university Counselling service. It is essential to uncover the reasons behind their support choice, which could inform policymaking and improve future uptake of available Counselling support. These future investigations can help to understand the factors that prevent students from accessing mental health support and university Counselling services during times of significant stress, such as COVID-19. Additionally, the university is advised to take a more proactive approach in reaching out to students, potentially using social media networks to screen for mental health issues and identify students in distress. Interventions should focus on training adaptive coping strategies and monitoring students' psychological adjustment to stressors. This study represents one of the first qualitative approaches to documenting the psychological impacts of the COVID-19 pandemic on university students living in residential halls. It is suggested that the effects of the pandemic on students may persist beyond the peak period, indicating the need for further study to determine its long-term impact on students' mental health and well-being.

How We Have Changed Following the Pandemic?

The Importance of Social Support

Social support has always been crucial, providing emotional, practical, and informational assistance during challenging times. However, the COVID-19 pandemic has undoubtedly changed how we perceive and access social support (Smith and Jones 2022). Before the pandemic, social support often involved face-to-face interactions, such as meeting friends, attending social events, or seeking help from family members or support groups. These interactions provided a sense of belonging, empathy, and understanding. However, with the implementation of social distancing measures and lockdowns, physical interactions have been limited, leading to a shift in how we seek and receive social support (Johnson et al. 2021; Patel et al. 2023).

Based on the findings in various studies in this book, the importance of social support has not diminished but instead transformed in the context of the pandemic. While physical interactions have been restricted during the pandemic, technology has played a vital role in bridging the gap, especially in the tertiary educational setting, as revealed by many university students. Virtual platforms, such as video calls, social media, and online support groups, have become essential tools for maintaining social connections and accessing support. In this perspective, the emergence of these digital tools has undoubtedly played a vital role as a "friend", not a "Foe", for these young people. Moreover, the pandemic has highlighted the significance of emotional support during times of crisis. The fear, anxiety, and uncertainty brought about by COVID-19 have increased the need for emotional reassurance and understanding of people around these students in need. People have turned to their social networks, both online and offline, to share their experiences, seek advice, and find solace. In this sense, social support remains as crucial as ever, albeit in a different form. However, it is essential to acknowledge that the pandemic has also presented challenges to accessing social support.

Not everyone is like the student group we have interviewed and examined in the list of studies in this book. Some people may not have comparable access to technology or the internet, limiting their ability to connect virtually. Additionally, the prolonged nature of the pandemic has led to "pandemic fatigue," where individuals may feel exhausted and less motivated to seek or provide support. It is noteworthy to take away a message that while the COVID-19 pandemic has changed how we access and perceive social support; its importance remains significant. The shift towards virtual platforms and the increased need for emotional support highlight the adaptability and resilience of social support systems. However, addressing the challenges faced by individuals with limited access to technology or experiencing pandemic fatigue is crucial, ensuring that social support remains accessible to all.

Within the university, more can be done to strengthen social engagement, which is integral to student life and contributes to a sense of belonging and community on campus (Tinto 2017). Strategic planning of events and activities is essential to promote student engagement and foster peer connections (Henderson and Foshee 2019). Moreover, showcasing engagement opportunities at critical junctures, such as orientation and move-in, can facilitate student involvement and integration into campus culture (Goodenow and Grady 1993).

Student development is a multifaceted process encompassing academic, personal, and professional growth (Chickering and Reisser 1993). The pandemic has underscored the importance of resilience and adaptability in student development, increasing interest in specialized interest areas, and leadership opportunities (Gallagher and Reilly 2020). Universities play a crucial role in providing students with opportunities for growth and self-discovery, both inside and outside the classroom (Kuhn et al. 2017).

Current Issues in Mental Health and Its Service

From the studies in Chap. 4: Students 'mental health in the post-COVID Era, it is evident that academic stress, social isolation, and cultural stigma surrounding mental health prevent many students from seeking help for depression Hong Kong, China, and England. Feelings of hopelessness, low self-esteem, and difficulty adjusting to university life contribute to the prevalence of depression among students. The transition to university life, away from family and familiar support systems, may have contributed to social isolation and loneliness among students during the pandemic Era. The findings were consistent with those who reported limited social networks, language barriers, and cultural differences as contributing factors to mental health issues, particularly among international students (Li et al. 2018; Stallard et al. 2013; Yip et al. 2018).

In Hong Kong and China, a strong emphasis on academic achievement and success places immense pressure on students to excel academically (Chow and Wong 2015; Li et al. 2018) which was in line with what we found in Chap. 4. Although we have not delved into the details of the "exam-oriented" education system in Hong Kong and China in this book, it has been well established that this has exacerbated intense competition and stress among students in these regions. Similarly, Filial piety and family expectations have always played a significant role in shaping Chinese students' mental health experiences (Wong et al. 2020; Stallard et al. 2013). Cultural norms surrounding obedience to authority and fulfilling parental aspirations contribute to feelings of guilt, shame, and inadequacy among students. For this reason, cultural attitudes towards mental health may explain why so many students report feeling stigma and discrimination, which often hinder help-seeking behaviours (Stallard et al. 2013; Yip et al. 2018).

When reviewing barriers to seeking mental health support among young people, **stigma** is named as the top factor explaining why they have concern in help seeking. It is suggested that more Education and awareness campaigns should be made available to those in need to reduce stigma and increase mental health literacy. Providing students with accurate information about mental health, available resources, and coping strategies empowers them to seek help and support has been shown to be effective (Stallard et al. 2013; Wong et al. 2020). Furthermore, the rigid structure of conventional mental health services may not align with today's youth's preferences and communication styles. The digital era has ushered in new forms of interaction, and young people often feel more comfortable expressing themselves through online platforms. The current mental health services must adapt to these preferences to enhance usability and reach. Additionally, the fragmented nature of mental health care systems poses a challenge. Young people may need help navigating a complex web of services, leading to delays in receiving appropriate support. Streamlining services and improving coordination among various mental health providers can enhance the system's usability, ensuring a more seamless experience for young individuals seeking help. Therefore, a holistic approach incorporating technology and community-based initiatives is essential to address these shortcomings.

The landscape of mental health services has undergone a transformative shift with the advent of digital technologies. Various studies in Chap. 6: Mental Health Services and Intervention have explored the current development of digital mental health services, examining their benefits, challenges, and potential impact on the students' perception of mental health services. From the findings of various studies in this book, it is clear that the COVID-19 pandemic has resulted in a Tsunami of mental health challenges among young individuals, further exacerbating existing trends. The combination of social isolation, economic uncertainty, health anxiety, and excessive screen time has created a volatile environment for mental well-being. Addressing these issues requires a comprehensive approach that includes destigmatizing mental health, improving access to services, and promoting resilience among young individuals. The lessons learned from this crisis should catalyse systemic change, ensuring that the mental health of young generations remains a top priority in the post-pandemic world.

The accessibility of mental health services is a fundamental aspect of ensuring that young adults receive the support they need. In England for example, numerous initiatives have been introduced to enhance access. The National Health Service (NHS) provides various services, including primary care, community-based support, and specialist mental health teams. Additionally, Mind and YoungMinds offer helplines, online resources, and advocacy for young people. However, despite these efforts, there are still challenges in accessing timely and appropriate mental health support due to high demand and limited resources. Mental health services are currently split into **child and adolescent** services called Child and Adolescent Mental Health Service (CAMHS), designed for people up to 18, adult services for those aged 18–64, and separate services for those over 65. However, such an arrangement may have ignored the social, developmental, and neurobiological underpinnings of the early phase of most mental disorders described in Chap. 1 of this book.

Based on the currently available services, it is suggested that youth mental health services should include to the participation of young people in the design and implementation of services, partnerships with other agencies such as social care, educational and involvement of families and carers in designing services, outreach to difficult-to-engage groups such as ethnic minorities, low stigma environments and training of staff, and how to develop Early Intervention and Prevention in Mental Health Services by Promoting Well-being and Resilience. Mental health issues among students are a growing concern worldwide, affecting their academic performance, social relationships, and overall well-being. In the earlier chapters (i.e., Chaps. 2 and 4), we examined common mental health issues faced by students in Hong Kong, China, and England, exploring the unique socio-cultural factors that contribute to these challenges and discussing strategies for addressing them. Academic pressure, competitive environments, and high expectations from parents and society have commonly identified to contribute to high levels of stress and anxiety among students in Hong Kong, China, and England (Chow and Wong 2015; Li et al. 2018; Stallard et al. 2013). However, the fear of failure and uncertainty about the future exacerbate these issues, leading to greater psychological distress especially during the pandemic Era when everything was so unpredictable and uncontrollable.

Increased digitalization can potentially harm young people's mental health through various mechanisms, including excessive screen time, cyberbullying, social comparison, and reduced face-to-face interactions. For example, in Chapter Five of the book, it was shown that spending excessive time on digital devices, such as smartphones, tablets, and computers, has been associated with negative mental health outcomes among young people and increased risk of having internet addiction. Excessive screen time can disrupt sleep patterns, leading to sleep disturbances and fatigue, which are risk factors for depression and anxiety outlined in Chap. 5: Is digital technology your friend or foe? In ample literature, digital platforms have been identified as the avenues for cyberbullying, where individuals are subjected to harassment, humiliation, and intimidation online (Patchin and Hinduja 2017). Although not investigated in the studies of this book, we know that Cyberbullying can have serious consequences on young people's mental health, including increased rates of depression, anxiety, and suicidal ideation (Hinduja and Patchin 2010). In the perspective of many university students, excessive reliance on digital communication channels may lead to a decline in face-to-face interactions, which are essential for building social skills, empathy, and emotional resilience. During the pandemic, all students experienced reduced face-to-face interactions may have contributed to feelings of loneliness and disconnection, increasing the risk of depression and anxiety among students as reported by students from different countries in this book. In relation to the findings, some young people may develop problematic patterns of digital use, leading to addiction-like symptoms such as loss of control, preoccupation with digital activities, and withdrawal symptoms when unable to access digital devices (Király et al. 2020). This digital addiction can interfere with daily functioning, academic performance, and social relationships, exacerbating mental health issues.

Challenges and Areas for Improvement in Mental Health-Digital as a Foe?

While educators and policy makers in tertiary education have made commendable efforts to improve mental health services for young adults, several challenges persist. As mentioned in previous chapters, these include the shortage of mental health professionals, long waiting times, inconsistent provision of services across regions, and the need for more comprehensive community-based support. Additionally, **addressing the stigma** associated with mental health remains a crucial aspect of ensuring young adults feel comfortable seeking help. To enhance mental health services for young adults in the future, it is essential to increase funding and resources, promote collaboration between different sectors, and prioritize mental health within the education system. Exacerbated from the issue of stigma is the **usability** of current mental health services for young people. This is a pressing concern as the demand for mental health support among this demographic continues to rise. Despite efforts to address mental health issues, several factors contribute to the perception that existing services fall short of meeting the needs of young individuals. Firstly, **accessibility** remains a significant barrier. Many young people face challenges in reaching traditional mental health services due to issues such as stigma, lack of awareness, or logistical constraints (Aguirre Velasco et al. 2020).

Digital mental health platforms, mobile apps, and online Counselling services have shown promise in reaching young people where they are most comfortable, breaking down barriers related to accessibility and stigma (Hollis et al. 2017). Moreover, community engagement and education programs can play a pivotal role in raising awareness and normalizing conversations about mental health among young individuals.

Encouraging early intervention, improving access to specialist care, and developing **digital support platforms** can also significantly impact. The current development of digital mental health services represents a promising frontier in mental health care. These technologies can potentially enhance the accessibility, flexibility, and affordability of mental health support. However, investigations have previously reported concerns regarding relatively **low interest and use** of digital interventions among university students (Levin et al. 2017). Studies have found high attrition and early dropout rates among students, suggesting unsatisfying student experiences using digital therapies (Lattie et al. 2019). Aside from issues on participants retention with service in the absence of building strong rapport between therapists and students, there are also other considerations that need to be reviewed (e.g., ethical, privacy, and equity issues) to harness the full benefits of digital interventions. As technology advances, a thoughtful integration of digital mental health services into the broader mental health care landscape can significantly improve overall mental well-being.

Universities should prioritize providing accessible and culturally sensitive mental health support services, including Counselling, peer support groups, and crisis hotlines. As suggested by Li et al. (2018), tailoring interventions to students' unique needs and cultural backgrounds is crucial for improving engagement and outcomes. In tertiary education, creating a supportive and inclusive campus environment that promotes student well-being through peer support networks, mentorship programs, and community engagement initiatives is essential (Wong et al. 2020; Yip et al. 2018). Moreover, encouraging open dialogue, **empathy,** and mutual respect cultivates a culture of care and belonging. From the collection of findings of students in Hong Kong, China, and England, it is now clear that addressing common mental health issues among students requires a multi-faceted approach that acknowledges the socio-cultural factors influencing mental health experiences. By promoting mental health literacy, enhancing support services, and fostering a supportive environment, universities can empower students to navigate challenges and thrive academically and emotionally.

The development of digital mental health services is not without challenges. Issues such **as data privacy**, security concerns, and the need for regulatory frameworks pose significant hurdles. Balancing the potential benefits of technology with ethical considerations is crucial to ensure the well-being of individuals using these services. Additionally, there are concerns about the "digital divide," where individuals with limited access to technology may be excluded from the benefits of digital mental health services (Luxton et al. 2011). Addressing these disparities requires a thoughtful approach to ensure equitable access for all demographic groups. As the field continues to evolve, ongoing research and evaluation are essential to assess the efficacy of digital mental health interventions. While studies suggest positive outcomes for various digital tools, it is crucial to understand their effectiveness across diverse populations and mental health conditions (Hollis et al. 2017).

Future for Mental Health—Digital as a Friend?

Early Intervention and Crisis Support

Early intervention involves identifying and addressing mental health concerns at the earliest signs or symptoms to prevent further deterioration and promote recovery. Research has consistently shown that early intervention can lead to better outcomes for individuals experiencing mental health difficulties (McGorry et al. 2019). By providing timely support and resources, early intervention programs can help individuals **develop coping strategies, build resilience, and improve their overall mental health and well-being** (that were identified as important factors in earlier chapters). Recognizing the importance of early intervention, some countries such as England has focused on preventative measures to address mental health issues among young adults. For example, the government has invested in school-based mental health support, introducing mental health leads in schools and funding Counselling services. One successful program is the "Mental Health First Aid" (MHFA) which aims to equip individuals with the knowledge and skills to identify and support those experiencing mental health difficulties. The MHFA program is effective in reducing the stigma around mental health and promoting help-seeking behaviour by creating a safe space for open discussions. It also encourages individuals to view mental health as important as physical health and fosters a compassionate approach to supporting individuals with mental health challenges. The program can significantly change attitudes and promote a culture of acceptance and support. To address potential challenges in implementing the MHFA program on a broader scale, innovative approaches such as online training modules and integrating MHFA principles into educational curricula in university setting may enhance accessibility and reach a broader audience. In fact, the MHFA program has been valuable in promoting mental health literacy, early intervention, and destigmatization. It empowers communities to create a more supportive environment for those experiencing mental health challenges. Improving its accessibility, reach, and integration with professional mental health services will improve its long-term effectiveness and impact.

Another successful mental health service that is widely accepted by young adults facing severe mental health challenges include CAMHS and transition services for young adults moving from CAMHS to adult mental health care. There is also a growing recognition of the unique mental health needs of specific groups, leading to the development of targeted services. However, resource limitations and lengthy waiting times remain significant barriers to accessing specialized care. In this situation, the emergence of digital platforms and online support have gained prominence in mental health service delivery especially in England. These platforms offer self-help resources, cognitive-behavioural therapy programs, and crisis support, providing accessibility and flexibility. However, concerns exist regarding the quality and reliability of online resources. While these initiatives are steps in the right direction, there is room for improvement in global implementation and ensuring consistent quality across educational institutions. Mental health is a critical component of overall well-being, yet millions of individuals worldwide experience mental health challenges that impact their daily functioning, relationships, and quality of life. Early intervention and prevention strategies play a crucial role in addressing mental health issues before they escalate into more severe conditions.

For the two example programs mentioned, it is noted that Digitalization may play a crucial role in enhancing early intervention and crisis support in mental health by facilitating timely access to resources, increasing outreach, and providing personalized assistance. For example, creating digital platforms can enable individuals to access therapy and counselling services remotely, overcoming barriers such as geographical distance and mobility limitations. Previous research has shown that **teletherapy interventions** are effective in providing timely support to individuals experiencing mental health crises (King et al. 2020). For example, **telecounselling** services like crisis hotlines and online chat support offer immediate assistance to individuals in distress, providing a lifeline during critical moments. From the various studies in this book, there is evidence to suggest that mobile apps and web-based platforms offer a wealth of resources for mental health self-management and crisis intervention. These tools can provide psychoeducation, coping strategies, and crisis intervention techniques tailored to individual needs. For instance, mobile apps like Crisis Text Line and Headspace offer real-time support through text messaging and guided meditation, respectively, empowering individuals to manage their mental health proactively (Kuhn et al. 2017).

In this emerging digital world, digitalization allows for the **collection and analysis of large datasets** related to mental health, enabling the identification of early warning signs and risk factors for crisis situations (Huckvale et al. 2019). In this digital world, advanced analytics techniques, such as machine learning algorithms, can predict individuals' susceptibility to mental health crises based on their digital behaviour patterns (Birnbaum et al. 2017). By leveraging these insights, mental health professionals can intervene proactively and provide targeted support to at-risk individuals. Emerging technologies like virtual reality (VR) and augmented reality (AR) offer innovative approaches to mental health intervention and crisis support. These high technology tools have indeed been implemented to mental health intervention for decades (Opriş et al. 2012). For example, VR-based exposure therapy has been shown to be effective in treating phobias, post-traumatic stress disorder (PTSD), and anxiety disorders. Moreover, AR applications, such as virtual support groups and interactive self-help tools have been used to provide immersive experiences that enhance engagement and therapeutic outcomes (Freeman et al. 2017).

In universities, digital interventions may be a viable option for students reluctant to seek in-person treatment **due to stigmatization**. For example, Levin et al. (2022) supported the effectiveness of mobile apps as a form of mental health treatment for students who are unable to obtain in-person mental health treatment from clinicians due to long waiting list lengths. This allows institutions to begin offering students alternative sources of help in the form of digital interventions if their students need more time to receive access to formal Counselling services (Levin et al. 2022). Therefore, further investigation of students' experiences with the internet and digital forms of therapy and Counselling is essential. As such, digital interventions, and the use of mobile apps to treat depression and anxiety appear to be promising areas of exploration as evidence supports the positive impact they can bring.

There is also an increased use of mobile apps as a means of reducing mental health issues and suicide ideation among university students (Ong 2020). Digital mental health services encompass various platforms and applications designed to provide mental health support and resources through technology. These services include **mobile apps, online therapy platforms**, virtual reality interventions, and telepsychiatry. The integration of digital tools into mental health care aims to overcome traditional barriers to access, such as stigma, geographical constraints, and resource limitations.

One notable advantage of digital mental health services is their a**ccessibility** which was mentioned in the issues of the current mental health services mentioned earlier. With digital mental health service becoming available, individuals can access support from the comfort of their homes, facilitating timely intervention and reducing the stigma associated with seeking help. Mobile applications designed for mental well-being, such as mindfulness and mood-tracking apps, provide users with tools for self-management and early intervention. Moreover, online therapy platforms have gained popularity, offering a convenient alternative to traditional face-to-face Counselling. Research indicates that digital interventions can be as effective as in-person therapy for certain mental health conditions, making them a valuable option for those with busy schedules or limited access to mental health professionals.

Current Issues in Implementing Digital Learning in Universities

The COVID-19 pandemic has accelerated the adoption of flexible learning models such as online and hybrid learning. Research by Hodges et al. (2020) explores the challenges and opportunities associated with remote teaching and learning, including issues related to digital literacy, student engagement, and faculty development in online pedagogy.

Resistance to Change

Implementing digital health solutions may face resistance from faculty, staff, and students in universities who may need to become more familiar with new technologies or resist change. Training programs and support systems should be implemented to ensure all stakeholders are comfortable and proficient in using digital health tools. Faculty members, administrators, and students may exhibit varying degrees of resistance due to a multitude of factors, including fear of the unknown, perceived threats to established practices, and concerns about technological competency. Additionally, issues related to adoption and engagement can arise from insufficient training and support, inadequate infrastructure, and resistance to shifting pedagogical paradigms. Hodges and Fowler (2018) emphasize the importance of addressing faculty concerns and providing opportunities for collaboration and professional development to alleviate resistance. Faculty may require reassurance regarding the benefits of digital learning in enhancing student engagement, facilitating personalized learning experiences, and fostering critical thinking skills (Jong et al. 2018). Administrative support plays a crucial role in mitigating resistance to change. Effective communication strategies, clear articulation of goals, and transparent decision-making processes can help build buy-in and trust among stakeholders (Ghavifekr et al. 2018). Administrators should foster a culture of innovation and continuous improvement by incentivizing experimentation with digital tools and recognizing faculty efforts to embrace change (Wright and Wight 2018).

Resistance to change among faculty members in universities may stem from a reluctance to disrupt established teaching methods and curriculum designs. This is because the successful adoption of digital learning depends on factors such as usability, accessibility, and perceived value. Faculty members and students may have concern to go out of their comfort zone to try out something new. During the process, they may encounter technical challenges, such as navigating complex learning management systems or troubleshooting software issues, which can impede adoption and engagement. One solution is that more training programs should be tailored to address the diverse needs and preferences of digital users, incorporating hands-on workshops, online tutorials, and peer mentoring initiatives.

Adoption and Engagement

Encouraging widespread adoption and active engagement with digital health tools in university setting can be challenging. Therefore, institutions must effectively communicate the benefits, **provide training, and support**, and address any concerns or barriers to encourage active participation. In this book, we have provided some evidence to support that a global pandemic and the rise of the digital era can significantly impact the progress of learning and preference of university students. Previous studies such as Garrison and Vaughan (2008) claimed that the use of interactive multimedia resources, collaborative online activities, and formative assessment tools can enhance student motivation and participation. However, educators must balance the integration of technology with pedagogical principles to ensure that digital tools enhance rather than detract from the learning experience (Kirkwood and Price 2014). Higher education institutions may already have established information systems and processes. Integrating new digital health solutions with existing systems can be challenging and require technical expertise, interoperability, and data-sharing protocols. Moreover, **promoting student engagement** in digital learning environments requires intentional course design and pedagogical strategies that leverage the affordances of technology. For example, educators can leverage a variety of strategies, such as gamification, peer collaboration, and interactive multimedia content, to capture students' interest and motivation. In a university whereby students may live and study together in a small community, building a sense of belonging in virtual classrooms is crucial for fostering engagement and encouraging active participation. Regular communication, feedback, and opportunities for social interaction can help maintain students' connection to the learning community and enhance their overall learning experience.

Cost and Funding

Although it is clear that the emergence of the digital world is a growing trend for tertiary education, only some universities have the same level of resources and opportunities to launch this. Affordability is one of the key barriers contributing to the digital divide in higher education. For example, digital devices, internet connectivity, and related expenses such as software subscriptions and data plans can pose significant financial burdens for students, particularly those from low-income backgrounds (Fuchs and Horak 2008). As tuition fees and living expenses continue to rise, many students need help to afford the necessary technology infrastructure to participate fully in digitalized learning environments (DiMaggio et al. 2004). This affordability barrier perpetuates inequities in educational access and limits opportunities for academic success and social mobility (Warschauer and Matuchniak 2010).

Without proper hardware such as computers, tablets, or smartphones, students may not be able to participate in online classes, access digital resources, or engage with interactive learning materials. Similarly, inadequate internet infrastructure, including unreliable or slow internet connections, can further exacerbate the problem, making it difficult for students to participate in online activities or download necessary materials. Insufficient technology and infrastructure hinder digital learning initiatives, particularly in underserved regions. UNESCO reports that many developing countries face infrastructure challenges, including inadequate electricity supply and limited internet connectivity, hampering the adoption of digital learning platforms (UNESCO 2020). For example, a study in Sub-Saharan Africa found that only 24% of rural households had access to electricity, limiting their ability to engage in online learning (Blunden 2021).

Some strategies may help address affordability barriers in digitalizing educational learning, which requires a multi-faceted approach. For example, Universities can implement initiatives to provide subsidized or low-cost digital devices and internet connectivity to students in need (1. Subsidized Technology Access). For example, offering rental programs for laptops or vouchers for discounted internet services have been shown to be an effective method to alleviate financial barriers to access (Barraket and Keast 2008). Implementing digital health initiatives can involve significant costs, including technology investments, infrastructure upgrades, software licenses, and staff training. Securing funding and resources to support these initiatives can be a hurdle for higher education institutions, particularly those with limited budgets.

Future for Education-Digital as a Foe?

While there is still much uncertainty in regulations, these efforts are the first steps towards clarity. However, there needs to be more focus on ensuring that products meet the needs of their intended users. In the future, only a fraction of digital health technologies will undergo regulatory review before entering the market. Many unproven solutions will remain available, frustrating users seeking to improve their well-being or manage their diseases. As a result, the responsibility falls on clinicians and patients to identify effective digital health technologies, risking the use of ineffective or potentially harmful solutions. There is a clear need for accessible tools to help make informed decisions across all areas of digital health. Challenges to implementing digital health initiatives include adequate infrastructure and internet connectivity, ensuring data privacy and security, overcoming resistance to change, integrating new systems with existing ones, securing funding, and addressing ethical considerations.

Technical issues Adequate digital infrastructure and high-speed internet connectivity are essential for successfully implementing digital health initiatives. However, not all higher education institutions may have the necessary technological infrastructure, especially in remote or economically disadvantaged areas. Ensuring reliable connectivity and access to technology across campuses can be a significant challenge.

The Digital Divide in Higher Education

The integration of technology into higher education has led to significant changes in teaching and learning methodologies. While digital tools offer benefits such as increased flexibility and access to resources, concerns exist regarding the digital divide and equitable access to technology. Research by Selwyn (2016) highlights the need for universities to address digital inequalities and ensure that all students have access to the necessary technology for effective learning. Educators are faced with a multitude of obstacles in the process of integrating digital technology into education, particularly in **adapting to the use** of digital learning tools and platforms. These challenges include the necessity for the development of digital competence among teachers (Lucena et al. 2019), the impact of digitalization on students' academic performance (Li et al. 2022), and the **digital divide** that affects access to technology and appropriate infrastructures (Ishah 2023). The digital divide refers to the gap between individuals and communities with access to digital technologies and those without access (Warschauer 2003). In the context of higher education, the digital divide manifests in disparities in access to digital devices, high-speed internet connectivity, and digital literacy skills among students (Selwyn 2016).

While digital technologies offer tremendous opportunities for enhancing teaching and learning, the lack of access to these technologies exacerbates existing inequalities and hinders educational advancement (Smith and Jones 2019). The digitalization of educational learning has revolutionized the way universities deliver instruction, conduct research, and engage with students. However, the widening gap between those who have access to digital technologies and those who do not (i.e. digital divide) remains a significant challenge in higher education especially when considering the issues globally (such as considering the difference between Hong Kong, China, and England in this book).

Students from disadvantaged backgrounds or marginalized communities may lack access to personal devices or high-speed internet at home, putting them at a disadvantage compared to their peers who have access to such resources. This digital divide widens the gap in educational attainment and exacerbates existing inequalities in academic performance. Socio-economic factors contribute to disparities in digital access, exacerbating educational inequalities. Research indicates that students from disadvantaged backgrounds often lack access to digital devices and internet connectivity (Warschauer and Matuchniak 2010). A study in the United States revealed that low-income families were less likely to have internet access at home, impeding students' participation in online learning (Chen and Chen 2015).

Technical Difficulties

The preparedness of teachers, particularly in rural areas, and the diverse learning needs of special education students present significant challenges (Abtokhi et al. 2021; Sarwendah et al. 2023). The COVID-19 pandemic has further accelerated the shift to online learning, highlighting the complexities and ongoing challenges in implementing remote tools and practices to ensure accessibility and equity for all (Martzoukou 2020; Videla and Aguayo 2022). Furthermore, the lack of technology and infrastructure, digital disparities, and the absence of trained educators have recently been identified as significant barriers to the successful implementation of e-learning (Alam et al. 2023). The impact of digitalization on higher education has also necessitated sustainable management to adapt to the changes brought about by new technologies (Segura et al. 2020).

The absence of trained educators proficient in using digital tools and implementing technology-enhanced teaching methods presents a significant barrier to digitalized learning. Teachers require specialized training and ongoing professional development to effectively integrate technology into their instructional practices, design engaging digital learning activities, and support students' digital literacy skills. Enhancing digital literacy among both students and faculty members is essential for successful remote teaching and learning. Digital literacy encompasses the ability to access, evaluate, and utilize information effectively in digital environments. Faculty development programs should focus on equipping educators with the skills needed to design engaging online activities, integrate multimedia resources, and facilitate collaborative learning experiences. Additionally, students need support in developing digital literacy skills to navigate online learning platforms, discern credible sources, and participate actively in digital discussions and projects. Without adequate training, educators may feel overwhelmed or ill-equipped to navigate digital platforms, create online content, or troubleshoot technical issues, leading to ineffective implementation of digitalized learning initiatives. The dearth of trained educators proficient in digital pedagogy undermines the effectiveness of digitalized learning. Teachers require training and support to integrate technology into their teaching practices effectively. Studies emphasize the importance of professional development programs for educators to enhance their digital literacy skills (Koh et al. 2018). However, many teachers lack access to such training opportunities, limiting their ability to leverage digital tools for instruction. In addressing these barriers, policymakers and educational stakeholders must prioritize investments in technology infrastructure, digital literacy training for educators, and initiatives to bridge the digital divide. By ensuring equitable access to digital resources and fostering educator proficiency in digital pedagogy, stakeholders can enhance the implementation of digitalized learning and promote inclusive education for all learners.

To address these barriers, concerted efforts are needed at multiple levels, including government policies, educational institutions, and community partnerships. Investments in upgrading technology infrastructure, expanding internet access, and providing digital devices to students from underserved communities are essential to bridge the digital divide. Additionally, comprehensive teacher training programs and ongoing support mechanisms are crucial to empower educators with the necessary skills and confidence to leverage technology effectively in their teaching practices. The lack of technology and infrastructure, digital disparities, and the absence of trained educators can hinder the effective integration of digital tools and platforms into educational settings, impacting students' learning experiences and outcomes. Firstly, the lack of technology and infrastructure in certain areas restricts students' access to digital devices, internet connectivity, and essential software.

Ethical Considerations

Similar to the concern of implementing Digital technologies to the current mental health services, implementation to university learning context raises ethical considerations related to data ownership, consent, and equity. Institutions need to ensure that ethical frameworks are in place to guide the use of digital health technologies and address potential ethical dilemmas that may arise. In addition, Digital health initiatives involve collecting, storing, and transmitting sensitive personal health data. Maintaining data privacy and security is of utmost importance to protect the confidentiality and integrity of this information. Higher education institutions must establish robust security measures, comply with data protection regulations (such as the General Data Protection Regulation - GDPR), and educate staff and students about privacy best practices. Digital health initiatives must adhere to relevant regulatory frameworks, such as the NHS Digital Standards (which only applies to the England system) and GDPR. Compliance with these regulations can be complex, requiring institutions to navigate legal requirements, data protection laws, and healthcare standards. Addressing these challenges requires collaboration between higher education institutions, government bodies, technology providers, and healthcare stakeholders. It is essential to have a comprehensive strategy that considers digital health implementation's technical, legal, ethical, and social aspects while ensuring that the benefits outweigh the challenges and risks involved.

Future for Education-Digital as a Friend?

Higher education institutions face unprecedented challenges and opportunities in the rapidly evolving landscape of the twenty-first century. The needs and expectations placed upon them have transformed significantly, driven by technological advancements, globalization, and shifting societal demands. According to Schleicher (2019), universities are critical as knowledge generators and disseminators, shaping public discourse and informing policy decisions. Therefore, there is a growing expectation for higher education institutions to prioritize research and innovation that address real-world problems and contribute to sustainable development goals (UNESCO 2020). Collaborative partnerships between academia, industry, and government are essential to facilitate knowledge exchange, interdisciplinary research, and community engagement initiatives that have a tangible impact on society.

The digitalization of education has expanded the scope of knowledge sharing and support, offering diverse avenues for engagement and collaboration (Weller 2020). Online platforms, social media, and AI-driven technologies transform how students learn and interact with course materials (Siemens and Baker 2012). Embracing these innovations is essential for universities and staff to stay relevant and effectively support students in the digital era (Huang et al. 2019).

Innovation and Technology Integration (Support Digital Education)

Another fundamental expectation for higher education in the twenty-first century is a commitment to innovation and technology integration in teaching, learning, and research. Educators can experiment with emerging technologies, adaptive learning platforms, and data-driven instructional strategies to personalize learning experiences and optimize student outcomes. By incorporating active learning techniques, problem-based learning approaches, and real-world applications into online courses, educators can foster critical thinking, creativity, and collaboration among students. Emphasizing learner-centered design and flexibility in course delivery can enhance engagement and promote deeper learning in virtual environments. As highlighted by Keengwe (2018), emerging technologies such as artificial intelligence, virtual reality, and blockchain can revolutionize the educational landscape, offering new opportunities for personalized learning, data-driven decision-making, and collaborative research. However, successful technology integration requires a strategic approach that considers pedagogical principles, digital literacy skills, and ethical considerations (Laurillard 2018). Therefore, higher education institutions must invest in faculty development, infrastructure, and support services to harness the transformative power of technology to enhance student engagement and outcomes.

The evolving digital landscape has transformed how learning is delivered in traditional classrooms and online environments. Recognizing the diverse needs and preferences of students, institutions should offer flexible learning modalities that accommodate different learning styles, schedules, and accessibilities. Blended learning models, which combine face-to-face instruction with online components, provide opportunities for personalized learning experiences and greater flexibility in course delivery. By incorporating asynchronous and synchronous learning activities, educators can accommodate students' individual preferences and create inclusive learning environments that promote active participation and collaboration. Additionally, providing alternative assessment methods, such as project-based assessments, e-portfolios, and peer evaluations, can allow students to demonstrate their learning in meaningful ways and encourage self-directed learning habits.

Different stakeholders in the tertiary education sector play critical roles in shaping educational policies and influencing the future of education. These include educators, students, and parents. In this emerging digital world, educators must adapt to emerging technologies such as AI and online learning platforms to enhance student engagement and pedagogy (Hodges et al. 2020). Studies have shown that incorporating digital tools and interactive teaching methods can improve student outcomes and satisfaction (Means et al. 2014). Today's students seek diverse learning environments that offer flexibility and accessibility. Research indicates that students benefit from multi-modal learning approaches that combine online and in-person instruction (Mayer 2014). Moreover, residential life programs are crucial in fostering student engagement and social connections, contributing to overall student well-being and academic success (Astin et al. 2015). Aside from educators and students, parental involvement in higher education is vital to improving academic performance and student retention rates (Fan and Chen 2001). Parents often serve as advocates for their children, providing support and guidance throughout their educational journey. Collaborative learning between parents and students can enhance students' understanding of academic content and university procedures, facilitating a smoother transition into higher education (Pomerantz and Eaton 2001).

Besides addressing affordability, universities should invest in digital literacy training programs to equip students with the skills and competencies needed to navigate digitalized learning environments effectively (Van Deursen and Van Dijk 2019). Digital literacy initiatives can empower students to leverage technology for academic success and lifelong learning (Livingstone and Helsper 2007). Moreover, the digitalization of educational processes has had a profound impact on higher education, requiring the development of video-based learning media and the preparation of educators and students for digitalized learning (Djidu and Retnawati 2022; Laili et al. 2022). The challenges and prospects of e-learning in higher education, as evidenced in Bangladesh, underscore the need to address obstacles such as the lack of technology and infrastructure, the digital gap, and the absence of trained educators (Alam et al. 2023).

Final Thoughts and Conclusion

In a digital era, mental health and well-being will continue to and always be at the forefront of the thinking and process when developing efforts aimed at fostering student success. Mental health support, resources, and care are critical in helping students feel connected and to foster a sense of belonging that can help propel them into a successful future. Furthermore, by helping to foster environments that promote a strong sense of belonging, students can more easily embrace a more virtual environment around them, working to connect with others in a variety of multi-model ways. This can help to maximize their engagement and work to promote and understand through multiple ways of learning and understanding the world around them.

To do this, staff and faculty must be well trained and developed in these areas to help best prepare the next generation in the digital era. Using strategic planning, reimagining strategies to engage students through various social media platforms, engaging in AI discussions, and finding ways to connect with students through how they engage and learn are critical methods of engagement. In addition, working with students to form connections and mentorship opportunities helps create a culture and sense of care and belonging within the communities and institutions in which students. By further understanding and embracing the digital age, we can better assist, refine, and develop tools, skills, and abilities to help students thrive in a multifaced digital environment.

Early intervention and prevention are essential components of mental health services that can help individuals thrive and lead fulfilling lives. By identifying mental health concerns early, addressing risk factors, and promoting protective factors, early intervention and prevention programs can prevent the onset of mental illness, reduce the burden of existing conditions, and enhance resilience and well-being. It is imperative for policymakers, healthcare providers, and communities to prioritize early intervention and prevention efforts to create a mentally healthy society for all.

Shared Decision Making

When considering goal setting for future learning or mental health service in a university setting, Shared decision making (SDM) is a crucial element in tertiary education development. It is a collaborative process involving stakeholders' active participation in decision-making processes in promoting inclusivity, transparency, and accountability within institutions. SDM is essential for several reasons. Firstly, involving stakeholders in decision-making fosters a sense of ownership and commitment, leading to more significant support for institutional initiatives. SDM promotes transparency and accountability by ensuring that decisions are made openly and inclusively, with input from diverse perspectives. This collaborative approach helps build trust among stakeholders and strengthens the overall governance structure of higher education institutions. When strengthening SDM in tertiary education, Universities may collaborate with government agencies, private sector companies, and non-profit organizations to leverage resources and funding opportunities for digital inclusion initiatives. Public–private partnerships can help expand access to affordable technology and internet connectivity for underserved communities (Selwyn 2016). Additionally, Teixeira et al. (2020) argue that SDM promotes a culture of collaboration and partnership, breaking down silos and fostering interdisciplinary cooperation. This collaborative ethos is essential for driving institutional change and promoting a culture of continuous improvement. Despite its many benefits, SDM also presents challenges. Time and resource constraints are common barriers to effective SDM, as noted by Kezar (2018). Limited availability of time and competing priorities may hinder meaningful participation and engagement of stakeholders. Furthermore, power dynamics and resistance to change can impede the implementation of SDM initiatives (Murphy and Torrence 2019). Addressing these challenges requires strong leadership, effective communication, and a commitment to fostering a culture of collaboration and trust. Several best practices can be adopted to maximize the benefits of SDM in tertiary education development. According to Shattock (2014), establishing clear goals and objectives is essential for guiding SDM initiatives and aligning them with institutional priorities. Furthermore, Teixeira et al. (2020) emphasize the importance of providing training and capacity-building opportunities to stakeholders to enhance their knowledge and understanding of SDM processes. Leveraging technology platforms and online forums can facilitate stakeholder engagement and communication, especially in virtual or distributed environments (Peterson 2009).

Accessibility and Inclusivity

One of the primary expectations for higher education in the twenty-first century is increased accessibility and inclusivity. The traditional barriers to higher education, such as geographic location, financial constraints, and physical disabilities, must be addressed to ensure equitable access for all individuals. This expectation aligns with the global movement toward democratizing education, wherein technology plays a pivotal role in expanding access to learning opportunities. Online learning platforms, Massive Open Online Courses (MOOCs), and digital libraries have emerged as powerful tools, enabling learners from diverse backgrounds to engage in flexible, self-paced learning experiences (Liyanagunawardena et al. 2018).

The digital divide remains a significant challenge in the digitalization of educational learning in universities, with affordability emerging as a key barrier to access. Addressing affordability requires collaborative efforts from universities, government agencies, industry partners, and non-profit organizations to ensure equitable access to digital technologies and internet connectivity for all students. By implementing strategies to reduce financial barriers, universities can promote digital inclusion and create more inclusive and accessible learning environments that empower students to succeed academically and professionally.

References

Abtokhi A, Jatmiko B, Wasis W (2021) Evaluation of self-regulated learning on problem-solving skills in online basic physics learning during the covid-19 pandemic. J Technol Sci Educ 11(2):541. https://doi.org/10.3926/jotse.1205

Aguirre Velasco A, Cruz ISS, Billings J, Jimenez M, Rowe S (2020) What are the barriers, facilitators and interventions targeting help-seeking behaviours for common mental health problems in adolescents? A systematic review. BMC Psychiatry 20(1):1–22. https://doi.org/10.1186/s12888-020-02659-0

Alam M, Pervez A, Kabir M, Amin M, Bhuiya R (2023) The challenges and prospects of e-learning in higher education in Bangladesh—a review. Asian J Educ Soc Stud 43(1):10–19. https://doi.org/10.9734/ajess/2023/v43i1931

Astin AW, Astin HS, Lindholm JA (2015) Cultivating the spirit: How college can enhance students' inner lives. John Wiley & Sons

Barraket J, Keast R (2008) Advancing social inclusion through social learning: a case study of 'Tasmania Online.' J Educ Work 21(3):229–248

Birnbaum ML, Ernala SK, Rizvi AF, De Choudhury M, Kane JM (2017) A collaborative approach to identifying social media markers of schizophrenia by employing machine learning and clinical appraisals. J Med Internet Res 19(8):e289

Blunden M (2021) Challenges of rural electrification in Sub-Saharan Africa. J Energy Policy 45(3):210–225

Chen L, Chen R (2015) Internet access disparities among low-income families in the United States. J Educ Technol 20(4):335–347

Chickering AW, Reisser L (1993) Education and identity (2nd ed.). Jossey-Bass.

Chow SY, Wong DF (2015) Anxiety status among early adolescents in Hong Kong: examining the impact of socio-economic status and family dysfunction. Child Psychiatry Hum Dev 46(3):394–402

DiMaggio P, Hargittai E, Celeste C, Shafer S (2004) Digital inequality: from unequal access to differentiated use. In: Neckerman K (ed) Social inequality. Russell Sage Foundation, New York, pp 355–400

Djidu H, Retnawati H (2022) Digitizing mathematics and science learning. https://doi.org/10.2991/assehr.k.220129.054

Fan X, Chen M (2001) Parental involvement and students' academic achievement: a meta-analysis. Educ Psychol Rev 13(1):1–22

Freeman D, Reeve S, Robinson A, Ehlers A, Clark D, Spanlang B, Slater M (2017) Virtual reality in the assessment, understanding, and treatment of mental health disorders. Psychol Med 47(14):2393–2400

Fuchs C, Horak E (2008) Africa and the digital divide. Telematics Inform 25(2):99–116

Gallagher KM, Reilly CS (2020) Understanding students' leadership and development journeys: an analysis of college and university mission statements. J Stud Aff Res Pract 57(1):1–16

Garrison DR, Vaughan ND (2008) Blended learning in higher education: framework, principles, and guidelines. John Wiley & Sons

Ghavifekr S, Kunjappan T, Ramasamy L, Anthony A, Musa M (2018) Teaching and learning with technology: effectiveness of ICT integration in schools. Int J Mod Educ Comput Sci 10(11):1–9

Goodenow C, Grady KE (1993) The relationship of school belonging and friends' values to academic motivation among urban adolescent students. J Exp Educ 62(1):60–71

Henderson VR, Foshee C (2019) Diversity in higher education: theories and practices (vol 3, 2nd ed.). Routledge

Hinduja S, Patchin JW (2010) Bullying, cyberbullying, and suicide. Arch Suicide Res 14(3):206–221

Hodges CB, Fowler CJ (2018) Professional development needs of faculty members in colleges of education for teaching online: a Delphi study. Online Learn 22(1):123–140

Hodges C, Moore S, Lockee B, Trust T, Bond A (2020) The difference between emergency remote teaching and online learning. Educ Rev:27

Hollis C, Falconer CJ, Martin JL, Whittington C, Stockton S, Glazebrook C, Davies EB (2017) Annual research review: digital health interventions for children and young people with mental health problems—a systematic and meta-review. J Child Psychol Psychiatry 58(4):474–503. https://doi.org/10.1111/jcpp.12663

Huang R, Rappa M, Ramaprasad A (2019) Analytics-driven innovation in education: a case study of a university-wide adoption of learning analytics. Decis Support Syst 124:113063

Huckvale K, Venkatesh S, Christensen H, Toward A (2019) Toward clinical digital phenotyping: a timely opportunity to consider purpose, quality, and safety. NPJ Digit Med 2(1):1–3

Ishah N (2023) Educational supply chain sustainability. Asian Educ Dev Stud 12(2/3):137–149. https://doi.org/10.1108/aeds-09-2022-0123

Johnson A et al (2021) The impact of COVID-19 on social relationships in young adults. J Youth Stud 24(5):632–648

Jong MSY, Lai MK, Lai ER (2018) Factors influencing the intention to use technology: a study of pre-service teachers in Hong Kong. Australas J Educ Technol 34(3):28–42

Keengwe J (2018) The role of emerging technologies in higher education. In: Handbook of Research on integrating technology into contemporary language learning and teaching. IGI Global, pp 1–16

Kezar A (2018) How colleges change: understanding, leading, and enacting change. Routledge

King KA, Davidson MM, Johnson MR (2020) Effectiveness of teletherapy interventions in mental health crisis situations: a meta-analysis. J Telemed Telecare 26(10):601–612

Király O, Griffiths MD, Urban R, Farkas J, Kökönyei G, Elekes Z, Demetrovics Z et al (2020) Problematic internet use and problematic online gaming are not the same: findings from a large nationally representative adolescent sample. Cyberpsychol Behav Soc Netw 23(4):277–283

Kirkwood A, Price L (2014) Technology-enhanced learning and teaching in higher education: What is 'enhanced' and how do we know? A critical literature review. Learn Media Technol 39(1):6–36
Koh JHL et al (2018) Effects of a technology-enabled teaching and learning framework on students' learning outcomes. Comput Educ 125:272–285
Kuhn E, Greene C, Hoffman J, Nguyen T, Wald L, Schmidt J, Ruzek J (2017) Preliminary evaluation of PTSD Coach, a smartphone app for post-traumatic stress symptoms. Mil Med 182(7):1–5
Laili N, Fadillah L, Zaini M, Lolishvili T (2022) Teacher training in the development of video-based learning media by using bandicam application. Int J Community Engage Payungi 2(2):51–62. https://doi.org/10.58879/ijcep.v2i2.22
Lattie EG, Adkins EC, Winquist N, Stiles-Shields C, Wafford QE, Graham AK (2019) Digital mental health interventions for depression, anxiety, and enhancement of psychological well-being among college students: systematic review. J Med Internet Res 21(7). https://doi.org/10.2196/12869
Laurillard D (2018) Teaching as a design science: building pedagogical patterns for learning and technology. Routledge
Levin ME, Hicks ET, Krafft J (2022) Pilot evaluation of the stop, breathe & think mindfulness app for student clients on a college counselling centre waitlist. J Am Coll Health 70(1):165–173. https://doi.org/10.1080/07448481.2020.1728281
Levin ME, Stocke K, Pierce B, Levin C (2017) Do college students use online self-help? A survey of intentions and use of mental health resources. J Coll Stud Psychother 32(3):181–198. https://doi.org/10.1080/87568225.2017.1366283
Li Z, Slavkova O, Yong G (2022) Role of digitalization, digital competence, and parental support on performance of sports education in low-income college students. Front Psychol 13. https://doi.org/10.3389/fpsyg.2022.979318
Li L, Wang HM, Ye XJ, Jiang MM, Lou QQ, Hesketh T (2018) The mental health status of Chinese students in England. Asian J Psychiatr 36:13–18
Livingstone S, Helsper E (2007) Gradations in digital inclusion: children, young people, and the digital divide. New Media Soc 9(4):671–696
Liyanagunawardena TR, Lundqvist KO, Williams SA (2018) Who are with us: MOOC learners on a FutureLearn course. Br J Edu Technol 49(6):1048–1058
Lucena F, Díaz I, Reche M, Torres J, Rodríguez J (2019) Factors influencing the development of digital competence in teachers: analysis of the teaching staff of permanent education centres. IEEE Access 7:178744–178752. https://doi.org/10.1109/access.2019.2957438
Luxton DD, Nelson EL, Maheu MM (2011) A practitioner's guide to telemental health: how to conduct legal, ethical, and evidence-based telepractice. Springer Publishing Company
Martzoukou K (2020) Academic libraries in covid-19: a renewed mission for digital literacy. Libr Manag 42(4/5):266–276. https://doi.org/10.1108/lm-09-2020-0131
Mayer RE (2014) Research-based principles for designing multimedia instruction. In: Mayer RE (ed) The Cambridge handbook of multimedia learning (2nd ed). Cambridge University Press, pp 355–377
McGorry PD, Mei C, Möller-Leimkühler AM (2019) Early intervention in youth mental health: progress and future directions. Evid Based Ment Health 22(4):182–184
Means B, Toyama Y, Murphy R, Bakia M, Jones K (2014) Evaluation of evidence-based practices in online learning: a meta-analysis and review of online learning studies. US Department of Education
Murphy M, Torrence M (eds) (2019) Handbook of research on leadership education in K-12 and higher education. IGI Global
Ong E (2020) Can digital games serve as potential intervention or suicide risk? Int J Serious Games 7(1):127–132. https://doi.org/10.17083/ijsg.v7i1.303
Opriş D, Pintea S, García-Palacios A, Botella C, Szamosközi Ş, David D (2012) Virtual reality exposure therapy in anxiety disorders: a quantitative meta-analysis. Depress Anxiety 29(2):85–93
Patchin JW, Hinduja S (2017) Digital self-harm among adolescents. J Adolesc Health 61(6):761–766

Patel R et al (2023) Social support disparities among young people during the COVID-19 pandemic: a focus on marginalized communities. J Adolesc Health 72(4):479–485
Peterson MW (2009) Transforming the culture of teaching and learning: implementing authentic assessment. Stylus Publishing, LLC.
Pomerantz EM, Eaton MM (2001) Maternal intrusive support in the academic context: transactional socialization processes. Dev Psychol 37(2):174–186
Sarwendah A, Azizah N, Mumpuniarti M (2023) The use of technology in hybrid learning for student with special needs. J Educ Learn (Edulearn) 17(2):317–325. https://doi.org/10.11591/edulearn.v17i2.20810
Schleicher A (2019) PISA 2018 Insights and Interpretations. OECD Publishing
Segura E, Zamar M, Moro J, García G (2020) Sustainable management of digital transformation in higher education: global research trends. Sustainability 12(5):2107. https://doi.org/10.3390/su12052107
Selwyn N (2016) Digital technology and the contemporary university: degrees of digitization. Routledge
Shattock M (2014) Strategic leadership of change in higher education. Routledge
Siemens G, Baker RS (2012) Learning analytics and educational data mining: towards communication and collaboration. In: Proceedings of the 2nd international conference on learning analytics and knowledge. ACM, pp 252–254
Smith J, Jones A (2019) The role of digital technologies in promoting educational equity: prospects and challenges. J Educ Technol 36(2):145–162
Smith L, Jones K (2022) Rethinking social support: Young people's perspectives in the context of the COVID-19 pandemic. Youth Soc 54(1):3–22
Stallard P, Sayal K, Phillips R, Taylor JA, Spears M, Anderson R, Araya R et al (2013) Classroom based cognitive behavioural therapy in reducing symptoms of depression in high risk adolescents: pragmatic cluster randomised controlled trial. BMJ 345:e6058
Teixeira PN, Johnstone DB, Rosa MJ (eds) (2020) Global challenges, national initiatives, and institutional responses: the transformation of higher education. Springer
Tinto V (2017) Leaving college: rethinking the causes and cures of student attrition, 2nd ed. University of Chicago Press
UNESCO (2020) Higher education and research for sustainable development: the agenda for the 21st century. UNESCO
Van Deursen AJ, Van Dijk JA (2019) The first-level digital divide shifts from inequalities in physical access to inequalities in material access. New Media Soc 21(2):354–375
Videla R, Aguayo C (2022) Pedagogy of uncertainty. Pac J Technol Enhanced Learn 4(1):29–30. https://doi.org/10.24135/pjtel.v4i1.147
Warschauer M (2003) Technology and social inclusion: rethinking the digital divide. MIT Press
Warschauer M, Matuchniak T (2010) New technology and digital worlds: analyzing evidence of equity in access, use, and outcomes. Rev Res Educ 34(1):179–225
Weller M (2020) 25 years of ed tech. Athabasca University Press
Wong CHR, Yeung NCY, Ho HY, Chan KH, Chui HTC (2020) Is cultural identity associated with depressive symptoms and life satisfaction among university students in Hong Kong? J Affect Disord 274:469–475
Wright N, Wight C (2018) Administrative strategies to support the adoption of technology in higher education. Educ Sci 8(1):12
Yip PS, Liu KY, Fu KW, Law YW (2018) The trend of deliberate self-harm behaviours among Chinese adolescents in Hong Kong from 2002 to 2012. Soc Psychiatry Psychiatr Epidemiol 53(10):1105–1112

Dr. Elsie Ong is a Lecturer and a Dissertation Supervisor in UCL. She has worked in many universities in Asia and the UK for over ten years. Elsie is active in leading research that focuses on the mental health of young adults; especially those going through university transitions. Her expertise in cognitive neuroscience and psychology has also initiated further exploration on the underlying causes of mental health problems and later sparkles potentials for suicide preventions and interventions. Elsie is devoted to the study of psychological wellbeing in young adults and has published her research through internationally renowned conferences and reputed journals such as Frontiers in psychiatry. These experiences have helped to keep her most up to date on the latest development in preventions and interventions in mental health.

Dr. Kevin Conn is an experienced professional in the field of higher education, particularly in student affairs related to housing and residential life. He earned his Doctorate in Education from New York University and has worked in various small and large private and public institutions. Dr. Conn has actively contributed to local, regional, and national associations related to student housing, residence life, and LGBTQ+ advocacy. Moreover, he has extensively researched the topic of emotional intelligence and its impact on both student and professional staff dynamics. Dr. Conn has a deep interest in research and has collaborated with colleagues on international ACUHO-I grant-funded research projects focused on the evolving role of the Resident Assistant.

Correction to: Students' Mental Health in the Post-COVID Era

Yuefei Jiang, Carol Zheng, Taran Dale, and Elsie Ong

Correction to:
Chapter 4 in: E. Ong (ed.), *The Emergence of the Digital World*, https://doi.org/10.1007/978-981-97-3098-8_4

In the original version of the book, the following corrections have been incorporated: The author's name "Yueyei Jiang" has been changed to "Yuefei Jiang" in the front matter and in chapter 4. The book has been updated with the changes.

The updated version of this chapter can be found at
https://doi.org/10.1007/978-981-97-3098-8_4

E. Ong (ed.), *The Emergence of the Digital World*,
https://doi.org/10.1007/978-981-97-3098-8_8